KNOW YOUR TYPE

D1560087

Ralph Metzner graduated from Oxford University and obtained his Ph.D. degree in clinical psychology from Harvard University, where he also pursued post-doctoral studies in psychopharmacology. He worked for many years in the area of psychedelic research and co-authored *The Psychedelic Experience* with Timothy Leary and Richard Alpert. He also wrote *The Ecstatic Adventure* and *Maps of Consciousness*. He has been a student of Actualism for ten years, and is currently on the faculties of the California Institute of Asian Studies and John F. Kennedy University, and in private practice in San Francisco.

KNOW YOUR TYPE

Maps of Identity

———◄►———

Ralph Metzner

ANCHOR BOOKS
Anchor Press/Doubleday
GARDEN CITY, NEW YORK
1979

The Anchor Books edition is the first publication of *Know Your Type*
Anchor Books edition: 1979

Grateful acknowledgment is made for use of the following material:

Excerpt taken from *Gurdjieff: Making a New World* by J. G. Bennett.
Copyright © 1973 by John G. Bennett. Reprinted by permission of
Harper & Row Publishers, Inc.

Excerpt taken from *Synergetics: The Geometry of Thinking* by
R. Buckminster Fuller and Edgar J. Applewhite. Copyright © 1975
by R. Buckminster Fuller. Reprinted with the permission of Macmillan
Publishing Co., Inc.

Drawings of body types from *The Body Reveals* by Ron Kurtz and
Hector Prestera. Copyright © 1976 by Ron Kurtz and Hector Prestera.
Reprinted with the permission of Harper & Row Publishers, Inc.

Drawing of the Enneagram of Fixations from "The Arica Training" by
John C. Lilly and Joseph E. Hart, in *Transpersonal Psyhologies*, edited
by Charles T. Tart. Copyright © 1975 by Harper & Row Publishers,
Inc. Reprinted by permission of the publisher and Dr. John Lilly.

The Self-Description Test of somatotype temperaments is reproduced
from "Physique and Self-Description of Temperament" by John B.
Cortes and Florence M. Gatti in *Journal of Consulting Psychology*,
1965, Vol. 29, No. 5, 432–39. Copyright © 1965 by the American
Psychological Association. Reprinted by permission of Professor Cortes
and the A.P.A.

The illustration of sexual types in Chapter 9, excerpted from *The
Circle of Sex* by Gavin Arthur. Copyright © 1966. Reprinted by permission of Lyle Stuart, Inc.

Library of Congress Cataloging in Publication Data

Metzner, Ralph.
  Know your type.

  Bibliography: p. 285.
  Includes index.
  1. Typology. I. Title.
BF698.M44   155.2'6
ISBN: 0-385-13162-3
Library of Congress Catalog Card Number 78–18142

This book is dedicated to my parents,
Wolfgang Metzner and
Jill Laurie Metzner

Contents

Preface   xi

Introduction   The Nature of Human Types   1

The Four Sources of Personal Characteristics. Personality, Character, Temperament. Stereotype, Prototype, Archetype. Interpersonal and Intrapersonal Understanding.

1 The Three Body Types   13

Research Findings on Somatotypes. Embryonic Basis of Somatotypes. Endomorphy-Viscerotonia. Mesomorphy-Somatotonia. Ectomorphy-Cerebrotonia. The Three Body Types in Religion and Culture. The Body Types and Evolution. Correlations with Astrology. Appendix: Somatotype Self-description Test.

2 The Four Humoral (Emotional) Types   37

Description of the Four Temperaments—Sanguine, Choleric, Phlegmatic, Melancholic. The Humors and Endocrine Types. A Modern Interpretation of the Humoral Typology. Emotional Balance and Relationships. Correlation with Body Types and Astrology. Appendix: Descriptive Self-test of the Four Humoral Types.

3 The Jungian Typology   55

Extraversion-Introversion. The Four Functions. The Four Functions and Time Consciousness. Empirical Findings Related to the Functional Typology. The Eight Functional Types. Individuation and the Development of the Functions. The Functional Types in Partnerships and Groups. The Jungian Types and Astrology.

4 The Evolutionary Typology of the Zodiac   75

Four Approaches to Astrology—Physical-Causal, Symbolic, Humanistic, Evolutionary. Sun, Moon, and Ascendant. Four Elements and Four Functions. The Three Air Signs (Libra, Aquarius, Gemini). The Three Water Signs (Cancer, Scorpio, Pisces). The Three Fire Signs (Aries, Leo, Sagittarius). The Three Earth Signs (Capricorn, Taurus, Virgo). Solar Progressions and Personal Growth. Appendix: Table of Sun's Progressions.

5 Planetary Types   111

Typology of the Lunation Cycle. Astrological Indicators of Planetary Prominence. Statistical Research of Michel Gauquelin. The Planetary Ruler. Edgar Cayce on Astrology. The Glandular Hypothesis. The Planetary Visions of Emanuel Swedenborg. Solar and Lunar Types. The Mercurial Type. Four Mental Types of the Mercury-Sun Cycle. The Venusian Type. The Martial Type. The Jupiter Type. The Saturnian Type. The Uranian Type. The Neptunian Type. The Plutonian Type.

6 Styles of Thinking   135

Visual vs. Nonvisual Thinking. Reflectivity-Impulsivity. Leveling-Sharpening. Field Dependence and Field Independence. Convergent and Divergent Thinking. Left-brain and Right-brain Thinking. The Left-right Polarity in Yoga, Mythology, and Folklore.

7 Political, Occupational, and Aesthetic Typologies   151

Personality Types and Political Attitudes. Vocational and Occupational Types. Executive Types and Managerial Styles. Personality Types and Aesthetic Styles. The Senses, the Elements, and the Arts.

8 Psychiatric Character Types   165

Development of Psychoanalytic Character Theory. The Hysterical Character. The Obsessive-compulsive Character. The Paranoid Character. The Masochistic Character. The Schizoid Character. The Dependent Character. The Psychopathic Character. Other Character Patterns. Character Disorders and Jung's Functional Typology.

9 *Types of Love and Sex*   183

Different Kinds of Love. Five Types on a Desert Island—A Test of Sexual Values. Personality Types and Sexual Behavior. Eastern Approaches to Sexual Typology. A Circular Typology of Sexual Preferences. The Development of Sexual Identities. Self-Evaluation of Sexual Identities. Interpersonal Relationship Balance.

10 *Oriental and Esoteric Typologies*   207

The Three *Gunas*. The Lunar Mansions of Hindu Astrology. The Twelve-year Cycle of Chinese Astrology. The Theory of the Seven Rays. The Arica Enneagram of Types. Gurdjieff's Typology of Human Development. The Science of Idiotism.

11 *The Typology of Numbers*   231

The Jungian Approach to Numerology. The Polarities of the Numbers. The Geometry of Consciousness. Symbolism of the Basic Number Series. Life-cycle Numbers. Personality (Name) Numbers. The Inner or Soul Name.

12 *Types of Consciousness—the Actualism Approach*   255

Sensitivity and the Human Energy Field. The Human Being as an Energy System. Types of Personality Consciousness and Their Polarities. On Transcending One's Type.

Epilogue   by Russell Paul Schofield   273

Appendix   A Typology of Ways of Growth   277

References   285

Index   295

Preface

Seven years ago I wrote a book called *Maps of Consciousness* to synthesize and integrate some of the major occult and oriental symbolic languages with current Western psychological formulations. The present book is a follow-up and extension of this bridging project, focusing particularly on individual consciousness and the typology of identity. During the intervening years I have been active as a student and teacher of the awareness techniques of Actualism, and also as a psychotherapist and astrologer. I have learned that differences in personality type are important for self-understanding and personal growth, as well as for interpersonal understanding and relationships. All types are within us; or, as the Roman poet said, "Nothing human is alien to me."

In studying and experimenting with the various type systems, I have come to realize that while these different maps of identity overlap greatly, they are not, in their present or past forms, identical to one another. They cannot be totally equated, however tempting it may be to assume or attempt this. The infinite spectrum of human variability may be analyzed and classified in numerous ways that are, hopefully, useful in coming to a better understanding of oneself and others. But these mappings cannot be taken as the last word or the final systematic truth about human individual differences. I trust and wish that this attempt at a synthesis will provide some hints and clues to the continuing puzzle of man's identity and the nature of his evolutionary design.

I would like to express my appreciation to the students at the California Institute of Asian Studies and John F. Kennedy University who took my courses on Human Typology and taught me a great deal. I would also like to express my gratitude to Russell Paul Schofield for contributing the Epilogue to the chapter on Actualism; and to Angeles Arrien, my love, for her unfailing support and encouragement in all phases of the work.

Introduction

The Nature of Human Types

Descriptions of human types are as old as man's inclination to reflect on human nature and to understand his relation to the universe. As a result, some symbolic typologies come down to us from very ancient times and the mythology and folklore of many cultures contain disguised allusions to the varieties of human temperament. For instance, the legend cycle of the twelve labors of Hercules has been interpreted as a series of tests and initiations for individuals with different dispositions. The marvelously humorous description of twenty-seven varieties of pigs found in the fifth book of the *Tumuripo*, the pre-Christian Hawaiian Chant of Creation, provides an intriguing allegory of human variability (Melville, 1969).

The sacred texts of the major religions often describe in legendary form the spectrum of human differences. In the Judaeo-Christian tradition, the story of the twelve tribes of Israel, descended from the twelve sons of Jacob, may be considered a kind of typology, and in the New Testament, the twelve disciples of Christ are said to exemplify the major human types. Another example is the typology of the three *gunas* described in the core sacred text of Hinduism, the *Bhagavad Gita*.

In Western philosophic-psychological literature, interest in human types goes back to the time of Plato and Aristotle, and the medical typology of Hippocrates. Plato, in *The Republic*, described five kinds of government and social organization, each associated with a particular type of individual. Aristotle, in his *Nicomacchean Ethics,* discussed many trait qualities of human nature as undesirable polar extremes, clustered around the golden mean of a virtue. Courage, for example, was the mean of which rashness and cowardice were the opposite polar extremes; meanness and prodigality were the excessive ends of a continuum, in which liberality was the golden mean. This kind of analysis has served as the prototype of many subsequent trait descriptions.

Despite this tradition, however, many contemporary westerners feel uncomfortable with the notion of human types, as if it were somehow undemocratic, and incompatible with their belief in human equality. But our equality is one of rights and privileges before the law, of social and economic opportunity, not of personal qualities, attributes, and temperaments. We use simple type systems all the time, and our minds can hardly avoid the cognitive necessity of categorizing people. We constantly classify by *stereotypes* of age (young, old, middle-aged), sex (male, female), intelligence (bright, dull), race and nationality, or by stereotypes of appearance (good-looking, plain, ugly), or psychological attitude (normal, neurotic, crazy). Perhaps the most common stereotype is a gross like-dislike categorization: "nice guy" vs. "bum," "sweet girl" vs. "bitch," or whatever the currently fashionable terminology is.

Types based on single dimensions or traits, such as most of those mentioned above, are generally misleading because they are overly simplistic, and encourage moralistic labeling in terms of "good" and "bad." This kind of evaluative bias has crept into many type-trait analyses. For instance, the famous Berkeley studies in the fifties of the authoritarian personality (Adornoa et al., 1950) implicitly contrasted the authoritarian fascist type with a "better" democratic personality type. Similarly, the recent study correlating "Type A" behavior with coronary disease (Friedman, 1974) depicts this pattern as pathological and its opposite as healthy, even though the latter may be associated with other diseases or problems.

It makes more sense to regard types as *clusters of traits,* or groups of personal qualities that constitute the pattern of an individual's nature. There is a hierarchy of levels of analysis: A type consists of several traits, which are made up of habits, which in turn are composed of series of specific stimulus-response patterns. For example, the extraverted type might consist of traits of dominance, sociability, aggressiveness, vitality, confidence, and so on. One of these traits—say, aggressiveness—might be analyzable in terms of specific habits of rude verbal behavior, discourteous gestures, making noise, rough physical contact, and others. These in turn could be further specified in terms of particular reflex-arc patterns of sensory stimulus and motor response.

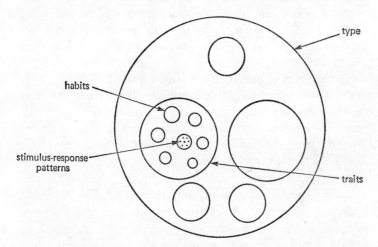

Physiological psychology confines itself to this last, most finely discriminative level of description and analysis. Behavior theory and behavior therapy largely focus on habits. The vast majority of personality research and psychiatric theorizing concerns itself with traits. Relatively few psychologists have been willing to take the leap to the next level of abstraction and simplification where, as ordinary laymen, we all regularly function. Notable exceptions to this are William Sheldon, Carl Jung, Wilhelm Reich, and psychologist Hans Eysenck, all of whom have made major contributions to typology that we will be discussing in this book.

The Four Sources of Personal Characteristics

Contemporary psychology attaches great importance to the distinction between phenotype and genotype. Phenotype is the "phenomenal type," the collection of traits and behavior patterns that appear outwardly in everyday life. Genotype is the "genetic type," the inherited biochemical constitution that, in combination with environmental factors, causes the outward phenotypical behavior. Personality tests and observations generally measure only the phenotype; inferences regarding the genotype require special, very rigorous laboratory and statistical procedures (for example, comparisons of twins with other pairs).

The question of the relative contribution of heredity vs. environment to the types discussed in this volume cannot therefore be easily decided. Generally, the assumption is that type structures, as well as traits, are fairly stable over time. In some theories, including Sheldon's somatotype theory and Eysenck's factorial system, causal explanations are offered in terms of underlying physiological-biochemical processes (for example, embryonic development or autonomic reactivity). This begins to approach analysis of the genotype system. However, we can only say that as far as psychology and current natural science are concerned, there are two main sources of personal qualities: heredity and environment, or nature and culture.

Taking a somewhat larger perspective, we know that belief in reincarnation has been a central feature of the esoteric traditions of most major religions. In modern times, the reincarnational point of view has been presented by occultists and psychics such as Edgar Cayce, Rudolf Steiner, and Alice Bailey. Steiner, in an essay on the esoteric basis of temperament, described temperament as a blending of inherited tendencies with tendencies derived from past life experiences—the ancestral pattern and the reincarnational pattern. If we are willing to consider, with an open mind, the occult point of view, we may add reincarnation as a third source of personal characteristics.

A fourth line of influence would be the astrological: the pattern of extraplanetary forces and energies. These may be regarded as an extension of environmental conditions beyond planet Earth. The planetary influences may not be of a causal nature, but rather indicative, as Jung suggested, of a kind of synchronistic correspondence. Nevertheless, for a more complete view of human nature they would have to be taken into account.

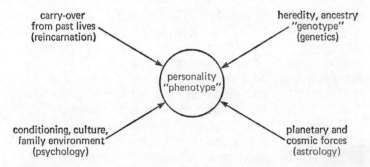

carry-over
from past lives
(reincarnation)

heredity, ancestry
"genotype"
(genetics)

personality
"phenotype"

conditioning, culture,
family environment
(psychology)

planetary and
cosmic forces
(astrology)

The sources of qualities, influences, and correspondences relating to human personality development may be diagrammed as above. To this model we must add, though we can hardly include it in the diagram, the role of the immortal Spirit, or Self. The occult tradition teaches that the incarnating Spirit enters by choice into the personality of each lifetime, choosing the time and place of birth, and hence the planetary conditions, as well as the parents and the familial-cultural context of personal development.

Personality is therefore not a passive recipient or victim of inevitable influences coming from the four sources that have been described. Such is the ancient conception of fate. Rather, we say that personality is shaped, molded, and blended by the creative hands of Spirit, using the qualities, elements, and attributes emanating from the four sources: heredity, cultural conditioning, incarnational history, and cosmic-planetary patterns.

Personality, Character, Temperament

The words used to describe variations in human nature are interesting clues to implicit belief-systems. The three terms "personality," "character," and "temperament" are generally used interchangeably, though their original meanings are very different.

"Personality" comes from *persona,* the mask used by actors in the Greco-Roman theater. The mask was held in front of the face and used "for sounding" (*"per-sonare"*). The term *persona* is also used by Jungians in the more specialized sense of a social mask or role that we play for others. Thus personality implies a pattern of outwardly apparent behavior, a role, a performance, a façade, something *expressed.* The question naturally arises: If personality is the outer mask, who is the actor? What is the Self that is expressing through the *persona?*

The term "character" is derived from words relating to tools used for writing and engraving. "Character" is still a synonym for "letter" (in the alphabetical sense). Thus this word connotes a mark being made, of something *impressed* on the world and on others. "Having character" is akin to having strength of character, or backbone. Again, the question that may be posed is: If character is the engraving or mark, who is the engraver? What is the Self that places its characteristic stamp or impression on the world?

The word "temperament" comes from the Latin *temperare,* to mix or blend in certain definite proportions. We know it in the concept of finely tempered steel, or the well-tempered clavichord, in which each tone is produced by a blend of three slightly different strings. On the planetary scale, an agreeable blend of humidity and warmth is referred to as a temperate climate. Temperament is historically associated with the medieval theory of the four humors, which needed to be blended harmoniously, and in the right proportions, for health and a balanced temperament. Incorrect or immoderate proportions would manifest as ill temper and bad humor. Evenly balanced, moderate qualities bring about what we call *temperance* in the individual. And again, one may well ask the question as to the nature of the Self who is blending the proportionate humors and qualities, and strengthening the supple alloy of temperament in the crucible of aware experience.

With each of these terms there is the definite implication of something or someone higher—the Spirit, or Higher Self, or Creator Self, or Atman, or Essence—for whom personality and character and temperament are the outer manifestations, or vehicles of expression. In ancient teachings, the personality is seen as self-extension, created by the immortal Self within. Each human being is a multidimensional, creative being, who has created personality vehicles at different levels of consciousness for self-expression.

We see that one of the values of thinking in terms of personality or character types, when considered in this light, is to point us toward our innermost being and to shift our perspective toward a more objective, inclusive point of view. We are not just a personality, any more than we are merely physical bodies. We *have* personalities, characters, bodies. We are *in* them, as aware, creative beings, although in various states of dissociated consciousness, ranging from normal lapses of awareness to severe psychopathology, we may be unaware of, and not in, our bodies and personalities.

Some other terms that are used at times in reference to human variability are "disposition," "constitution," and "individuality." Disposition is literally an arrangement, the way something is put together, how the parts are positioned. Constitution similarly connotes setup, organization, or makeup; it is generally used in reference to the physical aspects of man's function and structure. Individuality, which originally and literally means that which is undivided, indivisible, has come to be the term used for the integrated psychophysical totality: the unique, indivisible wholeness that results from the union, the *yoga*, of the personality self with the Higher Self.

Stereotype, Prototype, Archetype

We have already discussed some of the ways in which type classifications become destructive stereotypes. The danger of stereotypes lies in (1) their simplicity, which belies the complexity of human nature, and (2) their rigidity, which is not in accord with the ever-changing nature of life processes. Stereotyping is so notoriously insensitive and therefore damaging to interpersonal relationships that it has become the base of common expressions of verbal abuse. To call someone a "racist" or a "sexist" is not only to call attention to their stereotyping behavior, but also to practice insult and verbal aggression.

The obvious faults of stereotyping human behavior along simplistic trait categories should not, however, blind us to the real value of an awareness of the typical personality characteristics both in oneself and in others. Functional typology classifies people according to their goals and roles (rather than according to inherent qualities of worth or worthlessness), and has much to recommend it. We may categorize the managers in a business organization according to their characteristic managerial styles; or we may classify individuals according to the pattern of their personal relationships. We do not say one is better or worse than the other, but examine instead how well they accomplish their own purposes and goals. This can lead to enhanced respect and tolerance for individual differences of both purpose and method. Acknowledging that type categories are abstractions and that no individual ever fits one perfectly, we can nevertheless accept them as useful conceptual tools, a kind of symbolic code to facilitate interpersonal relationships.

In addition, since much human learning takes place by way of imitation, we can learn a great deal by studying individuals of different types than our own, and modeling our behavior after those who exhibit qualities we desire. Traditionally, one of the functions of the hero myth and of legends of gods and goddesses has been to provide the *prototypes* for given qualities of consciousness. In Greek astromythology, it was stated that the followers of Zeus tried to be like Zeus; those who admired Aphrodite or Hercules followed the examples set by their divine or semi-divine prototype. Zeus was the prototype of the warrior teacher, Apollo was the prototype of enlightened wisdom. In Indian mythology, Siva is the prototype of the yogi in deep meditation. These figures represent a higher, more evolved level of being that man can aspire to and emulate. Receptivity to the inspirational power of mythic prototypes is something the modern rational intellect has unfortunately lost, and would do well to try to recapture.

The concept of *archetype* (literally, chief or main type) has come to be particularly associated with the work of Carl Jung. In Jungian psychology archetypes are fundamental patterns of experience and activity found in the collective consciousness of the entire human species. They may appear in the consciousness of an individual—for example, in dreams—as thought-forms, symbols, personified figures, or ritualistic processes. They also appear, with uncanny frequency and regularity, in the myths, legends, folklore, and religious symbolism of every culture.

In their writings, Jung and his followers have described many archetypes: the Great Mother, the Anima, the Mandala, the Hero, the Wise Old Man, the Trinity, the Fish, the Tree of Life, and so forth. It must be emphasized that Jung distinguished between the archetype itself and its symbolic representation in dreams and myths. Thus, for example, Isis, Kali, Mary, and Demeter are all symbols, in varying forms, of the Great Mother archetype. The archetype itself is purely formal, according to Jung, existing as a pattern; it is comparable to the axial system of a crystal, around which the crystal forms itself.

Some of the typologies discussed in this volume, including the zodiac and planetary symbolism of astrology, and the number symbols used in numerology, are archetypal in the sense that they are based on fundamental structural-functional constants of the human collective psyche. Archetypes are normally outside of the range of individual awareness, but it is clear that in certain states of consciousness, in dreams, meditations, or visions, we do have direct personal access to them.

Archetypes contain the innate wisdom and vast creative power of the Spirit. It is not surprising that a number of cultures, including the American Indian, developed the practice of the vision quest, in which one sought for a direct experience of one's own archetypal symbol or totem. These primal forms represent essence qualities and features of the higher dimensions of our total being. In dreams, meditations, and states of heightened perception, they filter through to the everyday level of psychological functioning. Mythic prototypes and archetypal symbols function to awaken and inspire human awareness, tuning our minds, our feelings, our senses to the subtle energies of our own Higher Self, and to the evolutionary design of life on Earth. In this way they are not only conceptual tools that facilitate psychological understanding, but also spiritual tools that stimulate one's growth toward individuality and wholeness.

Interpersonal and Intrapersonal Understanding

The use and value of a typing system can be approached from two perspectives: interpersonal and intrapersonal. Interpersonally, a better understanding of individual differences leads to greater tolerance and respect for different individuals. In college classes where I have taught these typologies, I have suggested that for each type system the students try to categorize or type five individuals with whom they are well acquainted: themselves; their parents; their best friend, spouse, or lover; and their worst enemy. This has led to valuable insights and sometimes real breakthroughs in interpersonal communication. The reader might also like to apply the typologies in this way. In some instances a simple self-test is provided. In most cases, it is not hard to apply the type system directly both to oneself and to others. People who feel they have no enemies are encouraged to think of the person with whom they would least like to be stranded on a desert island. In the classes, we found that the "enemy" was sometimes of a very different type, with a kind of personal energy that clashed with the person's own. Not infrequently, however, the enemy turned out to have a very similar, if not identical, personality pattern. Recognizing this can lead to provocative, eye-opening insights, especially also in relationship to one's parents, who may have been temperamentally very different from their child and from each other.

In a recent paper on Jung's typology Osmond, Siegler, and Smoke state that according to his own account, Jung's purpose in constructing his typology

> was to understand the differences between his own outlook and those of Freud and Adler. He attributed the failure in mutual understanding among the analysts to differences in temperament, and hoped that his typology would enable them to see that each had a different but equally valid psychology based on his own type. . . . He felt that people were so imprisoned in their own type that they could not fully understand the viewpoint of someone of another type [Osmond et al., 1977, p. 206].

Thus his typology was originally constructed to help resolve interpersonal differences. In his own work and that of his followers, however, the emphasis shifted from the interpersonal to the intrapsychic. People were seen as having all the four functions, in different degrees, rather than being of one set functional type. Similarly, in Sheldon's body-type system, people are recognized as having each of the three structural traits, with one dominant. In astrology also, while there is a typology of zodiac signs, the personality pattern as portrayed in the horoscope is composed of planets and points in several, if not all, of the signs.

From the intrapsychic point of view, the question and task concerns the degree to which the person has balanced or equalized the component elements of his psyche. In Jungian terms, for instance, one asks to what degree the individual has integrated his inferior function. In teachings of evolutionary-spiritual development it is an ancient tradition that one needs to round out one's talents and abilities, develop one's underdeveloped function, integrate the head, the heart, and the body.

Wholeness involves a synthesizing and unifying of opposite and apparently contradictory or unrelated elements within the psyche.

An interesting and productive paradox is posed here. On the one hand there is the goal of rounding out, synthesizing, expanding one's range of awareness and ability. On the other there is the goal of finding one's particular mission, one's unique and special purpose in life, and actualizing that specific plan. For instance, should an individual choose a teacher or therapist to work with who is of the same type, or a very different type? If there is not an affinity, there may not be much relationship or communication. On the other hand, by working with someone very different one could learn much about the less developed side of one's nature. Yogananda, in his *Autobiography of a Yogi,* provides a fascinating portrait of a devotional type as disciple of an intellectual type.

I leave it to the reader to consider and evaluate the apparent incompatibility in the two statements of the evolutionary goal. My own view is that both are true and valid goals: One can be rounded out and well balanced, and yet also be a specialist with unique mastery in a chosen field of endeavor. With either program, however, by knowing one's own type one comes to a better understanding of one's strengths and limitations. A true and valid type system provides a map of the psychic space in which an individual lives and functions. Objectivity in regard to the manifestations of personality and character allows one to transcend limited and conditioned points of view. Recognizing one's own personality self and the unique integrity of the immortal Self leads also to the recognition of the special and precious uniqueness of the other, any other with whom we relate. And in knowing our type, we can affirm and validate the motto of the wisdom oracle of ancient Greece, inscribed over the entrance to the temple of Apollo:

"Man, Know Thy Self."

1

The Three Body Types

Intuitively and colloquially, we recognize the relationship between physique and temperament. We speak of the "fat and jolly" character, epitomized in the round merriment of Santa Claus and in numerous other figures of literature and legend, from Shakespeare's comic Falstaff to the pot-bellied, laughing Buddhas of Chinese Zen. On the other hand, the "thin, nervous" type is also well known, and recognizable in literary and historical figures such as the brooding Hamlet; the thoughtful, dignified Lincoln; or the miserly Scrooge. Shakespeare's Julius Caesar expressed a commonly felt discomfort with the nervous tension of the ectomorph when he said, "Let me have men about me that are fat; sleek-headed men, and such as sleep o' nights. Yon Cassius has a lean and hungry look; he thinks too much. Such men are dangerous."

Many attempts were made, by researchers in the past hundred years, to establish a scientific base for the belief, held since ancient times, in a relationship between body build and personality. It was William Sheldon, psychologist and physician, who made the most extensive and successful investigations. He developed a method, called somatotyping, of classifying people according to their ratings on three scales—endomorphy, mesomorphy, and ectomorphy. The method was tested and validated on thousands of individuals.

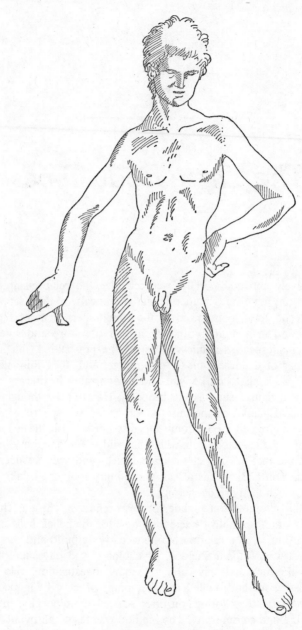

Ectomorph.

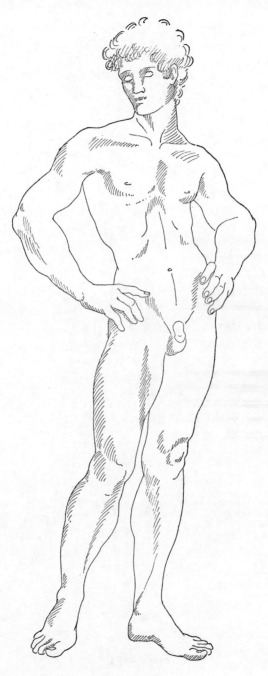

Mesomorph.

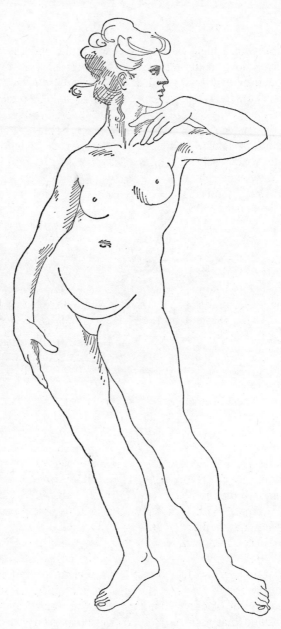

Endomorph.

A person with a high score on the first scale, endomorphy, and relatively low on the other two, is the classic endomorph with a round or oval body outline, protuberant belly and buttocks, and soft, fleshy features. A man with a high score on mesomorphy has the classic muscular, athletic physique, with broad shoulders and narrow hips giving a roughly triangular body outline. A female mesomorph is the buxom, voluptuous type, with broader pelvis giving the "hourglass" figure. A person high on ectomorphy and low on the other two has a relatively flat, linear body outline, with a long, somewhat fragile structure and finely chiseled features.

There are, of course, numerous variations, mixtures, and in-between types. For example, a person high on both endomorphy and mesomorphy—that is, fat *and* muscular—would be recognized as the thick-set, stocky type. A person of mixed mesomorphy and ectomorphy would exemplify the various gradations of svelte and slender figures in the female, or characteristics of wiry strength, physical speed, and agility in the male. Sheldon found that endomorphy, and endomorphic-ectomorphic mixtures, were more common in women, whereas mesomorphy and endomorphic-mesomorphic mixtures were more often found in men.

Sheldon and his successors developed quite precise and reliable measurements of body characteristics, involving indices of depth of fat tissue, length of muscles and bones, surface-mass ratios, height-weight ratios, and others. One basic measure is the trunk index, which compares the relative sizes of the upper torso (thoracic trunk) and lower torso (abdominal trunk). In the mesomorph the thoracic is larger; in the endomorph the abdominal is larger. With a little practice it is relatively easy to classify oneself and others on an approximate basis.

Sheldon also developed several secondary measures of constitutional type. One of these is *dysplasia,* the degree of somatotypic inconsistency among the different regions of the body. For example, a highly dysplasic individual may have the head-neck area typical of one somatotype and the legs of another. Sheldon found that there is more dysplasia in groups of psychotic patients than among normal individuals.

Another secondary component is called *gyandromorphy* (the "g index"), the degree to which the physique possesses qualities usually found in the opposite sex. A male high in this component possesses a soft body, broad pelvis, wide hips as well as other more feminine features such as long eye lashes and smallish face. Another secondary component, to which Sheldon attached great importance, is the *textural aspect* (the "t component")—the degree of fineness of skin texture and hair. Sheldon felt that this could be regarded as an index of "aesthetic pleasingness." Personology, which is a system of psychological trait analysis based on facial features, regards fineness of skin texture as a basic indicator of psychological sensitivity (Whiteside, 1974).

The work of Sheldon established three distinct temperamental attitudes correlated with the body types, and these correlations have been confirmed in many subsequent studies. It is important to remember, however, that correlation does not imply causation. We cannot say the body type *causes* the temperament, or vice versa. We do know that the different physical types have tendencies or proclivities in certain directions.

These tendencies can, and often are, masked or compensated for by the person's deliberate efforts. An example would be the ectomorphic "ninety-seven-pound weakling" who takes a Charles Atlas course, or the endomorphic fat lady who goes on a diet. Glandular imbalance or disease conditions can also mask the basic constitution. In Sheldon's system the measures of somatotype are presumed to be fairly stable over time, provided there is a fair degree of nutritional constancy and no gross pathology.

Generally, the norm of desirability and current cultural ideal tend toward the middle or mesomorphic part of the spectrum. Other cultures, and other historical periods, have had different structural ideals. The high valuation of mesomorphy in our Western culture has caused much anguish to those who happen to possess more endomorphic or ectomorphic physiques.

Before proceeding to a description of the types, it is suggested that the reader take the simple self-description test derived from the work of Cortes and Gatti given in Appendix

A to this chapter. This provides comparative evaluation of the temperamental qualities associated with the three types. After taking the test, it can be scored using the key found in Appendix B. One ends up with three numbers, representing the relative proportions of the endomorphic, mesomorphic, and ectomorphic characteristics in personality.

Research Findings on Somatotypes[1]

1. The basic finding of a correlation between physical type and temperament has been replicated several times, in different groups, including male and female college students, convicts, schoolchildren, even nursery-school children.

2. Sheldon and Eleanor Glueck of Harvard University found that juvenile delinquents tended to be more mesomorphic and less ectomorphic than nondelinquent adolescents. This finding has also been replicated. Note that it does *not* imply that mesomorphs are more delinquent than ectomorphs.

3. The mesomorphic delinquents were found, by interview and ratings, to be generally more energetic, impulsive, aggressive, and extraverted, and less submissive to authority than nondelinquents.

4. Sheldon found that ectomorphs, as a group, generally have a higher subjectively felt need for sex, as expressed in imagined choice situations. This does not necessarily imply greater sexual activity or potency. It is simply an indication of how important sex is to the person.

5. Psychological masculinity is positively correlated with mesomorphy, and structural femininity in males (gyandromorphy) is negatively correlated with mesomorphy. Physical lifting strength is markedly greater in mesomorphs than in the other types.

6. The Allport-Vernon test of values measures a person's relative interests in six classes of values: theoretical, economic, political, aesthetic, social, and religious. Males generally obtain

[1] The studies summarized here are described in Hall and Lindzey (1970), and Cortes and Gatti (1972).

higher scores on the first three (theoretical, economic, political); females generally score higher on the other three (aesthetic, social, religious). Researchers found that mesomorphic types generally scored higher on the three "male" value systems, and low on the "female" values. This was true for both men and women. Thus muscular mesomorphic females tended to score higher on male values than on female values.

7. The "need for achievement" test developed by David McClelland measures this motive by looking at the themes of stories, written by the subject in response to pictures of people in everyday, but ambiguous, situations. It has been found that, in both delinquent and normal groups, mesomorphs had higher than average need for achievement, whereas ectomorphs had significantly lower than average. People with a high need for achievement, measured in this way, have independently been shown to have high psychological energy, to be enterprising and willing to take risks (though not extreme chances).

8. In investigation of the body type of psychotic individuals, Sheldon found that three major classes of psychiatric disorder could be related to the three body types; endomorphs were more prone to the manic-depressive type of emotional disturbance; mesomorphs were more likely to have paranoid or delusional types of psychosis; and ectomorphs were more likely to develop the schizophrenic withdrawal syndrome.

Embryonic Basis of Somatotypes

It was Sheldon's belief that the three different body types developed out of relative dominance of one of the three layers of the developing embryo. He named the three types of physique on that basis.

To recapitulate the process of embryonic development briefly: the fertilized egg-cell divides into two cells, then four, eight, sixteen, and so forth, until it becomes a ball or mass of cells known as a morula. As the cells continue multiplying, this mass becomes a hollow sphere, known as a blastula. This in turn caves in and becomes cup-shaped—and at this stage is

EMBRYONIC DEVELOPMENT

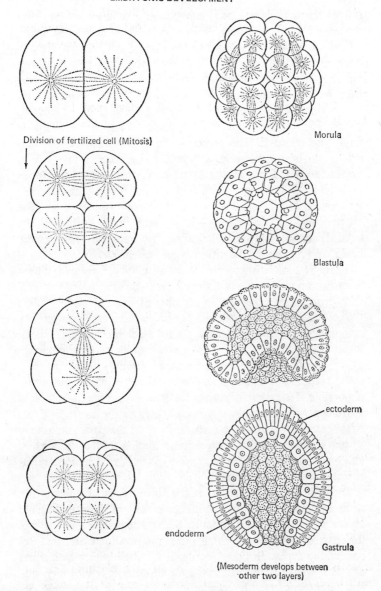

Division of fertilized cell (Mitosis)

Morula

Blastula

ectoderm

endoderm

Gastrula

(Mesoderm develops between other two layers)

called a gastrula. Within this gastrula, the germ cells are arranged in three layers, which eventually differentiate to form the major organ systems of the body. The innermost layer, called the *endoderm,* gives rise to most of the internal visceral organs, including the entire digestive tract, liver, pancreas, and bladder, as well as the respiratory system, and the thymus, thyroid, and parathyroid glands. The middle layer, or *mesoderm,* is the origin of the circulatory system (heart, blood vessels, spleen), as well as of the muscles, bones, connective tissue, kidneys, and adrenals. The reproductive system is generally considered to be mesodermic, although some sources relate it to the endoderm. Even in the latter case, however, the arteries and veins of that system would of course be mesodermic. The outermost layer, known as the *ectoderm,* becomes the outer coverings of the body—skin, nails, hair, teeth, and the central nervous system (including the sensory systems, the brain, and its glands, the pituitary and pineal).

There is some disagreement among embryologists in regard to the autonomic nervous system. The two branches of this system (sympathetic and parasympathetic) control and regulate the mostly involuntary internal functions such as digestion, circulation, reproductive activity, heat maintenance, and others. Some authorities attribute these nerve systems to the ectoderm, along with the central nervous system (brain, spinal cord, and sense receptors). There is, however, some evidence indicating a possible derivation of sympathetic nerves (which stimulate movement, constrict blood vessels, energize the heart, activate stress responses) from the mesoderm. And the parasympathetic system (which mediates digestion, dilation of blood vessels, and generally pleasurable relaxation) is at least functionally associated with the endoderm.

Thus Sheldon theorized that the three types of constitution were grounded in the predominance of one of these embryonic layers and their related systems. Some scientists do not accept this part of his theory; which does not invalidate the findings concerning types. In other words, it is possible to classify and describe people according to the threefold typology of physique and temperament without relating the types to embryonic development. It does seem to make a good deal of intuitive sense to think of the endomorph as gut-dominant ("viscerotonic"), the mesomorphic character as muscle-dominant ("somatotonic"), and the ectomorph as nerve-dominant ("cerebrotonic").

There is also some anatomical evidence that supports the embryological hypothesis.[2] Autopsies have verified that endomorphs have significantly longer and larger guts, as well as bigger livers, pancreases, thymuses, and stomachs, while ectomorphs have the smallest digestive organs. Heart, kidneys, adrenals, muscles, and bones are large and prominent in mesomorphic bodies. Ectomorphs are the lowest in size of bones and muscles, though they are the tallest of the three types. Their brains and sense organs are the same absolute size as those of the other types, and therefore of relatively greater size when compared to the other organ systems of their bodies.

It is a useful exercise in body awareness to *tune in* to the consciousness of the organ systems associated with the three types, or embryonic layers. One can simply sit quietly, let one's mind dwell effortlessly on the respective systems, and observe the thoughts, feelings, and sensations that rise up into awareness. Without wanting to prejudge the perceptions that may occur, one does appear to experience ease and relaxation from the endomorphic organs, energy and movement from the mesomorphic, and sensitivity and alertness from the ectomorphic. Generally, one gets the least impression from the organs associated with the least developed of the three components.

Endomorphy-Viscerotonia

The endomorphic type basically comes across as a calm, easygoing, affable, sympathetic, affectionate person. His humor is of the amiable, jovial kind. Not all endomorphs are neces-

[2] The anatomical and embryological evidence is described in detail in Appendix II of *Delinquency and Crime* by John B. Cortes and Florence M. Gatti (1972).

sarily good-humored, though, some being more of a lethargic, heavy, dense disposition. They have the ability to cry "real crying, sobbed up wholebelliedly from the depths of the abdomen," as Sheldon picturesquely phrased it. The viscerotonic is close to the soil, earthy, practical, and rooted in a realistic acceptance of the world.

As the endomorphic body consciousness is focused in the digestive system, there is an emphasis on food intake. This may be sublimated to a gourmet's appreciation of the aesthetics of fine cuisine, or, in coarser types, may deteriorate into hoglike, pot-bellied gluttony. Obesity and flabbiness can be real problems if the vegetative tendency is not checked by exercise.

Viscerotonics like to drink, as well as eat and smoke, but do not seem to become alcoholics as often as the other two types. They can handle more food and drink than others. They also tend to sleep a lot, and generally appear overrelaxed, slow, or even sluggish in their reactions compared to the quick, nervous cerebrotonics. Viscerotonics also have good thermal adaptability, enjoying both warm and cold weather.

Psychologically, the endomorphs tend to relate to life experience in a passive, receptive, dependent manner, regarding it as something to be absorbed and assimilated. This attitude makes for tolerance and acceptance of individual difference, as well as qualities of warmth and forbearance. However, it can also degenerate into excessive complacency and lack of motivation, a tendency to drift along with indiscriminate amiability toward all and everything. Some endomorphs come across with a kind of puppylike affection that strikes others as smothering and sentimental. They need to cultivate discrimination in the way they handle their emotional expression.

The focus on digestion, assimilation, and intake leads to a characteristic attitude of physical resilience and courage. Their whole demeanor seems to say, "I can take it." They have intestinal fortitude, a gutsiness that takes on the world even if their physical bodies spread under the burden and their feelings become depressed. Their solidity and predictability give them an air of trustworthiness, and they are generally trusted by others.

At its best, the endomorphic type has a vast capacity for acceptance and Taoist fluidity. They can be a combination of massive calm strength and good-humored conviviality. Endomorphic women have the exuberant ampleness portrayed in Rubens' paintings, or the soft sensuousness found in a Renoir nude.

Mesomorphy-Somatotonia

The mesomorphic type is action-oriented—they are the actors, the athletes, the executives, the achievers, the fighters. They love a vigorous life of challenges, obstacles, hardships to overcome. They are interested in making an impact on the world, in doing rather than merely experiencing. With body consciousness dominated by the muscular and circulatory systems, they are into movement and physical expressiveness. Compared to the viscerotonics, they are less interested in interpersonal relationships and affections, and are therefore often perceived by others as insensitive and arrogant.

Physically, mesomorphs are typically strong, well-proportioned, and exude a confident, energetic optimism. They tend to be morning people, who love walks and other forms of exercise, bright weather and mountains, and rough, dynamic forms of play. Of the three types, mesomorphs are the most athletic, with a marked preference for energetic, competitive sports such as tennis, speed sports such as skiing, and strength sports such as football. (The preferred sport of the endomorph appears to be swimming, and of the ectomorph long-distance running and similar solitary sports.) Mesomorphs do have a tendency to drive themselves to the degree of becoming subject to ulcers and coronary problems. Here we may find the go-getting achievement obsession that has recently been called Type A behavior and linked with heart disease.

The humor of the somatotonic is basically cheerful, bright, and enthusiastic. They are able to inspire others, but they also like mental contests and arguments. However, they are not as guarded and fearful as cerebrotonics: Somatotonics generally have an open, guileless face and attitude. Overeating can make them fat, and they can thus be mistaken for endomorphs. High blood pressure is also common in this type. From watching children at play, Sheldon concluded that mesomorphs seem to be more tolerant of noise generally, and also contribute more noise than others.

Their strong external orientation, if not balanced by conscious cultivation of inner values, can cut them off from their own subjective feelings and inner perceptions. Thus they tend to have relatively sparse dream recall. If they get involved in a religious, philosophic, or spiritual pursuit, they typically tend to adopt it with a wholehearted enthusiasm bordering on fanaticism. If they lack the ectomorphic traits of analytic and objective mentality, their subjective thinking can become self-righteous and self-justifying to the point of delusion and paranoia.

Unless they also have a strong endomorphic component in their temperament, mesomorphs generally have difficulty accepting the flow of life's changes, particularly the natural processes of growing old. As they idealize youth, they do not age gracefully. Mesomorphs tend to cultivate physical beauty and often produce the most pleasing kinds of physique: the balanced, powerful musculature in the male, and the voluptuously curved limbs of the female.

The great strength of the somatotonic character is the confident, energetic expression of willpower in action—the qualities of vitality and enterprise. However, somatotonics need to develop their sensitivity to inner states, which will increase their responsiveness and consideration toward others. In this way they can forestall the buildup of stress conditions in their heart and emotional nature.

Ectomorphy-Cerebrotonia

Ectomorphs are nerve- and skin-oriented in their body consciousness. Their nerves seem closer to the surface then those of the other two types, with less padding by either fat or muscle, like exposed "feelers," sensitized to the point of being raw. The nervous reaction of the ectomorph to life experience is strong, even vehement, compared to the easygoing affability of the endomorph and the dynamic mobility of the mesomorph. As a result ectomorphs tend to withdraw into a protective seclusion, either physically or psychically. Often this comes across to others as a dislike for people, which, in part, it is. But it is primarily a deeply felt need for privacy, to enable their high-strung nervous systems to handle the often overwhelming influx of perceptions and sensations, both pleasant and unpleasant.

Because of the conflicting surges of sense impressions and emotional reactions to them, the ectomorph often has difficulty balancing and stabilizing the energy distribution processes of his body. He or she may become diabetic (too much blood sugar) or hypoglycemic (not enough sugar). Eating habits and sleep patterns may be erratic, leading to chronic lassitude and physical debilitation. The level of nervous tension and anxiety is usually high; skin problems and bowel problems are not unusual. Basal metabolic rate and thyroid activity are often elevated; and thus ectomorphs never seem to gain weight, no matter how much they eat.

According to Sheldon's observations, cerebrotonics generally have poor voice control and can rarely sing well. He attributes their inability to project their voices to a "paralysis of over-awareness" and inhibition. This kind of cerebral overcontrol seems to afflict ectomorphs particularly in emotional situations such as Shakespeare's Hamlet described, where "conscience does make cowards of us all; and thus the native hue of resolution is sicklied o'er with the pale cast of thought." Hamlet was a typical ectomorph.

The ectomorph's hyperactive nervous system has a difficult time handling the powerful forces of sex. While the reproductive organs themselves stem from the mesoderm, the nerves associated with them come from the ectoderm. Hence the sex drive, to ectomorphs, often seems like an uncontrollable, almost demonic force that threatens to overwhelm or engulf them. Sexual problems are not uncommon. They don't seem to be capable of the leisurely, placid affections of the endomorph, or the active aggressiveness of the mesomorph. Ectomorphs' sensual feelings are strong, but inhibitors and conditioning influences are also strong—hence one may find a pattern of initial shyness followed by strong potency, or of sexual activity only under certain specific, limited conditions of privacy or relaxation.

While ectomorphs have keen perceptual abilities, they also have very active minds, which cause them to make judgments about whatever they perceive. Though brain/mind oriented, cerebrotonics may or may not be very intelligent, literate, or knowledgeable. Nor is intelligence necessarily correlated with cerebrotonia. Each of the three types seems to have a different kind of intelligence.

Cerebrotonics do have a tendency to be critical, superior, judgmental, and suspicious. They are guarded and cautious in their expression, and typically come out with thoughts and ideas that are surprising and unexpected to others. You never know what they are thinking, though you know they are thinking something. Their sense of humor, which is basically verbal and often takes the form of wit, can become laced with sarcasm and ridicule. They need to cultivate the endomorph's warm exchange of feelings in emotional relationships to soften the harsh edges of judgmentalism with tolerance and love. They could also benefit by the development of some of the mesomorph's initiative and forthrightness to overcome their anxious sense of distance and detachment.

The ectomorph's great strength lies in his keen capacity for objective observation; in quick, sensitive learning and communication; and in clear understanding of facts and information. Physically, ectomorphic women have a slender, delicate, almost fragile beauty; and the men at best a quality of lean, electrical masculinity and wiry strength.

The Three Body Types in Religion and Culture

Perhaps the most concise summary statement about their respective attitudes to life is that the endomorph *lets it happen,* the mesomorph *makes it happen,* and the ectomorph *watches it happen.*

We may imagine the scene of an accident, at which a representative of each of the three types happened to be present. The mesomorph would be the one to quickly jump in, take charge, and take action. The endomorph would offer expressions of sympathy and encouragement. The ectomorph would observe and comment on the situation.

Sheldon found that sleep positions could be used as a useful discriminator among the types. Ectomorphs tend to sleep curled up on their sides, in a fetal position. Endomorphs sleep in a limp, sprawling mass. And mesomorphs sleep with much vigorous movement and thrashing about—they seem to dream with their muscles, like many mammals.

From the point of view of growth and individuation, one would see that all three attitudes are valid phases of self-expression that need to be blended according to the nature of the situation for balanced relationships and activity. The endomorph's flexibility and acceptance can balance the aggressiveness of the mesomorph and the detached rigidity of the ectomorph. On the other hand, the energetic enthusiasm typical of the mesomorph could in many situations benefit and complement the endomorph's indolence and the ectomorph's withdrawal and anxious distance. Finally, the discriminative perceptiveness typical of the ectomorphic character is often a needed counterpoint to the endomorph's sentimental mushiness and the mesomorph's bluntness and insensitivity.

Sheldon felt that the world's major religions seemed to have favored one or another of the types at different periods. Taoism and Buddhism seem to have been generally more viscerotonic in their attitudes, for instance, and more endomorphic representations are found in the religious art of this Far Eastern tradition. While we have seen pot-bellied Buddhas, we have never had a pot-bellied Jesus.

Aldous Huxley, in his *Perennial Philosophy,* took up this theme and pointed out the correlation between the three body types and the traditional three ways to deliverance or spiritual enlightenment, as expounded in the *Bhagavad Gita:* the "way of works" corresponding to somatotonia, the "way of devotion" to viscerotonia, and the "way of knowledge" to cerebrotonia.

He felt that Indian Buddhism, along with Hindu Vedanta and traditional Christianity, was definitely contemplative-cerebrotonic in its attitude. On the other hand, Confucianism, with its emphasis on familial, worldly values, could be seen as more viscerotonic (along with Far Eastern Buddhism); and Islam, with later Christianity, as emphasizing the somatotonic element (as, for example, in "Holy Wars" and the "Church Militant").

In a somatotype study of 124 historical paintings of Christ, carried out by Sheldon and some of his students, it was found that his average score was 2–3–5, or predominantly ectomorphic. The picture changed, however, in the twentieth century. After World War I, Christ paintings depicted him with a higher mesomorphic component. Traditional Christian teachings of restraint and sensory inhibition can be seen as a religious formulation of a cerebrotonic attitude.

In Hinduism there is a doctrine of *three gunas* (discussed in more detail in Chapter 10), which has a remarkable parallelism to the three somatotypes. The gunas are thought of as the interweaving strands of energy that make up the universal substance at all levels, from macrocosmic to human. *Sattva* is the quality of radiant awareness, *rajas* the quality of action and movement, and *tamas* the quality of inertia and mass. At the level of human consciousness the sattvic mentality was said to be calm and clear; the rajasic mind restless and driven by impulses; the tamasic mind slow, heavy, and obscure. Someone with an excess of *rajas* (somatotonia) would be hyperexcitable, violent, even manic. Someone with an excess of *tamas* (viscerotonia) would be prone to depressive, lethargic states. Someone with an excess of *sattva* (cerebrotonia) was said to manifest extreme sensuality and curiosity.

The problem of racial types has also been examined from the somatotypic point of view. Robert Lenski (1976) has analyzed Sheldon's original published data and divided the sample into different geographical-racial groupings. Some interesting differences in body-type distributions were found, which could form the basis for a constitutional study of national character. The group called Nordics were found to be predominantly mesomorphic and ectomorphic, and low in endomorphy. By

contrast, European Jews, Alpine, and mixed Alpine-Mediter-
ranean groups were found to be predominantly meso- and endomorphic, and lower in ectomorphy. The differences are not
very great, but seem to fit some of the classic conceptions of
national temperament.

The Body Types and Evolution

Sheldon proposed that endomorphy-viscerotonia was the primary, or oldest component of constitution from an evolutionary perspective:

> The elemental business of digestion may probably be
> taken as the first and oldest biological function. In the
> beginnings of life, among the simplest animals and
> throughout the plant kingdom, this function appears
> to constitute, together with reproduction, both the
> ends and the means of existence. The entire body of a
> tree may be described as a specialized digestive, re-
> productive and circulatory apparatus. The body of an
> ameba may be in some ways less differentiated and
> specialized than that of a tree, but the ameba's sun of
> life appears so clearly to rise and set in the pursuit of
> basic viscerotonic activities, that motivationally an
> ameba would probably have to be described as a
> 7–1–1 [*Varieties of Human Temperament,* p. 256].

The body or soma could be regarded as a kind of fortified
carriage built around the viscera, and thus somatotonia is called
the second component. The organs of movement and physical
structure developed greatly in various ways throughout animal
evolution before cerebral dominance came into existence.

> The first beginnings of an animal skeleton are simply
> a hardening or toughening of swimming appendages
> which by vibration assist protozoa in locomotion and
> hence in the pursuit of food. As the ladder of animal
> complexity is ascended the chief changes encountered
> at precerebral levels are changes in the direction of

greater complexity and efficiency of bodily movement.
The skeleton with its muscular attachments develops
into many experimental forms, serving both as an aid
to locomotion and prehension, and as a defense
against predatory attack [op. cit., p. 268].

The third component, ectomorphic cerebrotonia, seems to
function principally as a restraining, screening, and selectively
inhibiting mechanism toward visceral and somatic function. Ec-
stasy for cerebrotonics is freedom from, and transcendence of,
the demands and impulses of the viscera and soma. As a result,
their greatest danger is dissociation from objective reality. Ectomorphs are much more prone to schizophrenia than the other
two types. "The freedom of the forebrain is likely to be
purchased at the price of a biological losing of the way" (Sheldon, op. cit., p. 276). A. T. W. Simeons has written persua-
sively of the psychosomatic distress symptoms caused by the
dissociative activity of the neocortex in *Man's Presumptuous
Brain.*

A striking convergence exists between these speculations
concerning human evolution, first published by Sheldon in
1942, and the recent formulations of the tri-une brain by
neuroanatomist Paul MacLean. According to MacLean's researches, described in Carl Sagan's book *The Dragons of Eden,*
the brain may be considered a three-level structure surrounding
the primitive neural chassis of brain stem and spinal cord.

The first structure, called the reptilian complex, evolved several hundred million years ago and is found in all reptiles and
subsequent species. It is most closely connected to the neural
chassis, in which digestive functions are controlled. It mediates
territoriality, aggressive behavior, ritual, and the establishment
of social hierarchies. The second brain structure MacLean calls
the limbic system, and evolved in mammals around 150 million
years ago. It is associated with motion and emotion, and with
sex, smell, and memory. The third level of brain organization is
the neocortex, found principally in advanced mammals (including dolphins and whales), primates, and man. It is the
locus of the anticipatory functions and hence of anxiety and in-

ventiveness. Speech, symbolism, reason, and perception all seem to be connected to this level of the brain.

There is clearly a provocative degree of correlation between this theory of brain evolution and Sheldon's ideas concerning the evolution of the constitutional components. Sheldon's remarks concerning trees can be applied equally well to reptiles: A snake is essentially a digestive tract with some additional systems. The viscerotonic tendency to habit formation has an echo in the reptilian brain's proclivity for ritualistic behavior. The mammalian brain is evidently the stage for evolution's experiments in motion. The verbal emphasis of the cerebrotonic fits with speech localization in the neocortex.

However, there are also some discrepancies. Emotion, linked by MacLean to the mammalian brain, is associated in Sheldon's model with the first, or viscerotonic, component. Future research will have to determine whether there is in fact a reliable functional-structural relationship among the layers of embryonic development, the evolutionary layering of brain systems, and the constitution of character types. The suggested correspondences are summarized in Table 1.

TABLE 1

Suggested Correspondences with Constitution

constitutional type	viscerotonic	somatotonic	cerebrotonic
embryonic layer	endoderm	mesoderm	ectoderm
primary function	digestion	movement	perception
dominant organs	viscera	muscles/bones	brain/nerves
attitude	acceptance	activity	observation
gunas	tamas	rajas	sattva
brain structure	reptilian	mammalian (limbic)	primate/human (neocortex)

Correlations with Astrology

Some astrologers, notably Ruth Hale Oliver, have worked out correspondences of the body types with the astrological symbolism of the planets. The idea here is that there is a natural affinity between each of the types and certain of the planets. These planets would then be expected to be strongly accentuated in a person's natal chart, either by rulership, angular position, strength of aspect, or midpoint configuration. As yet, these correlations are theoretical and symbolic only, since the empirical research to validate them has not been done.

The "endomorphic planets" are those classically referred to as female in polarity: Venus, the Moon, and Neptune. Jupiter, although not female, is also included in this group, because of its expansive influence. It is said that people with Jupiter near the ascendant, especially in water signs, are prone to obesity. Similarly, medical astrology associates Venus with the kidney-bladder system and venous circulation; the Moon with the lymphatic system; and Jupiter with the liver and, to a lesser degree, the pancreas.

The "mesomorphic planets" are those that are classically known as male in polarity: Sun, Mars, Pluto, and Jupiter again, if in supportive aspects to these masculine planets. The Sun rules the heart and arterial system, Mars the muscular system, Pluto the reproductive system. Saturn could also be considered part of this group, since it rules the skeletal system and connective tissues.

The "ectomorphic planets" are those generally considered neutral or bipolar in their expression. Here we have Mercury, which rules the nervous systems and brain; Uranus, which also affects the perception and communication systems of the body; and Saturn again, in its association with the skin, and also with mental constructs.

In a later chapter we shall see that there is also considerable correspondence in the psychological symbolism of the planets and what has been said of the three constitutional temperaments.

Appendix A   Somatotype Self-description Test[3]

1. Most of the time I feel _____, _____, and _____.

calm	relaxed	complacent
anxious	confident	reticent
cheerful	tense	energetic
contented	impetuous	self-conscious

2. When I study or work, I seem to be _____, _____, and _____.

efficient	sluggish	precise
enthusiastic	competitive	determined
reflective	leisurely	thoughtful
placid	meticulous	co-operative

3. Socially, I am _____, _____, and _____.

outgoing	considerate	argumentative
affable	awkward	shy
tolerant	affected	talkative
gentle-tempered	soft-tempered	hot-tempered

4. I am rather _____, _____, and _____.

active	forgiving	sympathetic
warm	courageous	serious
domineering	suspicious	soft-hearted
introspective	cool	enterprising

5. Other people consider me rather _____, _____, and _____.

generous	optimistic	sensitive
adventurous	affectionate	kind
withdrawn	reckless	cautious
dominant	detached	dependent

6. Underline *one* word in each set of three that most closely describes you.

assertive, relaxed, tense	confident, tactful, kind
hot-tempered, cool, warm	dependent, dominant, detached
withdrawn, sociable, active	enterprising, affable, anxious

[3] Adapted, with permission, from Cortes and Gatti (1965).

Appendix B   Key to Self-description

ENDOMORPHIC	MESOMORPHIC	ECTOMORPHIC
dependent	dominant	detached
calm	cheerful	tense
relaxed	confident	anxious
complacent	energetic	reticent
contented	impetuous	self-conscious
sluggish	efficient	meticulous
placid	enthusiastic	reflective
leisurely	competitive	precise
co-operative	determined	thoughtful
affable	outgoing	considerate
tolerant	argumentative	shy
affected	talkative	awkward
warm	active	cool
forgiving	domineering	suspicious
sympathetic	courageous	introspective
soft-hearted	enterprising	serious
generous	adventurous	cautious
affectionate	reckless	tactful
kind	assertive	sensitive
sociable	optimistic	withdrawn
soft-tempered	hot-tempered	gentle-tempered

Key to Temperament Test

Count the number of adjectives that you selected in each of the three categories. For example, if your totals are 10/6/5, you have predominantly endomorphic traits. A 6/10/5 means you are high in mesomorphic traits. The three numbers should add up to 21.

2

The Four Humoral (Emotional) Types

A classification of human temperaments based on body fluids, the "humors," was in widespread usage throughout Western civilization for close to two thousand years. To this day, a man's sense of "humor" is considered one of the most important aspects of his character. The four principal terms used in this system have entered into ordinary language: We know the unemotional calm of the *phlegmatic* attitude; the cheerfully optimistic or *sanguine* disposition; the sullen depressiveness of the *melancholic;* and the flashing hot temper of the *choleric.*

It is generally believed that the division of men into four types, corresponding to the qualities of the four elements, originated with the school of Hippocrates in the fifth century B.C. The Roman physician Galen, in the first century A.D., delineated nine temperaments based on the elements: one normal, four of simple qualities (warm, cold, humid, dry), and four of compound qualities. During the medieval period, marked by such luminaries as the great alchemist-physician Paracelsus, the doctrine arose that the body contained four kinds of fluids or humors—black, yellow, white, and red—and that the relative proportions and mixtures of these humors brought about the four constitutional types. Imbalances, deficiencies, and excesses in the humors were held responsible for the various disease

Flegmaticus.
Vnſer complex iſt mit waſſer mer getan
Darum̄ wir ſubtilikeit mit mügen lan.

Phlegmatic: "Our constitution
    is made with water.
    Hence we have subtle
    and delicate moods."

Colericus.
Vnſer complexion iſt gar von feüer
Schlahē vn̄ kriegen iſt vnſer abenteüer.

Choleric: "Our constitution is
    made with fire. Combat
    and warfare is our ad-
    venture."

Melencolicus.
Vnſer complexion iſt von erden weych
Darüb ſeÿ wir ſchwärmütigkept gleich

Melancholic: "Our constitu-
    tion is rich with earth, so
    our temper is heavy and
    brooding."

Sangumeus.
Vnſer conplexion ſind von luſtes vil.
Darumb ſeÿ wir hochmütig one zpl.

Sanguine: "Our constitution
    is filled with joy. Hence
    we are happy without
    direction."

NOTE: From a fifteenth-century German calendar.

states—a doctrine that dominated medical practice for several hundred years.

Each of the four temperaments was described as a blend of two qualities and associated with a particular color, a specific taste, and one of the elements of classical alchemy.

TABLE 2
The Four Temperaments

TEMPERAMENT	QUALITIES	COLOR	TASTE	ELEMENT
sanguine	warm & moist	red	sweet	air
choleric	hot & dry	yellow	salt	fire
phlegmatic	cold & moist	white	bitter	water
melancholic	cool & dry	black	sour	earth

These types could be arranged in a fourfold figure as follows, showing how the combinations of the qualities of heat and moisture gave rise to the four temperamental blends.

	Cold	Hot
Dry	melancholic	choleric
Moist	phlegmatic	sanguine

The fifteenth-century English scholar Robert Burton, in his treatise *The Anatomy of Melancholy,* advanced the idea that "choler," or angry humor, derived from the gallbladder; and "melancholy" (literally, "black choler") was associated with the spleen. Words such as "galling" or "splenetic" still convey some of these associations. After William Harvey discovered the circulation of the blood, various attempts were made to correlate differences in blood flow, size of blood vessels, and blood pressure with the different types. For example, the German philosopher Immanuel Kant (eighteenth century) described the sanguine type as "light-blooded," the choleric as "warm-blooded," the melancholic as "heavy-blooded," and the phlegmatic as "cold-blooded." Popular psychology still retains some of these physiological associations, as, for example, in the stereotype of the cold-blooded killer.

After the discovery of the nervous system, differences in its functions were brought in to account for type differences. Thus, the nineteenth-century German psychologist Wilhelm Wundt, focusing on reactivity to stimuli, set up a definition of the types according to the *strength of reaction* and the *speed of reaction*.

	Slow	Quick
Strong	melancholic	choleric
Weak	phlegmatic	sanguine

Another psychologist, Elsenhans, was apparently the first to propose that the humoral temperaments have to do primarily with feeling states, as distinct from mental or nervous attitudes. He defined the types according to the strength of feeling or emotion, and the degree of mobility of feeling (which he described as either "alternating" or "persistent").

	Persistent	Alternating
Strong	melancholic	choleric
Weak	phlegmatic	sanguine

This association of the humors with emotional consciousness represents a major clarification. In other words, we are dealing here with a fourfold typology of feeling or emotion, not necessarily with the overall constitution or personality of man. Even if we do not accept, as modern scientists do not, the idea of only four basic body fluids, advanced concepts of psychosomatic medicine and esoteric teachings of ancient times converge in the belief that the fluid or water component of the body does relate to the emotional nature. The state of the circulatory and glandular systems is known to be profoundly affected by emotions. Conversely, the emotions are influenced by disturbances and changes in these systems. The well-known effect of the menstrual cycle on feminine mood might be cited as one obvious example. Another would be the effects of fear and anger on heart rate and adrenalin secretions.

In the classical tradition, the red humor of the sanguine type was the blood (the word "sanguine" means "of the blood"). Thus we would expect heart consciousness to predominate in this type, which fits with the "warmth" and "sweetness" traditionally associated with the sanguine disposition. The white humor of the phlegmatic type has generally been associated with what are now called lymph fluids, as well as phlegm, mucus, and other intercellular fluids. Physiologically, the flow and movement of lymph fluids is much slower than that of blood, since the lymphatic system does not have a pump circulation, as the arterial system does. This lends some credibility to the association of lymph or white humor with the calm, almost sluggish temperament of the phlegmatic.

The humor of the choleric type was known as yellow bile and could probably be identified, in modern terms, with the secretions of the adrenal glands, situated on top of the kidneys. The role of adrenalin in the fight-flight reactions of the body is consistent with the reputed fiery aggressiveness of the choleric nature; and the role of the adrenal cortex in regulating the level of mineral salts is interesting in view of the traditional "salty" taste of this type.

The term "melancholic" literally refers to "black choler" or "black bile." Probably this would correspond to what is now called bile—the secretion of the liver, stored in the gallbladder. In line with this association would be the "bilious" angry moods of the melancholic and his "jaundiced" disposition. We can see from these examples that the association of humors or fluids with emotional states is sufficient to warrant further in-depth study and research on these factors. Reliable measurements of the actual physiological variables involved would be prerequisites to that kind of serious research. However, it is possible to study and recognize the four temperaments without reference to the underlying physiology.[1]

[1] A check list of adjectives descriptive of the four temperaments is in the Appendix to this chapter.

Description of the Four Temperaments

The *sanguine* type has the most positive connotations and associations in mass-mind ideas and ideals. Here is the classic heart-person—warm, jovial, outgoing, and emotionally expressive. Their disposition is often referred to as loving or "sweet." They are generally kind to strangers and affectionate with friends. They have a playful, optimistic outlook on life in general, and like to laugh a lot. Their sense of humor is of the warm, convivial, laughing-with variety. This kind of person responds with eager empathy to the feelings of others. They often have moist, limpid eyes that easily brim over with feeling, they can weep profusely if their feelings are hurt, and they glow with inner merriment.

It is worth noting the distinction between *empathy,* which is a more conscious kind of "feeling with" someone, and *sympathy,* which is more of an automatic unconscious reaction based on identification with another. Sanguine types given to excessive sympathetic reactions can get caught up in sentimental dramatics, and may then come across to others as cloying or smothering. Here their fluid emotional responsiveness becomes a splashy or gushy kind of overreaction. Such behavior is sometimes popularly described as "all wet." It tends to lack realism and objectivity.

According to Rudolf Steiner, the sanguine temperament is one in which the astral element predominates. This manifests as a mobility of interest and attention, a quick passing from one subject to another. "We are able to recognize the entire outer physiognomy, the permanent form and also the gestures, as the expression of the mobile, volatile, fluidic astral body" (Steiner, 1944, p. 35). The eyes light quickly upon something and quickly turn to something else. The form is usually slender and supple, the gait elastic and springing, the facial expressions mobile and changeable.

Generally, the sanguine types are pleasant to be around and are therefore well liked. Their easygoing sociability makes them popular at social functions and gatherings. They have a basically hopeful and debonair attitude, which makes them charming as friends and congenial as associates.

The *choleric* type is ardent and excitable, burning with adrenalin energy and overbrimming vitality. Their emotional outflow is passionate, electric, impulsive, sparkling, and enthusiastic. They are able to inspire others with their idealism, but may also attack them with sharp emotional barbs if others do not meet their expectations. This is the type whose eyes flash with anger. In interpersonal relations they do not have the easy give-and-take attitude of the sanguine, and are less prone to either sympathy or empathy. For this reason they usually come across as more egocentric. They are the classic "hotheads."

Cholerics see life in terms of conflict and struggle, and at times appear to relish a rough-and-tumble approach to relationships and human interactions. They are fighters more than lovers. Their speech and manner are not sweet but rather "salty," often to the point of aggressiveness. Their sense of humor tends to be sharp, more the laughing-at variety, sometimes even cutting. They relish slapstick and other active forms of humor.

In Steiner's interpretation of the four temperaments, the choleric is dominated by will and the need for ego assertion. The eyes maintain a strong, assured gaze, and may often be coal black. Facial features are sharply cut, the walk is firm and steady. "When he walks on the ground, he not only sets his foot on it but he treads as if he wanted to go a little bit farther into the ground" (Steiner, op. cit., p. 35).

In their actions, cholerics are decisive, quick and energetic, but also impulsive and erratic. They seem to live with a high degree of nervous tension, which periodically discharges in almost explosive fashion. Some cholerics express these nervous-emotional outbursts outwardly: there is a quality of emotional violence that can burn others. The more inhibited or introverted cholerics (tending toward melancholic) hold the explosions in and discharge them via the body, leading to various psychosomatic stress ailments, such as ulcers, inflammations, or hypertension.

People of the *phlegmatic* type are popularly regarded as unemotional, which they are not. Their emotions do not have the fiery intensity of the choleric, or the spontaneous warmth of the sanguine: It is a more calm, even-flowing kind of energy. Along with that kind of physical energy, their predominant state of consciousness, or temper, is also even and steady, like a wide river or a calm, unruffled lake. Their emotional responses are slower to develop, but when they do, are more persistent and consistent, less fluctuating and erratic. They evaluate a situation in what they consider a realistic fashion and base their feeling responses on these considered attitudes. What to the phlegmatic person is a realistic perspective often causes them to become somewhat "bitter," as if they had the feeling of having tasted life's bitter essences.

While not as sympathetic as the sanguine type, they are also not sentimental; in fact, they tend to be somewhat uncomfortable with maudlin emotionality. However, they are basically kind in their outlook, and considerate, even generous toward their friends. The more detached, selective attitude of the phlegmatic is at once his strength as well as his potential weakness, if it becomes uncaring coldness. Their sense of humor tends toward what is known as "dry wit," a kind of light banter with undertones of sarcasm. Their eyes do not have the sparkle of the choleric or the moistness of the sanguine, but they may have a kind of cool clarity, as they look at the world with a calm, steady gaze. In situations of emotional upheaval and turmoil, the phlegmatic is a pillar of strength, capable and resourceful.

The *melancholic* temperament, though associated in the popular mind with depressive states of consciousness, is not necessarily all negative. Some writers have attempted to avoid the clinical connotations of the term "melancholy" by calling this type "nervous," which however has other misleading associations. In modern terms, the melancholic type is "cool"—that is, he does not become overexcited or let his emotions run away with him. As with the phlegmatic, the emotions are steady, even to the point of fixity. But they are very strong feelings: this type often has deep and complex emotions and motivations. They tend to get locked into long-lasting depressive emotional states, lacking the choleric's volatility and the sanguine's capacity for rebound. Melancholics are prone to guilt and feelings of rejection.

The melancholic's basic emotional attitude toward life is pessimistic. They expect the worst to happen and in consequence of their thinking it often does, thus confirming their beliefs. Their taste of life is "sour," giving the face its characteristic "sour grapes" expression, with downturned corners of the mouth and furrowed eyebrows.

Steiner's view of the melancholic temperament was that it is dominated by the physical body, and that the sense of oppression and despair comes from a feeling of not being able to master the physical realities of the body and the world. "The person is not able to bring about flexibility where it should exist. The inner man has no power over his physical system; he feels inner obstacles" (Steiner, op. cit., p. 32).

Their approach to human relationships is generally sober and serious; they regard them as something to be pondered and worked out. Rarely do they have a well-developed sense of humor, and when they do, it is likely to be of the "black" kind; they are apt to laugh at catastrophes (the German *Schaden freude*). Their eyes tend to guard their feelings rather than express them, though when they do express, there is often surprising depth and intensity of feeling. They can display remarkably steady nerves in the face of danger and a kind of cool courage.

The Humors and Endocrine Types

Around the turn of the century, the new discoveries of the endocrine glands and their hormones led some researchers to believe that a typology based on the glands would be better than one based on the old idea of "humors." A physician named Louis Berman published a book in 1921 called *The Glands of Personality,* which put forward this idea. Occultists such as Max Heindel and the Rosicrucian School also looked on the endocrine glands as major determinants of character. Some astrologers and psychics, including Edgar Cayce, have related variations in endocrine functioning to planetary influences, thus providing a possible causal link between planets and personality.

Studies of the effects of the glands revealed emotional aspects and personality differences that seemed to parallel some of the distinctions of the old humoral doctrine. A fairly clear correspondence exists between what was called the "adrenal character" and the choleric temperament. The role of adrenalin in the "fight or flight" syndrome led to a characterization of the adrenal type as active, dynamic, vigorous, and aggressive. Physically, this type was said to be often swarthy or freckled, with a broad, irregular face, a low hairline, and a fair amount of hair on the face.

The characteristics of the "thymus type" bear some resemblance to the sanguine. This gland, generally thought to control growth in children, also seemed to have some mysterious connection with processes of regeneration and degeneration (currently, it is believed to be involved in the body's immune-defense systems as well). Thus the active thymus type was said to have a perpetually youthful appearance, with delicate teeth and bones, silky hair, and a kind of childlike softness and playfulness.

Speculations regarding the role of the spleen in negative emotions go back to the Middle Ages—whence the term "splenetic." Endocrine theorists associated both the spleen and the pancreas with the lymphatic system, and described these types as watery, round, passive, and moody. There is some resemblance here to the phlegmatic disposition, which in fact was sometimes called "lymphatic" as an alternative.

The "thyroid character" of the endocrine theorists, based on descriptions of people with overactive thyroids, had no obvious counterpart in the humoral classification. These people were said to have a lean, bright-eyed vitality and restless nervousness; persons with underactive thyroids were described as cold and slow, which fits in part the melancholic character.

Other character descriptions, such as those linking masculinity to dominance of the anterior pituitary and femininity to the posterior pituitary, do not seem to have stood the test of further empirical findings. The basic failing of the endocrine doctrine was the fact that no concrete evidence was ever brought to bear on the question of whether there actually were excesses or deficiencies in the activities of the glands in certain

recognizable types. It may be that in the future more sophisticated biomedical techniques will be able to provide measurements that will answer such questions.

TABLE 3
Humoral and Endocrine Associations
with the Four Temperaments

TEMPERAMENT	TRADITIONAL	PHYSIOLOGICAL	ENDOCRINE
sanguine	red humor	blood/heart	thymus
choleric	yellow humor	adrenalin	adrenals
phlegmatic	white humor	lymph	spleen
melancholic	black humor	bile/gall-bladder	hypo-thyroid

A Modern Interpretation of the Humoral Typology

The contemporary psychologist Hans J. Eysenck of the University of London has been one of the few serious scientists to give
any credence to the humoral classification of types. First, he
proposed that one regard the four types not so much as
discrete, boxlike categories but rather as resultants of two continuous dimensions, which can be described as varying along
two independent axes. Thus the Wilhelm Wundt model would
define the two dimensions as intensity of reaction (equated
with dry-moist) and speed of reaction (equated with hot-cold).
The Elsenhans definitions would translate as two dimensions
of strength or *intensity of feeling* (dry-moist) and changeability
or *mobility of feeling* (hot-cold).

Such a transposition has the advantage that one can place an
individual at his place on the grid and compare positions with
another individual. Thus, in the example to follow, A is warmer
and more variable but less intense than B, even though both
are in the choleric quadrant. Similarly, C is more cool—that is,
less changeable—than D, whereas D is more intense than C,
though both are phlegmatics.

Eysenck's own translation of the two co-ordinate axes was in
terms of the personality traits that he has developed on the
basis of a large number of research studies and tests. In his system, the hot-cold axis is equated with extraversion-introver-

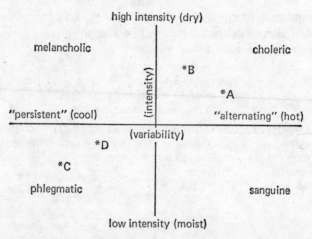

sion, and the dry-moist dimension to neuroticism or instability vs. emotional stability. People scoring high on neuroticism
on his test are said to be emotionally overreactive and labile:
They tend to have psychosomatic complaints and are subject
to various worries and anxieties. People scoring high on extraversion are said to be active, sociable, impulsive, and expressive. Thus the following graph would result:

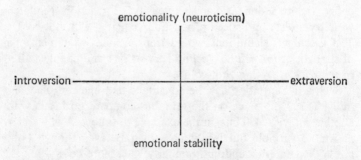

In this schema, the choleric is an extraverted neurotic and
the melancholic an introverted neurotic. Eysenck's researches
with his tests of extraversion and neuroticism, which have been
run on hundreds of different groups, have identified the following correlations, among others (Eysenck & Eysenck, 1969):

1. Prisoners, criminals, and psychopaths score high on extraversion and neuroticism—that is, they fall in the extreme of the choleric segment.

2. Anxiety neurotics, alcoholics, and depressive patients are in the extreme high introversion and high neuroticism area—that is, melancholic.

3. Successful managers, some industrial workers, scientists, and mathematicians, tend to score in the introverted, less neurotic segment of the scales—that is, phlegmatic.

4. Sportsmen, parachutists, and salesmen, on the average, fall more into the extraverted, less neurotic—that is, sanguine quadrant. These connections can be found even in children; for example, sanguine children learn to swim more quickly than others of their age group.

Eysenck's theories and findings are interesting and thought-provoking. It is clear that, as measured by his tests of extraversion and neuroticism, the differences and correlations described do exist. Whether these two traits can in fact be completely equated with the old hot-cold, dry-moist dimensions remains to be seen.

One major criticism of this formulation is that emotionality is equated with neurotic disturbance or predisposition, making two of the types (the choleric and the melancholic) pathological. This goes against the old tradition, which is backed by common-sense observation and intuition, that it is imbalance, through either deficiency or excess, in *any* of the four qualities or "humors" that produces physical or psychic disturbances. Eysenck's own findings actually indicate that this is an unfortunate categorization. For example, several experiments showed that university students, as a group, scored higher on neuroticism and lower on extraversion—that is, in the melancholic segment—than average adult groups; and academic achievers also tended to be in the "introverted neurotic" area. It is really only in the *extremes* that these tendencies would become neurotic or pathological. The average, well-balanced person would score more toward the middle of the intersection of the two coordinates.

Robert Burton spoke of the "justly constituted man" as one

who had the four humors in an even-tempered proportion. Wilhelm Wundt thought that one could *be* one or the other character type, according to the situation. This is perhaps an ideal that most people are not flexible enough to attain, responding instead more according to their type predisposition. But these are emotional states or conditions that we all can experience at different times. One can think of learning or growing to develop and express the humoral qualities that one does not possess by native disposition.

Emotional Balance and Relationships

The emotions are essentially fluid manifestations; in the body they are related to the major liquid systems, including the blood, the lymph and the glandular systems. One might use the analogy of different bodies of water: The feelings of the choleric are like a spurting fountain or hot spring; those of the sanguine are like a deep, fast mountain stream; those of the phlegmatic are like a wide, slow river; and those of the melancholic are like a dark, still pool. The following figure summarizes and synthesizes both the traditional and the modern versions:

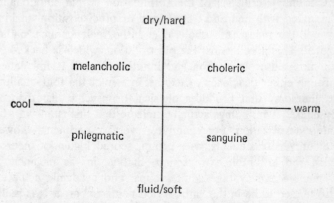

The intense, expressive, dynamic qualities of the sanguine and choleric are generally experienced as emotionally "warm," tending to "heated." The passive responding of the other two is generally felt as being more "cool," which may become "cold"

if it is extremely indrawn. The phlegmatic and the sanguine share a quality of fluid flexibility, which is appropriately correlated with "moistness" and contrasts with both the sharp, angular, nervous reactions of the choleric and the rather fixed emotional attitudes of the melancholic. It is interesting to note that it is fluidity of emotions that corresponds to emotional stability in the Eysenck tests. The ability to *flow with* one's changing, surging emotions is actually a kind of steadiness, whereas "dryness" has a tendency to become fixed, brittle, or rigid.

In order to bring about the inner balance required for individuation or wholeness, we need to synthesize the qualities of heat-fire with the qualities of moisture-water. If there is excess of fire, we may get, as in the choleric, a gaseous dissipation of energies, which is manifest as lack of focus and lack of human concern. If fire is out of balance with water in the sanguine type we get a suffocating, smothering steam, and sentimental overconcern. If there is excess of water and not enough fire-warmth, we may find a cold, heartless attitude in the phlegmatic, a "dampening" of spirits and vitality. Lack of fluidity and/or warmth in the melancholic results in fixed moods of cold, dark depression, or excessive anxiety.

In emotional relationships there are actual changes and exchanges of "fire" and "water." There is the physical warmth or even heat of emotional-physical contact, ranging all the way to the "heat" of sexual attraction and passion. We may experience cold fear when there is no contact, or an element of rejection or violation in the relationship. As feelings are communicated verbally or nonverbally, there are fluid changes in the body: The heart rate may speed up in adrenal excitement, or slow down in vagal relaxation.

By identifying one's approximate position on the graph and the corresponding positions of people with whom one relates, some valuable insights can be gained. Generally, it is easier to relate to people in adjoining quadrants—for example, the sanguine with the choleric or phlegmatic—and most difficult to relate to those from the opposite sector because they are most different. Thus the sanguine types, with their warmth and outgoing optimism, have the most trouble understanding or relating to the somewhat rigid and distant cool pessimism of the melancholic. Personally, being of a generally phlegmatic disposition, I can empathize fairly well with sanguines and melancholics, but find it more difficult to synchronize my natural pace with the speed and fiery energy of cholerics. Their erratic abruptness seems to irritate my nervous system; whereas, no doubt, my slow deliberateness irritates theirs.

In marriage relationships one often finds the opposites paired, as if each spouse were seeking some kind of emotional balance by relating with his or her complementary opposite. Being aware of the differences in natural-response tendencies and temperamental energies can make one more understanding of and tolerant toward differing behavioral manifestations and expressions. Difficulties in communication that are otherwise extremely frustrating can, with enlightened awareness of these innate differences, be resolved into productive and creative synergistic companionship.

Correlation with Body Types and Astrology

Traditionally, each of the four humoral types was associated with one of the four planets: the sanguine with Jupiter, because of the expansiveness; the choleric with Mars, because of the fiery quality; the phlegmatic with the Moon, because of the association with the lymph system; and the melancholic with Saturn. Modern astrologers would extend this list, bringing Venus in with the sanguine character, because of the heart-love qualities; and adding Mercury in with the melancholic, because of the tendency to nervous tension (Mercury rules the nervous system in astrology).

The figure opposite shows how the four humoral types might be related to the body types discussed in the previous chapter. These correlations are based on descriptive similarity only, and would need to be validated by empirical research. The melancholic has many of the qualities of the ectomorph, but some of the latter are also part of the choleric disposition. Endomorphs appear to be a blend of phlegmatic and sanguine. Mesomorphs have qualities both of the choleric and the sanguine.

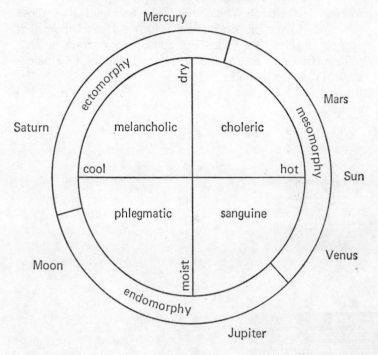

Appendix: Descriptive Self-test of the Four Humoral Types

I	II	III	IV
warm	hot and fiery	calm	cool
easygoing	excitable	even-tempered	sober
playful	vital	slow	black humor
talkative	restless	persistent	serious
sympathetic	aggressive	considerate	reserved
sociable	egocentric	careful	anxious
hopeful	ardent	reliable	depressive
carefree	impulsive	controlled	brooding
sweet	salty	bitter	sour
optimistic	idealistic	realistic	pessimistic

Total
Score____   ____   ____   ____

Directions: Go through the list of adjectives and mark those that apply to you moderately well with a (1), and those that apply strongly with a (2). Then add up your scores in each column. Category I = sanguine, II = choleric, III = phlegmatic, IV = melancholic.

3

The Jungian Typology

First published in 1921, the theory of types formulated by Carl Jung has become one of the most widely used and discussed in psychological circles. The terms "extraversion" and "introversion," though not invented by Jung, have become indelibly associated with his name. His ideas concerning the four functions —thinking, feeling, intuition, and sensation—though they leave much to be desired in terms of clarity and consistency, have the kind of broad appeal that suggests a basically valid pattern is being described.

Extraversion-Introversion

According to Jung there are two fundamental attitudes governing the flow of psychic energy, or libido, in relationship to the world. In the extraverted attitude—which, if it becomes dominant and habitual, governs the extraverted type—the flow of energy, of interest and attention, is *outward,* toward the world of objects. Thus this type is affirmative, sociable, confident in action, and expressive in communication. In the introverted attitude, by contrast, the flow of energy, attention, and interest is *inward,* away from the objective world, toward subjective states of consciousness. Thus this type is comparatively asocial, preferring solitude or the company of a few friends and family;

they reflect on their experience before acting on it, and are generally not very expressive in communication.

Both attitudes, if carried to the extreme, have certain characteristic weaknesses. The extraverted type may be quite superficial, or overly concerned with appearances and surface impressions. He may get so caught up in objects and the demands of external situations that, as Jung puts it, he may "lose himself in the toils of objects," and have only minimal awareness of his physical body and interior states. The extremely introverted type, on the other hand, often feels the world of objects is somehow imposing or impinging on him in a disagreeable fashion. He does not handle interpersonal relationships very well, and appears gauche and awkward in social situations. Jung makes the important observation that introverts are usually undervalued by others because they fail to communicate the abundance and interest of their subjective lives. Their communications are fragmentary and lack the easy flow of warmth toward the other.

This is not to say that introversion is the same as neuroticism. The two dimensions are independent. Jung suggested, and the research of Eysenck and others has generally confirmed, that the two types, if they become neurotic, are predisposed to two different kinds of neurosis. The extravert neurosis is hysteria, with its exaggerated emotionality and excessive clamoring for the attention and interest of others. With the introverted type, the typical form of neurosis is what Jung called "psychasthenia," now more commonly referred to as anxiety neurosis, which is marked by extreme sensitiveness and chronic fatigue.

According to Jung, both attitudes are always present in everyone, and only the dominance of one brings about the polarization into the two major types. The nondominant attitude is also operative, but *unconsciously*. Thus in the conscious extravert, there is said to be an unconscious flow of energy from the object back to the subject. The conscious introvert is similarly unaware of the hidden flow of energy with which he invests the object out there, which he only feels as impinging on him.

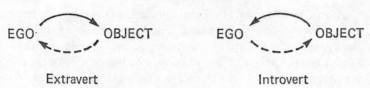

Extravert   Introvert

The unconscious attitude, of which the person has little or no awareness, reveals itself in primitive and distorted ways. The extravert's unconscious (and hence underdeveloped) introversion makes him vulnerable to irrational, regressive internal processes and images; the introvert's unconscious (and hence primitive) extraversion causes him to come across as childish and awkward in social and reality relationships.

The Four Functions

In addition to the two primary attitudes, each person is dominant in one of four functions. Each of these functions may be extraverted or introverted: Thus we have eight basic functional types. Some Jungians also consider the second strongest function that a person manifests: If this is done, we arrive at sixteen types.

The *thinking* function is concerned with principles, reason, order, logic, and meaning. The thinking type prefers to organize his life according to certain principles and formulae. While all types have thoughts, when the thinking function is primary, there is basically a thoughtful, considered approach to life.

The *feeling* function, as described in the Jungian literature, is concerned with values and relationships, with the appreciation of situations, persons, objects, and psychological states. The feeling type orders his life around the *relationships* he has with external or internal situations or events, and orients himself around the feeling tone of these relationships. Jung is at pains to distinguish feelings from emotions or affects, in terms of the greater physiological arousal of the latter. It must be said, though, that his writings in this particular area are neither clear nor convincing.

Strangely, Jung regards both thinking and feeling as "rational" or "judging" functions. Thinking, according to his theory, evaluates and judges something according to its truth or falsity. Feeling judges objects according to like or dislike. They are thought to be opposite to and incompatible with each other.

The other two functions, sensation and intuition, are said to be "irrational" or "perceptive" functions. *Sensation* is conscious perception of immediately present data, facts, and events. *Intuition* is defined as unconscious perception of possibilities and potentials. By intuition we get glimpses and hunches regarding the possible or probable future development of a situation or event. These two perception functions are also said to be opposite to and incompatible with each other.

The idea of two pairs of opposite functions, making up a fourfold pattern, or *quaternio,* was one that intrigued Jung greatly, and he found seeming parallels to it in many systems of mythological and religious symbolism.[1] Much of his psychological theorizing on the types is based on the assumption that a person who is thinking dominant invariably has feeling as his inferior or unconscious function and vice versa; and that intuitives always have inferior sensation and vice versa. Although it may often turn out that way, there is really no evidence to support such a neat schema as an invariable law. The four functions may vary independently of each other.

One might also question the classification of the functions as either judging or perceptive functions. There are thinking, feeling, intuiting, and sensing, as such, pure and simple. Then there is the evaluative process, which may attach to any of these four functions. Mentally, we judge and evaluate according to truth or falsity, clarity or obscurity, meaning or lack of meaning. The evaluation or judgment is not the same as the thought. Emotionally, we judge and evaluate our feelings and those of others in terms of good or bad, like or dislike, approach or withdrawal. We also judge and evaluate sensations according to conditioned reactions of pleasant or unpleasant, approval or

[1] The distinction between thinking and intuition is in many ways parallel to Nietzsche's well-known polarity of Apollonian vs. Dionysian.

disapproval. Even intuitive perceptions are evaluated according to whether we judge them exciting or dull, interesting or boring, useful or impractical.

The Four Functions and Time Consciousness

A brilliant contribution to the understanding of the Jungian typology appeared in a 1968 paper "The Many Worlds of Time" by Harriet Mann, Miriam Siegler, and Humphrey Osmond of Princeton University. Mann et al. start from certain concepts and observations developed by students of animal behavior—concepts such as von Uexküll's *umwelt,* the time-space world in which a creature lives. Extending this notion, they propose that each of the four types relates to time in a characteristic and different way. The feeling type relates primarily to the past, the sensing type to the present, the intuitive type to the future, and the thinking type to the line of temporal development from past, through present, to future.

"For the feeling type, time is circular: The past manifests in the present and then is immediately returned to the past as a memory" (Mann et al., 1968, p. 37). Feeling types are great collectors of memories—they cherish reminiscences, diaries, memorabilia, loyalties, folklore, heritage, tradition. They relate to and value present events and situations for the emotional resonance they generate with past experiences; they may anticipate its place in the past, noting it as "something to remember." Feeling persons can be loose and unreliable regarding appointments and timing, because to them the emotional value, the feeling atmosphere and its maintenance, are more important.

The thinking type relates to time as a measured, flowing stream. These people are interested in the development of the process, the causes leading to effects, antecedents leading to consequences. Time for them is linear rather than circular: They prefer the long-range overview, the historical perspective. Thinkers are often slow in deciding on a course of action because of their lengthy analyses of plans and methods, or their formulations of principles and reasons. For situations requiring administration, organization, and clear objectivity, this function is invaluable. In other situations, such as interpersonal relationships, the fluid, spontaneous responses of the feeling function are more appropriate.

The sensation type relates to the current, here-now reality, the tangible details of immediate, sense-perceived facts and events. Where it came from or where it's going are of less interest than "what's happening." This attitude makes the sensation type the most effective adaptors, the most skillful in dealing with the material aspects of the environment.

The intuitive type relates primarily to the future—they anticipate where something will lead, how something or someone will develop. Since they tend to get caught up in the excitement of their projected vision or dream, people of this type are often impatient with the demands of present reality and find it difficult to see things through to completion.

Recently, this group has extended their revision of Jung's typology to include also an analysis in terms of the psychological space, as well as time. In this new scheme, each combination of two functions is seen as having a different attitude to space, a different *umwelt*. Thinking/sensation combinations are called structural (or territorial). Their opposites are the intuitive/feeling types, called oceanic. Thinking/intuitive combinations are called ethereal; and their opposites, the sensation/feeling combinations, are called experial (or volcanic) (Malone, 1977; Osmond et al., 1977).

Empirical Findings Related to the Functional Typology

There are two tests that have been developed to empirically measure the functional types according to Jungian theory. One is the Myers-Briggs Type Indicator, the other the Gray-Wheelwrights Type Survey. Studies indicate that they correlate fairly highly with each other, and may essentially be regarded as measuring the same factors; the Myers-Briggs, however, has had more extensive validation and is considered more reliable, although it is also longer.

Both the Myers-Briggs and the Gray-Wheelwrights tests incorporate Jung's assumptions regarding opposite functions in the test items. Each question is a choice between two alternatives: introversion vs. extraversion, thinking vs. feeling, or sensation vs. intuition. Thus the test is constructed in such a way that responses would tend to fall into such categories of opposites, and a negative correlation between thinking and feeling, and between sensation and intuition, is presupposed, not observed. Even so, however, analysis of thousands of cases of the Myers-Briggs test by Strickler and Ross (1964) show that results do not necessarily support the idea of a bipolar distribution. A view that sees the four functions varying independently of each other is just as consistent with the data.

Despite the limitations of the tests, the following findings may nevertheless be taken as supportive of many aspects of the functional theory. They are reported in the Manual for the Myers-Briggs test (Myers-Briggs, 1962), and in the *Bulletin of Research in Psychological Type* (1977).

1. Males more often choose thinking over feeling, whereas females do the reverse. This is true of both adolescents and adults and probably reflects cultural sex-role conditioning.

2. On the Strong test of vocational interests, people interested in sales, finance, and business tend to be extraverted sensation or thinking types; those interested in the professions and sciences tend to be introverted intuition or thinking types; those interested in music or the arts are mostly introverted intuitives or feeling types.

3. On the Allport-Vernon test of values, "theoretical" was associated with thinking; "economic" and "social" with extraverted sensation; "aesthetic" with introverted intuition; "social" with feeling and sensation; "religious" with feeling and intuition.

4. Very high correlations are found between extraversion and talkativeness. Sheer quantity of verbal output is probably the simplest and most direct indicator of extraversion.

5. Intuitive types tend to have high scores on tests for autonomy and independence. Apparently they need freedom for

their intuition to function. This is also related to the fact that they have the highest job turnover rate of any type, especially if they are in mechanical or routine jobs. Intuitives also indicate a greater willingness to take risks than sensing types.

6. Extraverts and feeling types tend to gravitate toward jobs in sales and customer relations. Introverts, who are less comfortable with people, show the reverse pattern: They move out of sales jobs and into clerical jobs.

7. In a major study of practicing, creative professionals (research scientists, architects, writers, mathematicians), McKinnon found that an astonishing 96 per cent of them are intiutives. This compares with averages of 15 per cent intuitives in vocational schools, 40 per cent in high schools, and 65 per cent in colleges. In other words, the higher educational levels evidently select or elicit the intuitive capacity. The writers in the group tended more toward intuition plus feeling; the scientists more toward intuition plus thinking. This finding is an interesting corollary to Douglas Dean's (1974) research on the prevalence of ESP (a form of intuition) in highly creative and effective executives.

8. In a study of medical specialties, it was found that intuitives predominate in psychiatry, neurology, research, and teaching, whereas sensing types predominate in anesthesiology, obstetrics-gynecology, surgery, and general practice.

9. In high-school and college students, scholastic achievement, grades, and IQ are somewhat correlated with both introversion and intuition. This suggests that those unaware of or uninterested in their own inner states have greater difficulties with their academic studies.

10. Theology students tends to be predominantly intuitive-feeling types; business-school students are most frequently sensing-thinking types.

11. According to Eysenck's findings, in various psychomotor tasks extraverts perform with greater speed, but less accuracy, than introverts; extraverts also have more driving accidents. Other research, though, indicates that extraverts perceive time more accurately than introverts.

12. Extraverts work better in the afternoon and in groups; introverts work better in the morning and alone.

13. Introverts can be conditioned more quickly and thoroughly than extraverts. If we regard the process of socialization as a conditioning of controlled behavior patterns, we might say that the introvert's conditioning takes hold too well—hence their greater level of social inhibition, for example, their more inhibited communication (Eysenck and Eysenck, 1969).

The Eight Functional Types

Extraverted thinking. This type is interested in logical principles and systems that enable him to deal with external facts and data. Jung cited Darwin as an example, with his incredible drive to amass factual information. Scientists whose main involvement is in experiment and data collection, instrumentation and technological application, belong in this category. It is important, however, to remember that both intelligence and education are independent of type, so a person may be uninformed and his reasoning may be faulty, and yet display the qualities of this type. Extraverted thinkers like to impose order and efficient methods on the outer world. They are the administrators and managers, the systems men (or women) who can organize people and materials, whether in government bureaucracy, industrial corporations, applied technology, or professions such as law. Political leaders such as Thomas Jefferson, F. D. Roosevelt, J. F. Kennedy, Lenin, and Chou En-lai might be cited as examples of this type.

Introverted thinking. In this type the passion for order is turned inward. From observations of facts their thoughts turn to internal relationships of theory and conceptual explanation; unlike the extraverted thinkers, who move from facts to further sets of facts, extending their scope horizontally. The introverted thinker is the scientific or philosophical theorist, the type who is forever examining basic assumptions or formulating new abstractions to account for observations. Facts are intrinsically less interesting to him. Freud was an example of such a type, building elaborate theoretical systems concerning the consciousness of infants and children, but declining to observe them in the nursery. Mathematicians, dealing in pure abstractions, would perhaps be the most extreme expression of this type, and philosophers such as Kant, Schopenhauer and many others, would also be examples. They prefer to analyze the world, rather than run it.

Both thinking types often, though not always, have feeling as the inferior or least-developed function. Emotional growth has lagged behind intellectual growth in these cases, and emotional reactions may be childish and primitive, expressed in awkward fashion or not at all. Such "inferior feeling" types appear socially inept, or cold and unfeeling, or they may have intense, even fanatical, but invisible loyalties. If they do not develop their emotional awareness and sensitivity, these thinkers may get caught in unexpected outbursts or breakdowns as feelings that have been repressed erupt in crude or violent fashion. The story depicted in *The Blue Angel,* in which a professor degrades himself in an affair with a woman of ill repute, is a classic example of such a situation. The thinking type may also have sensation as the underdeveloped function, in which case we have the well-known "absent-minded professor" type, who can think profound theories but can't find his way home from the bus stop.

Extraverted feeling. This is the type known in earlier ages as "sanguine." They radiate warmth, good feeling, and pleasure in human relationships. They are relatively aware of their own feelings and relate to the feelings, not the ideas, of others. They handle relationships not according to principles or objectives, but according to emotional ideals and values. Being extraverted —that is, externally oriented—these ideals and values may often be those inculcated by family or social tradition. Jung gave the example of the woman who "loves" the "right kind" of man. The sensitivity to feeling is highly differentiated in this type, going well beyond the crude like-dislike reactions of inferior feeling. They deal in shades and nuances of feeling tones, and work hard to bring about harmony and positive feeling among people. It has been said that they seem to "lubricate their environment."

These types are drawn to professions such as nursing, psychotherapy, social work, the ministry, or restaurant work, where their nurturing tendencies find expression. Musical performers, dramatic actors, and entertainers also often belong to this group; their profession calls for the dynamic and enthusiastic projection of feeling. Among political leaders, one could cite Eisenhower, George Washington, Robert Kennedy, Mahatma Gandhi, and Mao Tse-tung as examples.

Introverted feeling. This type, according to Jung, is the hardest to fathom. Like the sanguine, extraverted feelers, they have strong emotions and live with their awareness primarily in the emotional realm. But unlike the extravert, they either do not express their feelings or express them only within the safe circle of close family, friends, or perhaps religious association. "Still waters run deep" applies to this type, which corresponds in many ways to the old idea of the melancholic. Like the extraverted feelers, these people ardently desire emotional harmony and peace, but they tend to withdraw into a private inner world to attain it rather than work it out with others. Taken to the extreme, this becomes the attitude of the recluse or monk, pursuing his religious devotions in hermitage or cell. Or it may take creative expression in poetry or music, especially the romantic variety (classical forms appeal more to the thinking function).

Both feeling types, if thinking is their inferior function, as it often is, tend either to reject thinking (for example, the socialite who says "I don't like to think"), or to adopt a prefabricated religious or political system, consisting of a few, rigidly held beliefs. When the "inferior thinking" is operative, they tend to think, and talk, in a rather critical, judgmental way that is both nagging and irrational. Mao Tse-tung, for example, often gave his lieutenants contradictory and confusing instructions. His inspirational feeling function, however, was a perfect counterpoint to Chou En-lai's brilliant administrative thinking.

Extraverted sensation. This type is dominated by the aim and desire to touch, grasp, experience, and physically act upon his environment and the people in it. They have a highly developed perception of and memory for details. They see and appreciate the texture of things. The people of this type are often found in manual occupations, working with tools and materials, doing things, shaping and manipulating external reality. They have a keen sense of practical values, including political and economic factors. Successful salesmen are usually of this type, as are many bankers and businessmen, especially those involved in production and marketing. (By contrast, investors and speculators have a strong intuitive component.)

There appear to be two subtypes here. On the one hand, there are the practical, *sensible* realists and workers, corresponding somewhat to the phlegmatic type of the ancients. On the other, there are those sensation extraverts who might be called *sensualists:* Their aim is sense enjoyment, whether it be refined aesthetic appreciation of the arts, the joy of physical movement in dance or athletics, or the pleasure-seeking of unabashed hedonism.

Introverted sensation. The introverted "sensors" also have the amazing, almost photographic capacity to absorb and retain detailed impressions. But they perceive and record subjective, inner events and impressions as well as, or better than, outer facts. They are more interested in and aware of internal factors, and hence may appear by comparison outwardly silent and unusually slow. They tend to base decisions and actions on their vast storehouse of accumulated factual data. Like the extraverted sensors, they like to rely on common sense in the handling of reality events and relationships, rather than on principles or considerations of others' feelings.

These introverted sense people are often regarded as passive, and they may indeed feel themselves to be "victims" of environmental forces. If extremely imbalanced, the introverted sensualist may drift into alcoholism or drug addiction as a way of satisfying the strong craving for sensation. However, even the apparently passive introverts can often be found engaged in small manual hobbies such as carpentry, cooking, repairing tools, or making things. If their creative energy is functioning this type may produce richly detailed and finely textured art, such as the novels of Thomas Mann or the drawings of Albrecht Dürer. If they are psychically gifted they may be superbly clairvoyant, like Joan Grant and her detailed descriptions of other lifetimes; or Emanuel Swedenborg and his encyclopedic descriptions of the worlds of angels and spirits.

Depending on which function is underdeveloped, sensation types may have irrational, inconsistent thinking; or they may be rough and inconsiderate in emotional relationships (the "ruthless realist"). If intuition is the inferior function, they are given to bizarre or suspicious fantasies, which, in the introvert especially, may take on a paranoid tone, as if people were out to influence him in a negative way.

Extraverted intuition. These people are the enthusiastic innovators. They are always conceiving or perceiving possibilities, and devising imaginative new ways of getting things done. They are the great initiators of projects, pouring enormous energy into them and inspiring others to share with or follow them. They are not necessarily good at following through and carrying things to a conclusion, unless they also have strong thinking or sensing. They get bored easily with any kind of routine; indeed, desire for change and excitement appear to be one of their primary motivations. Here we have the scientific inventor, the creative innovator in the arts and professions, the journalist with a "nose for news," shrewd investors and speculators playing their hunches, promoters, advertisers, agents, pioneers, adventurers, and explorers. We find here also the politicians with a flair for assessing future developments, or revolutionaries such as Joan of Arc, Leon Trotsky, Adolf Hitler, and Che Guevara.

Introverted intuition. This type also is innovative and creative, but more in relation to the inner worlds of ideas and symbols. These people are highly sensitive to subliminal stimuli, or subtle impressions from other planes of consciousness; thus they may have psychic perception and/or precognitive ability. Often too, their perception is tuned in with collective consciousness, seeing vast social and cultural panoramas of change, as with the prophets of the Old Testament, whom Jung cites as examples of this type. If they do not succeed in finding a creative expression for their far-out visions and insights, they may be branded as eccentric cranks or impractical dreamers. On the other hand, if they do have artistic ability, they may be able to formulate their intuitions with such vividness that people are deeply affected by them as, for example, in the visionary paintings of William Blake or Marc Chagall, or the almost mystical scientific intuitions of Teilhard de Chardin. Even when well organized and/or creatively productive, these people are often imbued with something akin to religious fervor concerning their favorite project.

Lack of practicality is probably the most common failing of intuitives, reflecting an underdeveloped sensation function. They become so preoccupied with the future that their ability to relate to the present is diminished. For example, they may be unpunctual, vague concerning details, or inefficient at managing money. If they are very closed off to here-now sensation, they become neglectful of the body and may have trouble handling sexual and other appetites.

Individuation and the Development of the Functions

Jung describes individuation as the process by which a person becomes a differentiated individual, distinct and different from the images and imprints of collective consciousness. It may also be described as the process of becoming "indivisible"—that is, whole, not torn by separative conditioning and imbalanced development of one part of the psyche compared to another.

A highly developed function is distinguished from a less developed function by the degree of *differentiation,* compared to which the inferior function appears crude, primitive, or immature. It is as if that aspect of the personality had not grown up as far as the primary function, and was still operating at a childhood level, whether infantile, prepubescent, or adolescent. The inferior feeling function, for example, operates in terms of simple like-dislike, good-bad, black-white reactions. The more developed feeling function of a primary feeling type has many shades of feeling tones, is aware of subtle nuances of emotional response, and can relate interpersonally with skillful attention to atmosphere, mood, tact, and timing.

Thus the development of the inferior, or weakest function, is seen as a key to psychic development and personal growth. Although it tends at times to erupt into consciousness in a primitive and regressive manner, it is also the door to the healing and creative potentials of the unconscious. It relates us to the instinctive or animal components of our psyche, which can reveal and release tremendous integrative power. For example, a dream of a wild, untameable animal may point to a person's image of his undeveloped part. Dreams of barbarians, of primitive or exotic people, often serve a similar function.

People will try to express their inferior function in some imaginative way. Intuitives, such as Jung, may choose, as he did, to engage the sensation function by working with clay or stone. Others may become involved in some form of body movement, body therapy, or martial art to develop sensation. Thinkers or intuitives, seeking to develop feeling, may take up music or painting. Hard-nosed scientific sensation types often find recreation and inspiration in fantastic, intuitive science fiction.

Jung's student Marie-Louise von Franz has pointed out that the common mythological theme of the King and his three sons can be related to this situation. Usually the third son is characterized as backward, awkward—a simpleton or a fool. He represents the least-developed function; the King or father, the primary function. Yet in the tales it is usually this idiot son, whom everybody ridicules, who wins the prize, or accomplishes the mission, to everyone's surprise. This is because the inferior function, through its access to unconscious material, can bring in the needed resources that will bring about balance and harmony in the psyche. The unconscious is a rich source of creativity and energy for healing/wholeness.

Jung also related this process to the universal mythic symbolism of the three and the four. The trinity, or threefold structure, becomes a quaternio, or fourfold mandala-like structure, which is much more stable and balanced. The four functions are then centered around an identity nucleus, of which they have become the instruments. This is the legendary "fifth essence," or *quintessentia*, of the alchemists: the essence of the four, in the One that is beyond them.

The Functional Types in Partnerships and Groups

Often, an individual will attempt to balance the functions not within himself, but in his relationship with others. The authors of the Gray-Wheelwrights type test claimed that their research indicated that most people tend to marry the opposite type, though they usually choose friends of the same type. For example, a thinking man may then fall into the habit of leaving the functions and activities natural to feeling—that is, social and family relationships, home environment and decor, to his wife, the feeling partner in the relationship. A wild, undisciplined, intuitive-creative person may team up with a practical, sensible realist; the latter in turn depends on the former for inspiration and excitement.

The question that arises is whether balancing the functions this way, in a partnership, inevitably maintains one's own intrapsychic imbalance. The relationship in which most of the thinking is done by the man and the feeling by the wife may in the long run leave both partners frustrated and dissatisfied with their own inner lack or incompleteness. Integrating and balancing the functions *within* one's own nature would seem to be an inescapable and essential aspect of the individuation process.

Another pattern, frequently found, is for a small group of people with a common goal or interest to distribute the functions among each other. A prime example, as pointed out by Humphrey Osmond, is given by the three architects of the Russian Revolution: Lenin was the thinker and the interpreter of Marxist doctrine, Trotsky the intuitive prophet and demagogue, and Stalin the hard-nosed sensation type, who took action and took over the power. This situation had striking parallels with the history of the struggle over the succession of Julius Caesar. Here Brutus was the thinking type, the principled moralist, Marcus Antonius the emotional, feeling type, and Augustus the ruthless sensation-realist who, again, took action and reaped the benefits.

A fictional example is also provided by the famous television series *Star Trek*. Mr. Spock plays the role of the imperturbably logical thinking type; Dr. McCoy represents the warmth and humanity of the feeling function; and Captain Kirk is the man of sensation and action, who must make decisions of the basis of the facts available to him.

Another example is provided in the early history of the psychoanalytic movement. Freud was the thinker, constructing complex theories that his students are still trying to disentangle more than fifty years later. Many of his early followers broke with him because they couldn't handle his rigid, doctrinaire style. Jung, an intuitive, developed psychological theories that are more intriguing and profound, but do not have the logical consistency and clarity of Freud's. Adler's work is that of a sensation type: brief, practical, concerned with that type's values of status and power. Reich was another intuitive, but extraverted, in contrast to Jung's introversion. Reich pioneered several new lines of research in psychology, body therapy, basic physics, cancer therapy—and was jailed for his eccentric ideas, which were too far ahead of their time.

The Jungian Types and Astrology

Several attempts have been made to translate the Jungian framework into the terms of astrological symbolism and vice versa. The positive (air and fire) signs are traditionally regarded as masculine and extraverted, whereas the negative (water and earth) signs are thought of as feminine and introverted. There is some empirical support for this association. Mayo, White, and Eysenck (1978) have published a study showing significantly higher extraversion scores for both men and women born with the Sun in positive signs, vs. those born with the Sun in negative signs. Similar findings (for males only) have been reported by Lim (1975) and Metzner et al. (1979). It has also been shown that introverts more often have Saturn near their Ascendant or Midheaven, whereas extraverts more often are born with Mars or Jupiter near their Ascendant or Midheaven (Gauquelin et al., 1979).

Some astrologers relate the four functions to the four quadrants of the horoscope, or groups of houses, as follows: first, second, and third houses—intuition; fourth, fifth, and sixth—feeling; seventh, eighth, and ninth—sensation; and tenth, eleventh, and twelfth—thinking. However, these distributions do not work particularly well. For instance, the sixth house, placed in the feeling quadrant, is strongly concerned with realism and details, rather than feeling. On the other hand, the twelfth house, placed in the thinking quadrant, is usually highly emotionally toned.

A more successful correlation can, I believe, be developed if the four functions are related to the four elements of the signs. Thinking is symbolized by the air signs—Gemini, Libra, and Aquarius—all of which are concerned with concepts, information, intellectual communication, and evaluation. The water signs are related to the feeling function, as emotions are reflected in the fluid systems of the body. Some have related the fire signs to feeling, but the emotionality of Pisces, Cancer, and Scorpio seems inescapable. The fire symbolism fits with the intuitive function—the pioneer spirit in Aries, the enthusiasm and enterprise of Leo, the perception of Sagittarius. The earth signs are the sensation types of the zodiac, known for their practicality, realism, and (especially in Taurus) their sensuality.

A recently completed study carried out by the author in collaboration with Richard and Jean Holcombe provides some empirical support for these generalizations. Using the Gray-Wheelwrights Jungian Type Survey and weighted scores of elemental predominance in the natal chart (number of planets plus Ascendant and Midheaven, in the four elements), the following relationships were found: a positive correlation between intuition and fire preponderance; a negative correlation between intuition and earth; and a positive correlation between sensation and earth.

TABLE 4
The Eight Functional Types

	INTROVERT	EXTRAVERT
Thinking (Air)	theorist, philosopher, mathematician, scientist	engineer, manager, administrator, lawyer
Feeling (Water)	recluse, mystic, poet, composer, melancholic	socialite, actor, performer, therapist, sanguine
Sensation (Earth)	painter, sculptor, novelist, clairvoyant	salesman, athlete, realist, sensualist
Intuition (Fire)	prophet, psychic, visionary, eccentric	pioneer, inventor, entrepreneur, adventurer

4

The Evolutionary Typology
of the Zodiac

The most ancient, and by far the most popular, human typology is undoubtedly the symbolic language known as astrology. Here we have a system that places human personality and behavior within a cosmic framework, a system of complex interweaving relationships among the Earth, the Sun, the planets, natural processes on Earth, and the social and personal lives of men and women.

The historical origins of astrology are veiled in mystery, but the available evidence indicates it has its roots in Babylonian, Egyptian, Chaldean, and perhaps even Atlantean schools of astronomer-priests and initiates. In their monumental scholarly study *Hamlet's Mill*, Georgio de Santillana and Hertha von Dechend have shown how thoroughly astrological concepts and images permeate much of the world's mythology and symbolic literature. There has existed in the West, since the time of the Greeks, a fairly cohesive and consistent system of astrology, which was intensively studied and analyzed by several of the founding giants of modern science, including Galileo, Kepler, and Newton, and which has undergone considerable development and refinement in modern times. Although empirical research in astrology is still at a minimum, the past ten years in particular have witnessed an extraordinary blossoming of serious interest in astrology by disciplined and intelligent minds, bringing a greater depth of understanding and a broader scope of interpretation.

We do not have space within this volume to discuss at length the various theories designed to explain the nature of the relationship between cosmic factors and human life. A survey of such explanatory theories is contained in my book *Maps of Consciousness,* and a review of the physical, scientific evidence for astrological influence can be found in *The Case for Astrology* by J. A. West and J. G. Toonear. We may review here briefly the four major kinds of astrological theory: physical-causal, symbolic, humanistic, and evolutionary.

Physical-causal explanations of astrology usually rely heavily on concepts and findings regarding the electromagnetic fields of the planets; the fact that the Earth and all the planets are within the Sun's field; and the observation that ionospheric and atmospheric disturbances and fluctuations on Earth are triggered or modulated by the angular relationships of the planets. Changes in the Earth's field are believed to affect the timing of births and the patterns of heredity. Examples of a physicalistic approach may be found in Gauquelin's work on "planetary heredity," and in Edmund van Deusen's book *Astrogenetics.*

Other astrologers prefer a purely *symbolic* approach—for example, deriving the meanings of the signs from the nature of the season that that sign encompasses. Thus Aries is fiery and youthful like spring, Cancer nurturant and fertile like summer, Virgo discriminating like the harvesting process in the fall, and Capricorn conservative and structured, as suggested by the containment of natural forces in winter. A good example of this approach may be found in *The Combination of Stellar Influences* by Reinhold Ebertin.

The *humanistic* approach to astrology, associated particularly with the writings of Dane Rudhyar, has aligned itself with humanistic psychology in its emphasis on individual growth and the search for meaning. Here the symbolism of astrology focuses on the individual's need for direction and perspective in the unfolding of his or her potentials.

Esoteric or *evolutionary* astrology—as found, for example, in the writings of Alice Bailey (1975) and some of the Edgar Cayce readings (Gammon, 1967)—extends the humanistic-symbolic framework into larger cosmic perspectives of karma and reincarnation. Here it is assumed that the human Spirit, or Higher Self, incarnates into personality form by choice, choosing the time, place, and conditions of its birth as well as the identities of its parents, teachers, and other significant people in the life. This choice is made on the basis of experiences and lessons learned in prior lifetimes for the sake of evolutionary growth and advancement in this lifetime. The planetary pattern at birth is seen as a kind of blueprint or design for the life about to begin unfolding. Following the ancient Hermetic principle of "as above, so below," a kind of resonance is established between the macrocosmic map of the heavens and the microcosmic map of individual consciousness.

This map is not deterministic or fixed: Like any map, it indicates lines of development and relationship, but the individual personality chooses whether to—and how to—pursue those developments and build those relationships. The person's evolutionary growth and gain really depend more on how these choices are made than on the initial set of inclinations and predispositions given at birth. The natal chart itself does not indicate the degree of awareness and responsibility with which the person has handled the talents that were given to him. Thus it is notoriously difficult, even for an experienced astrologer, to tell the difference between the chart of a gifted and that of a retarded individual without any other information.

The astrological language is comprised of three interrelated alphabets, or symbol systems. (1) The *first* is the series of ten planets, including the Sun and Moon, but not counting the Earth, since the horoscope is computed from a geocentric, (earth-centered) point of view. (2) The *second* alphabet is the set of twelve zodiac signs, marking the orbital path of the planets around the Sun (again, transposed to a geocentric point of view). The tropical zodiac, most commonly used, is structured around the Earth orbit's four cardinal points: the two equinoxes and the two solstices. The less frequently used side-

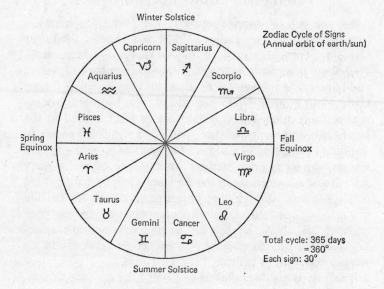

Winter Solstice

Zodiac Cycle of Signs
(Annual orbit of earth/sun)

Capricorn ♑

Sagittarius ♐

Aquarius ♒

Scorpio ♏

Pisces ♓

Libra ♎

Spring Equinox

Fall Equinox

Aries ♈

Virgo ♍

Taurus ♉

Leo ♌

Gemini ♊

Cancer ♋

Summer Solstice

Total cycle: 365 days
= 360°
Each sign: 30°

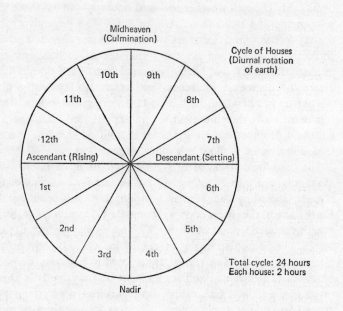

Midheaven
(Culmination)

Cycle of Houses
(Diurnal rotation
of earth)

10th   9th

11th   8th

12th   7th

Ascendant (Rising)   Descendant (Setting)

1st   6th

2nd   5th

3rd   4th

Nadir

Total cycle: 24 hours
Each house: 2 hours

real zodiac is structured around the twelve constellations, bearing the same names as the signs, which lie outside of the solar
system. (3) The *third* series is that of the twelve houses, derived
from the rotation of the Earth on its own axis, which, from the
perspective of an observer at any given point on Earth, yields a
pattern of daily risings, culminations, and settings of the Sun,
Moon, and all the planets.

In astrology as commonly practiced, there is a natural relationship among these three alphabets. The planets, which symbolize certain functions and structures of personality, are given
a particular qualitative expression or coloring according to the
sign in which they are placed. The house in which the planet-
sign combination is found indicates the area of earthly life in
which this particular function/structure is expressed or manifested. To give a simplified example, Mercury symbolizes the
mind. Mercury in the sign Virgo means that the mind is analytical and discriminating. Mercury in Virgo in the seventh
house, that of relationships, indicates a discriminative mind that
is used and applied in interpersonal relationships.

An additional, critical factor in interpretation is given by the
aspects, which are actually triangular relationships between
any two planets, and the Earth. Thus, in the above example,
aspects to Mercury in Virgo in the seventh house from other
planets could significantly amplify, attenuate, or modify its expression in the human personality.

Sun, Moon, and Ascendant

These three are generally considered the three primary symbolic indicators of personality structure and functioning. The
Higher Self, or incarnating Being, does not actually "appear" in
the horoscope. One could say that He/She is the One who designed the map for the growth and evolutionary unfolding of
the personality through life experiences. There is an interesting
and suggestive linguistic association between Sun and Soul
through *Sol,* the Latin name for Sun. The Sun astrologically
symbolizes the most enlightened part of one's identity—the

part that contains the essence of the lessons learned in all previous lifetimes, which is brought forward into this life as a natural, basic, effortless "chief feature." It is the dynamic light of one's innermost nature, and has a decidedly masculine connotation. The position and progressions of the Sun in the horoscope *illuminate* the areas of life symbolized by the houses that are occupied.

Whereas the Sun, with its powerful radiation, is dynamic (positively polarized) in relation to the Earth, the Moon, with its tidal pull on both planetary and physiological fluids, is a magnetic factor. Thus, astrologically, the Moon represents the magnetic, or feminine, side of the nature. It also represents that part of personality or identity that is related to the form or body— what might be called the instinctual nature. The Moon symbolizes primary need, as Noel Tyl has pointed out, whereas the Sun relates to primary drive or purpose. The Moon indicates the maternal line of inheritance, the early relationship with the mother, other relationships with women, and the domestic sphere—home, food, clothing, and creature comfort concerns in general. In women, and in men with a strong magnetic or feminine component, the Moon *can* be a more significant, outwardly evident factor in the chart than the Sun.

The Ascendant is the sign rising over the horizon at the moment of birth. Hence it symbolizes the quality of consciousness that is rising above the horizon of awareness during the life. It appears to indicate that which we are consciously striving to express as human beings, the personal qualities we are trying to project and develop. Alice Bailey referred to the Ascendant as the "sun of possibility," as distinguished from the Sun sign, the "sun of probability." The Ascendant relates more to the future, to promise and potential, than the Moon sign, which symbolizes our past, our hereditary "roots." Since our first area of self-expression is the physical body, particularly the face, the qualities of the rising sign are often expressed in the face and physical structure. Personal style, manner, speech and gesture, clothes, and color preferences are all likely to be related to the Ascendant sign.

The Ascendant marks the beginning of the first house, the

house of personal identity, self-projection, and development. In the circle of houses it lies opposite the Descendant, which marks the beginning of the seventh house, the house of interpersonal relationships and partnerships, both marital and professional. The sign on the Descendant in a horoscope often indicates the nature of the person one marries, the kinds of people one is attracted to, and the qualities of one's interpersonal relationships.

Four Elements and Four Functions

The symbolism of the four elements—earth, air, fire, and water —pervades ancient and medieval alchemical and occult teachings, and has tremendous usefulness and power, when applied in modern astropsychology. The four functions formulated by Jung as a psychological typology can be synthesized with the ancient esoteric teachings about man's higher bodies and levels of consciousness, and their relationship to the corresponding systems of the physical body. In delineating these relationships, I am drawing particularly on the teachings of Actualism, a modern consciousness school founded by Russell Paul Schofield. The relationship of the four types of function and consciousness to the four elements in astrology is also well described by Arroyo (1975) and Greene (1977).

The *physical* body is regarded as the lowest frequency, or densest vehicle of personality expression. It is constituted of "earth elements," the elements of the planet Earth. It is the body we use for personal expression in the time-space world of physical reality, the world of humans, creatures, plants, minerals, and concrete physical objects. Awareness focused at this level of consciousness is focused on the immediate data of sense experience and the practical realities of physical action. This level corresponds to the *earth element* in alchemy, to the sensing function in the Jungian system, and to the three earth signs—Taurus (construction), Virgo (discrimination), and Capricorn (organization)—in astrology.

The next "higher" body (that is, higher in frequency or vibratory rate, not higher in space or in value) is referred to as the *perceptual* in Actualism. In other esoteric systems it is also known as the etheric, lower astral, vital, or desire body. The perceptual dimension is the world of perception, intuition, nonverbal communication, vitality and power transmission, imagination and fantasy. In the physical body, these functions are related to the central and autonomic nervous systems, and especially to the solar plexus. When highly developed, by nature or by special training, perception may manifest as clairvoyance, clairsentience, precognition, or other kinds of psychic perception. It may also be manifest as a high degree of nervous vitality or as superactive imaginative and inspirational faculty. In alchemy this corresponds to the *fire element*, and in the Jungian system to intuition. Astrologically, intuition is sometimes associated with the water signs, as a kind of empathic feeling function, or emotional intuition. Direct perception, however, especially as it relates to trends and future possibilities, is more a Sagittarius (fire) function, and the other two fire signs also have strong symbolic connections to this dimension —Leo with vitality and imagination, Aries with power and inspiration.

Next in vibratory rate is the *emotional*, or astral, body, our vehicle in the world of feelings and emotions, from the negative states such as fear, anger, grief, and resentment, to states of pure joy, love, serenity, and rapture. At the physical level, emotions are linked to the fluid systems of the body—the blood, the lymph, and the glandular systems—and have the flow and wave characteristics of fluids. Linguistically, "emotions" are linked to the word "motion," and they do move and motivate us. Symbolically, we can relate the emotional function to the *water element*, and thus to the water signs in astrology, where we have family feeling and nurturance in Cancer, emotional depth and passion in Scorpio, and emotional duality and compassion in Pisces.

The next level is the *mental*, known as *manas* in Hindu philosophy. Sometimes the mental body has been referred to as the "causal body," because of the causal nature of thought, that process which conceives the realities in which we live. Noteworthy is the connection between the word "concept" as thought, and "conception" as the beginning of a new creation. Here is the world of ideas, thoughts, concepts, and intellectual/ verbal communication, as well as nonverbal communication, mental telepathy, and the meetings or conflicts of minds. In the physical body, the mind is, of course, linked to the brain systems, the nervous systems, and the lungs, which supply the oxygen necessary for brain activity. Alchemically, this is the *air element,* the atmosphere (literally, the "sphere of breath"), the winds and wings of thought. Astrologically, we find here the logical clarity of Gemini, the mental relatedness and balance of Libra, and the detached objectivity of Aquarius.

Above the mental level, there are three other levels of consciousness, designated by various names in the occult literature.[1] These higher levels are said to be "unobstructed": they are not subject to the conditioning influences that the four personality bodies are exposed to. Thus, in some writings (such as those of Swedenborg, for example), they are referred to as various grades or levels of "heaven." Present-day astrology does not have much to say about these higher levels of man's nature and design. Perhaps the outer planets—Uranus, Neptune, and Pluto—indicate some aspects of these higher dimensions. Possibly the stars and constellations beyond the solar system will need to be considered to delineate these higher, inner worlds.

It is interesting to observe that, in the zodiac, the progressions of the planets' paths along the ecliptic, and around the horoscope, follow the descending order of the levels of consciousness as we have just delineated them. If we start with one of the air signs (mental), and proceed counterclockwise in the usual way around the zodiac, we come next to water (emotional), then fire (intuitive-perceptual), and then earth (physical) before the cycle is repeated, starting with the next air sign.

In addition to the groupings of signs according to polarity (positive and negative), and the four elements, there is also a grouping according to the three modes (cardinal, fixed, and mutable). The cardinal signs are active, dynamic, expressive;

[1] See Chapter 12 for a further discussion of levels of consciousness.

they initiate and stimulate activity (mental, emotional, perceptual, or physical). The fixed signs are structured and resistant to change; they consolidate and contain thoughts, feelings, perceptions, and behavior patterns. The mutable signs are flexible, communicative, adaptive; they exchange and communicate ideas, emotions, intuitions, and material substances. Table 5 summarizes these symbolic associations.

TABLE 5
The Symbolism of Zodiac Signs

SIGN	POLARITY	ELEMENT	MODE
Aries	+	fire	cardinal
Taurus	—	earth	fixed
Gemini	+	air	mutable
Cancer	—	water	cardinal
Leo	+	fire	fixed
Virgo	—	earth	mutable
Libra	+	air	cardinal
Scorpio	—	water	fixed
Sagittarius	+	fire	mutable
Capricorn	—	earth	cardinal
Aquarius	+	air	fixed
Pisces	—	water	mutable

The Three Air Signs

Libra. The beginning of Libra is the autumnal equinox, when night and day are of equal length and the whole symbolism of this sign revolves around the principles of balance and equi-*librium*. The glyph of Libra, ♎, is said to represent scales, both those of justice and of equality, as well as the scales of weighing and measuring.

Weighing and measuring are mental processes, as when we ponder (literally "weigh") a situation, de*liber*ate, consider, or evaluate. Accordingly, the Libran mentality is oriented above all toward the examination and analysis of *relationships*. Traditionally, Librans are said to make good counselors, psychologists, and lawyers. Their unexcelled ability to consider, evaluate fairly, and accept views and opinions other than their own also gives them flair in diplomacy, public relations, and social functions. A Libran can say, "I disagree with you, but I may very well be mistaken."

Librans are the consummate harmonizers of the zodiac. Ruled by Venus, they love beauty in the realm of art and aesthetics, and strive for order and balance in interpersonal relationships. At a workshop in which I asked the natives of each sign to express nonverbally the essence quality of their type, the four Librans lay down on the floor with their feet touching, forming a perfect, four-pointed star. If the Moon is in Libra, the need for harmony is so physical and intense that these people may actually become physically ill in the presence of conflict or disorder. Often Librans will shy away from relationships of real depth because they fear the entanglement and confusion these would entail. There is a floating quality in many people of this type, who seem like birds gliding with outstretched wings above the Earth.

With Libra rising, the qualities of formal beauty are expressed in outer appearance. Here we find individuals of exceptional charm, grace, and refinement of manner. The women often have clear, delicate skin and a marked symmetry in structure—for example, a central parting of the hair. They seem to prefer pastel colors, especially blues, greens, and pinks.

Women with Libra Moon or Ascendant may be flirty social butterflies, or they may emanate a remote ladylike beauty that can become coldly intellectual. Men with Moon in Libra tend to idealize their women, putting them on pedestals and treating them like "fairy princesses."

There is another side to Libra, too, which is associated in part with its complementary opposite, Aries. If their sense of justice and fair play is violated, they can be tremendous fighters as was, for example, Mahatma Gandhi who had Sun in Libra. They work extremely hard for the social and personal principles they believe in. People born with Libra on the Ascendant, and thus an Aries Descendant, tend to attract Aries-like mates, who are very dynamic and hard-working individuals.

The crux of the Libra consciousness appears to be in the

area of balance. The normal expression of this is in the area of interpersonal relationships, where the individual seeks to find himself or herself through reflection from another, through caring, sharing, and balancing with a complementary type. At a higher turn of the evolutionary spiral, the lessons here involve the balancing of male and female *within* the nature, so that the dynamic decisiveness of the masculine Aries (ruled by Mars) is blended with the harmonious adaptiveness of Libra (ruled by Venus).

Aquarius. In ancient Egypt, according to Cyril Fagan (1971), the Nile flooded its banks shortly after the Full Moon was seen in the constellation Aquarius. The symbolism of an abundant flood of nourishing energy has been associated with this sign ever since. However, since it is an air sign, the flood of energy is primarily mental—showers of ideas, communications, inventions, concepts, suggestions, and observations. Sometimes the Water bearer is shown showering stars to the earth, symbolizing the light of knowledge and inspiration that he brings. In the classical Tarot, the card associated with Aquarius is The Star; in the New Tarot, he is called "The Wayshower."

The Aquarian mentality, at its best, is highly independent and original, as if inspired from an inner source of insight; compared to the Libran mentality, with its focus on interpersonal relationships, it is also rather impersonal. We find here a combination of intuition and objectivity that can lead to startlingly innovative points of view and contributions, recognized as scientific genius in Aquarians such as Galileo, Copernicus, Darwin, Swedenborg, and Thomas Edison. In the arts, this quality is exemplified by the fountain of melodic inspiration found in Mozart.

Aquarians seem to naturally adopt a kind of scientific attitude of detached observation and experimentation. It is as if they conducted life as an experiment, in which theories and ideas are constantly tested. On the one hand, this makes them open to and tolerant of widely divergent philosophies and attitudes. On the other hand, the experimental position, when carried into the area of human relationships, may strike many people as either eccentric and weird or uncaring and aloof. People who are willing to try new lifestyles, new inventions, new social forms, often have a strong Aquarius factor in their horoscope. Yet paradoxically, as Aquarius is the fixed air sign, these people can also be quite stubborn and fixed in their unconventional ideas and attitudes.

The humanitarian, social-welfare motivation is very strong in the Aquarian consciousness. They do not merely play with ideas, as Geminis tend to, they also want to solve problems and generate ideas that will improve the human condition. Thus they will often work in group projects and endeavors devoted to human and planetary service.

If the Moon is in Aquarius, this humanitarian sympathy becomes more of an instinctive, gut-level gregariousness. These are people who participate in clubs, social movements, interest groups, religious associations, or just neighborhood friendship cliques. Family relationships take on a quality of co-operative partnerships and teamwork. Husband and wife will want to be friends, even "buddies." This is the sign in which non-intimate same-sex friendships are cultivated, in contrast to its opposite, Leo, in which the focus is on sexual and creative polarization.

In outer appearance, the person with Aquarius rising or prominent looks like a friendly giant, often with wavy hair. They seem to be looking down on the world with a bemused and quizzical expression. They relish talk, especially on unusual and stimulating topics, and love games and surprises. They, like all the air signs, are somewhat uncomfortable with feelings, and may withdraw from intense emotional involvement into a kind a cloudlike state of abstractions and dreams. The core tension of the Aquarian consciousness relates to the need to find a place in the social order; to synthesize the prized independence of the ego with allegiance to a co-operative group venture for the purpose of enlightened humanitarian service.

Gemini. The symbolism of Gemini is indelibly linked to the numerous legends of twins found all over the world. In some mythologies, the twins are close and loving; in the Tarot, the card corresponding to this sign is called "The Lovers." In many other legends, the element of contest and struggle is emphasized, where one twin is righteous and true, the other evil and vindictive. Among the Greeks, the popular legend was the one of Castor, the mortal, and Pollux, the immortal, who were bound by such close ties of affection that when Castor died in battle, his twin brother, Pollux, begged his father Zeus to let him die too. It was arranged that they would spend alternate days on earth and in heaven, always together.

Thus it has been said that the basic dualism of Gemini is that of soul and form, or the immortal essence and the mortal personality. The idea of the good and evil brothers derives from this when the personality, not evil per se, becomes ensnared in the illusions of images and conditioning, and thus turns away from, or even against, its own inner lighted Self.

The Gemini glyph ♊ is said to represent the two pillars guarding the gate of Truth, which play an important part in the symbolism of Freemasonry. Gemini in astrology represents the brain-mind intellect, which is the key to making the choice between the way of truth and the path of falsehood. In the body, Gemini is related to the brain, with its two hemispheres; the nervous system, with its two divisions; and the two arms and hands, for making and expressing choices.

In the Gemini mentality, dualistic thinking reaches its highest expression. The Gemini mind has a restless hunger for ideas, facts, information, and communication. Among the Greeks and Romans, the Twins were the gods of the winds; sailors prayed to them to swell their sails. Far and wide, Gemini minds roam, like the winds, all over the earth, to seek knowledge and establish lines of communication. No other sign has such a versatile, quick, ingenious, curious, and adaptable mind, such phenomenal memory for facts, or such love and appreciation of the scintillating power of the word. In everything they do, Geminis always look for the connections, the linkages, and the demarcation of truth from falsity. Thus reporters, critics, writers, scholars, and lecturers are frequently Geminis. Examples of this kind of genius are the novelist Thomas Mann, and poets W. B. Yeats, Walt Whitman, Allen Ginsberg, and Bob Dylan. The fantastic art of M. C. Escher illustrates beautifully the polarizing duality of the Gemini vision.

When Gemini is rising, the birdlike nose, the vivacious, twinkling eyes, the gesticulating, fluttering hands, and, above all, the unceasing talk are the inevitable signs. Geminis move a lot, moving their bodies when they talk, traveling in order to talk to friends, writing letters, telephoning, communicating by every means at their disposal.

With the Moon in Gemini, the mind tends to be overactive, trying to analyze and verbalize, where gut-level, bodily intuitions would be better left alone. These people can overrationalize their feelings to the point of dissipation. They don't stay with their emotions long enough to let them mature. Here we find the man who likes a witty, intelligent, sister-type partner, a "girl" for a woman. And we find the women who are social butterflies, will-o'-the-wisps, flitting from one relationship to another.

The core test of the Gemini consciousness is to find and maintain the proper function of the mind, so that it does not get overextended and scattered into a thousand random ideas and facts, but rather serves as the mediating link between essence and personality. Directing awareness to the world of Spirit within, the mind can *also* comprehend and relate to the realities of the external world. Thus serving as bridge and mediator, it can bring about the union between the inner realms of consciousness-light and the outer realms of physical facts and events.

The Three Water Signs

Cancer. From immemorial times, the symbolism of the midsummer sign has revolved around the image of a protective shell or covering. To the Egyptians, this sign was the scarab, which protects its seed by rolling it into a sphere of earth. To the Babylonians, it was the tortoise, which, like the crab, carries its home wherever it goes. With these amphibian creatures, the most ancient animals of the zodiac, we also get the symbolism of primal origins in the nourishing mother sea, and the tentative emergence to land life.

In the human body, the sign Cancer is usually associated with the breasts, as providers of nourishment, and the stomach, as container of nourishment. However, medical astrologers have found that other covering and containing structures, including the uterus, the meninges, the pleura, and the sinuses are also ruled by Cancer. At another level, it is said that Cancer represents the physical form as the "home" of the Soul—thus again the idea of nurturing and protecting of the seed of life.

In the Cancer type, these two factors of nurturance and protection are particularly strong in the emotional (watery) realm of feelings and interpersonal relationships. Here we find the archetype of the Great Mother—not the sensual Earth Mother associated with Venus-Taurus, but the mother of nourishing, warm embrace, who represents the "bosom of the family." During the Cancerian phase of the precessional ages, around 8000 to 6000 B.C., the Great Mother religions were supreme throughout the ancient world (Stone, 1976).

Men and women with Sun in Cancer have a kind of emotional sensitivity that enables them to reach out and communicate, especially on a nonverbal level. If the childhood conditioning has been harsh and unfeeling, they learn to cover their anxiety and timidity with a defensive shield, which can become the notorious Cancerian reticence, shyness, or even crabbiness.

If the Moon is in Cancer (its natural rulership), the domestic-mothering consciousness is particularly emphasized, in a physical expression. This is the kind of woman whose life revolves around the home and who tends to mother everyone she comes in contact with. Carried to excess, this woman's maternal instincts can smother her own children. For men, Moon in Cancer characteristics are a bit difficult to handle, because of cultural images of masculinity. Cooking and other domestic arts may be pursued professionally, however, as well as obstetrics, pediatrics, or psychotherapy. Dr. Benjamin Spock, the renowned "baby doctor," is an outstanding example of Moon in Cancer.

As noted in Chapter 3, the emotional types of the Jungian

system tend to be oriented toward the past. Cancers likewise tend to have deep emotional identification with their roots in family, ancestry, and the traditions of tribe, race, or culture. Patriotism is often strong, and the awareness belonging to a family or tribe seems to nourish the emotional nature.

The novels of Marcel Proust and Hermann Hesse, the paintings of Rembrandt and Chagall, and the films of Ingmar Bergman, all of whom were Cancers, exemplify this extraordinary resonance to deep psychic currents from personal and collective memory. Buckminster Fuller, another Cancerian with tremendous sensitivity to the emotional currents of history, also expressed this consciousness in another way, by inventing, designing, and building shell-shaped (!) structures for people to live in.

If Cancer is rising, the person's face often has a kind of lunar roundedness and fullness to it, with a smallish nose and a compressed, thin-lipped mouth. These people don't speak much, and always seem to hesitate before responding to a question. Their personal style has a quality of curvedness, indirectness, or sideways relating (reminiscent of the sideways gait of the crab), rather than direct confrontation. Outwardly passive, they are inwardly (emotionally) very dynamic.

The Cancer type can become caught in a kind of tenacious, clutching overdependency on external emotional nourishment (that is, a mother complex), or can withdraw into moods of crusty defensiveness. He or she learns in time to overcome this dependency and timidity, by finding and tapping the sources of emotional nourishment and protection available from within, and relying on the inner support and unfailing strength that awareness of the Soul can provide.

Scorpio. This sign seems to have inspired both awe and fear since the most ancient times. On the one hand it was associated with sexual energy and regeneration, and on the other with secrecy, death, and destruction. The Akkadians called it the Stinger; the Egyptians and many other cultures referred to it as the Serpent; in India it was sometimes known as the Bee. The giant and brilliant red star Antares, which is in the center of the constellation Scorpio, has been considered warlike and violent in its influence. The Chinese, however, called it the "Fire Star," and thought it afforded protection against fires. During the Taurus-Scorpio Age approximately 4000 to 2000 B.C., Persian astonomers referred to Antares as the "Watcher of the West," one of the four great royal stars.

The theme of concealment and detection is basic to the Scorpio consciousness. This kind of individual conceals his own motives and feelings, but probes and investigates those of others. Scorpios are demonstrably drawn to psychiatry as a profession, as well as detection, investigation, intelligence, or probing the mysteries of nature in basic energy research (for example, Madame Curie). People with Scorpio rising are notorious for their penetrating, unsmiling gaze, which seeks to unmask others. They are impatient with superficiality, and desire to plunge into the full depth of an emotional experience. They do not speak readily about their own feelings, but when they do they are often brutally frank.

Emotional struggle and inner violence is another core theme of the Scorpionic consciousness. As it is the fixed water sign, emotional reactions are deep and persistent. The person often feels that his emotional nature is a bottomless well or cauldron, boiling with passion, whether sexual or violent. This intense, dramatic emotionality, when harnessed into artistic form, can have unbelievable impact, as exemplified by the novels of Dostoevski, or the paintings of Picasso, both of them Scorpios. It can also become the passionate zeal of the religious or political reformer, as, for example, with St. Paul, Martin Luther, Mohammed, Leon Trotsky, or Billy Graham.

When the Moon is in Scorpio, emotional reactions have a gut-level physicality that can be shattering in its intensity, whether pleasurable or painful. The tendency to emotional inflexibility makes it especially hard to handle feelings of jealousy, resentment, guilt, or rage. Unless the passions are lighted with awareness, these people may bear grudges or nurse revenge. Relationships tend to be stormy, punctuated by explosive excitement and clashing crises, with a strong emphasis on the sensual-sexual element. Both the heights and the depths of passion are experienced. Scorpio rules the generative and the eliminative organs. If Sun or Moon in Scorpio have stressful aspects, constipation or venereal problems are not uncommon.

Scorpio types are very aware of and concerned with the power aspect of sexual, emotional, and other relationships. They tend to be contemptuous of weakness of any kind. In the world of business or politics, fighting for territory or position, they make cunning, determined opponents. They can also be excellent physical or psychic healers, lending the strength of their will to uplift and support others. Or they may act as emotional "sappers," magnetically seducing and draining those with whom they relate, as in the legend of the Lady of the Lake, "La Belle Dame sans Merci." Charles Manson, for example, had five planets in Scorpio.

And yet Scorpio has the potential for extraordinary in-depth transformation and regeneration. The eliminative, catabolic processes, which it rules, function to *destructure* old, useless forms—a process that becomes destructive only if done blindly and violently. The generative power, if not limited to the physical sex act, can become transmuted into regenerative power, drawn inward and upward for spiritual renewal. The will of the warrior, when brought into accord with inner purpose, no longer runs rampant, seeking dominion over others, but fights the physician's battle against the enemies of the body, or the reformer's battle against the common enemies of man. Likewise the passionate grasping of the sensualist, concerned only with his own desires, can become the compassionate touch of the friend or therapist.

Pisces. If Cancer is symbolized by the flowing river and Scorpio by the deep pool, then Pisces is undoubtedly the ocean. Here the emotionality is vast and extensive, rather than forceful and intensive, as in Scorpio. Like Proteus, the shape-shifting sea-god of the Greeks, or like the many moods of the ocean itself, the Piscean feeling consciousness is changeable, elusive, fluid, unexplainable. There is duality and conflict of emotion, but not the seething turmoil found with Scorpio. The two fish swimming in opposite directions that represent Pisces symbolize the male and female, the outgoing and receptive aspects of feeling. There is great openness to others, emotional sensitivity to the point of vulnerability, and assumption of others' emotional loads. There is also a sympathetic outreaching to help and serve the weak and helpless. When carried to excess this can lead to a posture of false strength, and a need to have others be dependent to bolster one's own superiority.

The ability to touch the heart, inspiring emotional responses in others, is the great gift of the Piscean artistic temperament. We find it in the fluid harmonies of Chopin, the gentle serenity of Ravel, or the delicate sensuousness of Renoir's paintings. The oceanic-cosmic consciousness of Pisces, the feeling of oneness with all life, has been expressed in other ways also, as in the mystic scientific attitude of an Einstein, or a Luther Burbank. The Piscean soldier-statesman George Washington had prophetic visions on the battlefield. Mediumistic, psychic aptitudes are common with Pisces, and several of the best-known mystics, and channels of occult knowledge, including Rudolf Steiner, Edgar Cayce, and Meher Baba, have been Pisceans.

If Pisces is the rising sign, there is often a limpid, dreamy look to the eyes. Melancholy may be indicated by the whites showing above the lower lids. Their emotional sensitivity and impressionability make these people shy to the point of timidity and reclusiveness. They are gentle in expression, and seem to have an inward focus, as if listening to unheard melodies. Some Pisceans, especially lymph-dominant endomorphs, tend toward massive, whalelike body structures, as if carrying the sufferings of the world.

With the Moon in Pisces, there is deep identification with one's instinctive sympathetic reactions, especially those of grief and depression. Here we may find the character of "Deirdre of the Sorrows," lost in self-pity, weeping with cosmic pain. Escaping into drugs or alcohol, idealistic fantasizing, self-sacrificing martyrdom, or the victim game are some of the less constructive manifestations of this position. But as blind sympathy becomes aware empathy, these people are able to relate in interpersonal situations with unequaled delicacy and balanced sensitivity.

The mission of Pisces involves the fusion of magnetic (feminine) and dynamic (masculine) emotional energy and the practical application of sensitivity, so strong in its polar opposite, Virgo. Then the cosmic vision of the mystic can be earthed in the ministry of the healer-teacher, or the artistry of the poet-musician.

The Three Fire Signs

Aries. The symbolism of Aries revolves around the youthful vigor of springtime and the dynamic directness of the ram. Born in the season in which new life force germinates and emerges from winter's sleep, these people have a quality of overbrimming, vibrant vitality that sparks and inspires others. They are often found in leadership positions where their pioneering spirit and dynamic enthusiasm can generate new projects and enterprises. While there is a natural aptitude for leadership, it is not the team- or group-oriented kind, but more the highly personal style of leadership focused around a particular individual. Autocratic soldier-statesmen such as Charlemagne or Bismarck might be cited as examples.

Aries traditionally rules the head, and people born in this sign are idea-oriented, originators and innovators of new developments in art, science, or philosophy; Wilhelm Reich provides a good example of this pioneering spirit. Aries, however, rules the sensory-motor systems of the head, rather than the brain itself (which is ruled by Gemini), and thus the Aries mentality is not the cool, associative logic of Gemini, but more intuitive, direct, decisive, and action-oriented. It wants to bring forth, to show, to express the exuberant life force gushing out from within. Advertising, promoting, and acting are careers attractive to this type. In the traditional Tarot symbolism Aries corresponds to The Emperor, the autocratic ruler; in the New Tarot he is The Actor, the one who takes *action*.

There is a side of Aries that is ruled by Mars that exults in combat and fierce competitive struggle, whether in sports, politics, or business. Here the forthright expressiveness of the springtime ram becomes the forceful aggressiveness of the battering ram used in medieval warfare. The fighting-spirit of Aries manifests in quick, impulsive flashes of hot temper, not in the slow, smoldering fire of the Scorpionic warrior. Aries types face challenges with a direct, frontal view that tends toward narrowness and a certain amount of naïveté. The superior strength and energy of the warrior can lead to arrogance and to insensitivity to others' needs.

If the Moon is in Aries, the inner urge toward activity and self-expression becomes a restless need for constant physical stimulation and excitement. Such people have a volatile emotional nature, with quick, extreme mood swings. They are impatient, impetuous, and impulsive, but may hide their fiery forcefulness behind a calm exterior, especially if the Sun is in an earth or air sign. The men link up with women who are excitable and vital. The Aries-Moon woman comes across as the proverbial "ball of fire," with an explosive, passionate temperament, given to neither domestic contentment (*à la* Cancer) nor sweet romance (*à la* Taurus).

The physical appearance of someone with Aries rising is dominated by the head. Often it is large, with luxuriant and/or curly hair, and a relatively low hairline. The red hair and beard of Van Gogh is a classic example of Arian structure. The features are strong and forceful, with a pronounced emphasis on the middle of the forehead—sometimes a slight bulge is found here. They may have ruddy complexions, and tend to prefer reddish colors in clothes and decor.

It has been said that Aries is a ram on the outside but a lamb on the inside. The Greek myth of Phrixos told of the hero being carried to safety by a flying ram, with the fear of death behind him. Some astrologers feel that Aries consciousness is somehow haunted by past-life memories of Piscean cosmic oneness, submerging his identity. The Arian brash courage and assertive sensuality do seem to have an undertone of insecurity. It is as if the powerful thrust into extraverted objectivity is motivated, at least in part, by an unconscious fear of falling back into a kind of introverted subjectivity.

There is something impersonal about the Aries style of relating. Like the other fire signs, these people are more interested in the ideas and energies behind relationships than in feelings per se (which is more characteristic of the water signs). The Aries individual needs to learn some of the sensitive consideration of his opposite, Libra, so that he can channel his (or her) uncontainable, fiery energy into an acceptable social form, allowing self-expression in creative activity and personal relationships.

Leo. Whereas the energy of Aries is a fierce rushing, explosive and volcanic, the energy of Leo is a steady fire, the blazing warmth of the midsummer sun. The Aries personality can initiate and innovate, but is not usually strong on follow-through. The Leo personality, on the other hand, has a natural organizing talent that can pull together gigantic enterprises (for example, Henry Ford, Cecil B. deMille). Leo is ruled by the Sun, so in this sign the solar energy, the inner light-fire of a man or a woman, radiates with a generous, regal splendor that warms all who come within its field of influence. Aries wants and strives to be a leader, but Leo just assumes a position of authority and power naturally. At its best this character expresses nobility, confidence, true pride, and dignity. When debased or exaggerated, the type may express lazy self-indulgence and arrogant egotism. The dictatorial propensity is exemplified in Leos such as Napoleon, Mussolini, and Fidel Castro.

Leo rules the heart, pumping life force throughout the body. Leos often function as the heart of a group, inspiring and supporting their friends with generous recognition and praise. They require equal recognition and admiration for themselves, and can become quite distressed if this is not forthcoming. Because of this keen sensitiveness to social feedback, Leos are vulnerable to flattery and to exploitation by those who would take advantage of their gullibility.

Leo personalities are highly aware of their impact on others, and cultivate and develop the power of their personal projection. This is the core of the dramatizing tendency often noted in people of this type: They derive much of their sense of identity from the feeling of having an audience, of being onstage. An unusually high percentage of actors and celebrities, who function in the limelight, are Leos.

Especially if the Moon is in Leo, this dramatizing tendency can reach theatrical and even hysterical proportions. These people have an almost physical need to feel important and admired. In women we find the "queen bee" type, who likes to surround herself with the symbols and ceremonies of status and eminence, whether political, financial, or artistic. In men we find those who admire and attract powerful, regal women; or those who avoid relationships with women altogether, in order not to be dominated by them. And yet here, too, the ardent, warm-hearted nature of the Lion attracts and inspires friendships and love affairs.

In personal appearance, some of the indicators of a Leo Ascendant are broad shoulders, the leonine mane, the characteristic cock of the head, the blond or russet hair, and the high, nervous vitality. The personal style may be dignified and poised, or it can be abrupt and overbearing. Orange, gold, and yellows are preferred colors.

Leo represents the dynamic aspect of creative energy, the outpouring expression of vision and power. This is in contrast to Taurus, which represents the receptive aspect, the gathering of resources and building of structures to support creative activity. While many Leos are outstandingly creative in relationships with children, as teachers or counselors, they are not naturally drawn, as Cancer is, to parenthood. In family relationships there is high emphasis on playing the game, on social forms and rituals. In the arts too, the preferred mode of expression is one involving rich use of symbols, vivid colors, and flamboyant flights of imagination.

In the cycle of initiation legends known as the Labors of Hercules, the sign Leo is connected to the fifth Labor—the slaying of the wild Nemean lion. This is a task that Hercules had to accomplish by strangling him with his bare hands. One could say that the rampant lion, devastating the countryside, symbolizes the powerful personality, running wild, under the influence of egocentric images. Then the test of the Leo individual is to learn to handle these random destructive forces. Another version of the Leo initiation is given in the Tarot card

"Strength," which depicts a woman taming a lion with gentle hands: Here the rampant power of the personal ego (the lion) is integrated with Spirit through the gently persuasive influence of love.

Sagittarius. Chinese astrologers called the constellation the Horse, Indians referred to it as the Archer, and the western zodiac combines both symbols in the figure of the Centaur-Archer. The moving power of the horse together with the aiming vision of the archer indicate the essential duality of the sign, which is known as the mutable fire sign.

Sagittarius rules the thighs, the main power springs for movement in the body. One key feature of the personalities of this sign is their interest and involvement in *moving activities:* travel, adventure, outdoor games, and sports, especially those that require use of the legs (hiking, jogging, skiing, riding). Sagittarians are notable for their often worldwide journeys, their curiosity about and openness to foreign cultures and people. The cultural anthropologist Margaret Mead was an outstanding example. For some, the expansive moving activity is carried on entirely in the inner realms of consciousness: Here we find the wide-ranging philosophers and seekers, expanding the horizons of their awareness through mental and spiritual pursuits and practices.

The aiming vision of Sagittarius also manifests at several different levels. It can be the sharp perceptiveness of the teacher or counselor, the prophetic vision of the psychic, clairvoyant, or artist (for example, Nostradamus, William Blake), or the spiritual aspiration of the devoted believer. The mentality of Sagittarius does not have the factual emphasis of Gemini, or the objectivity of Aquarius, but is more concerned with beliefs and attitudes. Sagittarians endeavor to attain a philosophical perspective, whether through their own thinking or through adoption of an existing belief system that they can support and espouse. When they do commit themselves to a mental, spiritual, or political position, they tend to do so with emotional idealism, at times bordering on fanaticism. Winston Churchill and Charles de Gaulle, both visionary statesmen, were classic Sagittarians.

With some personalities of this type, the aiming arrow of the Archer manifests in sharp, pointed talk—the notorious Sagittarian bluntness that loves to shock hidebound attitudes and puncture inflated egos. Paracelsus' bold and brilliant mockery of the medical profession of his day, Jonathan Swift's biting, yet subtle satires, and Mark Twain's good-natured humor are varying examples of this kind of expression in the literary field. Sagittarians' speech in social interactions may be careless and brusque, but it is sincere and uncalculating.

When Sagittarius is the Ascendant one often sees a long, straight nose, eager, pulsing eyes, and either unusual height or ample thighs and hips. Always the adventurous spirit, the benevolent optimism, the love of outdoors, the casual, free-and-easy attitude, but also the love of argument and debate are characteristic. With the Moon in Sagittarius, these qualities are present also, and manifest particularly in relationships with family members. The combination of wanderlust and visual focus gives both men and women of this type somewhat of the "roving eye," and a tendency to be attracted to someone on "the other side of the fence," especially someone from a different culture or country.

Sagittarius is the wanderer and the truth seeker. Often they search in their youth and teach as they grow older. Their everyouthful enthusiasm makes them inspiring teachers. As they fuse the powerful flexibility of the centaur with the perceptive accuracy of the archer, they reach the place in consciousness to which they aspire, where purposeful evolutionary growth is supported by the inspirational vision of truth.

The Three Earth Signs

Capricorn. The symbolism and mythic connections of Capricorn are full of paradoxes. He is the sure-footed goat, scaling remote and difficult mountains, but he has the tail of a dolphin and is thought to be either escaping into or emerging from the sea. He is associated with cold midwinter, the preservation of fire through the long night of the winter solstice, and the birth of new light (including the Christmas festivals). The Romans associated the goddess Vesta, virginal preserver of the hearth fire and inventor of housing, with this sign, but the Greeks associated it with Pan, the goat-legged, horned deity who frolicked with lusty earthiness among the flocks and wood nymphs. By mythic transformation, Pan became the cloven-hoofed, horny devil of Christianity. The related Satyrs, with their rampant virility and exuberant song, gave birth first to the genre of comic parody known as "satire," and later to Greek "tragedy" (which literally means "goat song").

All of these associations are found in varying degrees in the Capricorn character. There is the core feature of achievement —the determination and ambition to accomplish high aims through mastery of skills. The Capricorn personality is hard-working, disciplined, practical, and conscientious. They set an objective and methodically plan the steps necessary to reach it. Many outstanding managers, executives, and political leaders have been Capricorns—for example, Ben Franklin, Martin Luther King, and Mao Tse-tung. This hard-line focus on material goals and results has given this sign somewhat of a reputation for being coldly rigid and calculating, qualities exemplified by Capricornians Joseph Stalin and Konrad Adenauer, who was nicknamed the "cast-iron chancellor."

Capricorns' drive to achieve and excel is not limited to the world of politics and business. They are deeply interested in laws, whether it be the laws of man, of nature, or of God. Several outstanding scientists, including Isaac Newton, Johannes Kepler, and Louis Pasteur, have been Capricorns. The superb organizational capability and versatile resourcefulness of this sign have also found expression in organized spiritual work by such figures as G. I. Gurdjieff, Albert Schweitzer, and Swami Yogananda. Always with Capricorn there is deep respect for tradition and for the values and practices that have passed the test of time, conserving the light of truth in the midwinter darkness of ignorance. In the body, Capricorn is related to the bones, maintaining the structural integrity of the whole organism.

The earthy side of Capricorn is often hidden behind the outer persona of responsible seriousness. Yet these people are capable of being very sensual in private, as well as very humorous. The quality of their humor may be lusty and ribald, as in the novels of Henry Miller, or impish and philosophical as with J. R. Tolkien, or sprightly playful with a gifted comedian such as Danny Kaye.

With the Moon in Capricorn, the serious reserve usually prevails, and the need for power and authority seems to mask a deep personal insecurity and shyness. Such people, though capable and resourceful, tend to be out of touch with their feelings, except in states of melancholy and depression. Their early home and family life is often somehow cold, lonely, and demanding. Considerations of status and career enter significantly into their choice of mate and the raising of their children.

With Capricorn on the Ascendant (unless overshadowed by a dominant angular planet), one recognizes the serious, almost austere demeanor, the air of melancholy, the features that are either bony-gnarled or heavy-set, and the wrinkles of concern on the forehead. They tend to prefer dark colors and a conservative, classical style in clothes.

Capricorn is the paternal counterpart to Cancer's maternal domesticity. Capricorns represent the patriarchal principles of authority, structure, and social tradition. During the Capricorn experience these souls learn to temper the rugged hardness of the mountains with the fluid warmth of the sea, so that authority does not become authoritarian, structure remains flexible, and tradition supports evolutionary growth.

Taurus. It was during the great age when the vernal equinox was in Taurus (approximately 4000–2000 B.C.) that several of the great civilizations of ancient times, at the prime of their development, celebrated the springtime forces of procreation in symbolic worship of bulls or cows. Egypt had the cult of Apis, who was considered an incarnation of the creator-god Ptah, and was shown with a golden disk between his horns. In the Assyrian and Chaldean civilizations, numerous statues of winged and crowned bulls guarded the temples, and the Sumerians revered Taurus as the "Bull of Light." The great star Aldebaran, the left eye of the bull, was regarded as the "Watcher of the East," opposite Antares in Scorpio. From this stellar reference we derive our expression "bull's eye."

Like the other earth signs Taurus is credited with common sense, practicality, and realism. In contrast to the vaulting ambition of Capricorn, Taurus operates more quietly to accumulate resources and establish foundations. His home is the blossoming fields of May, rather than the craggy mountains of December. Generally speaking, Capricorn is more interested in earthly power, Taurus in earthly wealth. In group projects, the Taurus type is generally the one to stabilize and consolidate the advances pioneered by an Aries, proclaimed by a Leo, or envisioned by a Sagittarius. Though they tend to rely on others to provide the initial impulse and inspiration for action, they are great builders and structuralists. Some of the most prolific thinker-writers have been Taureans, including Honoré de Balzac, Bertrand Russell, Robert Browning, Sigmund Freud, and Karl Marx.

The sensual side of earthiness is also found in Taurus, who is reputed to be the one zodiac type most addicted to the pleasures of the senses. The Roman astrologer Manilius called Taurus *dives puellis* ("rich in maidens"), because of the two clusters of "female" stars in that constellation, the Pleiades and the Hyades. The Greeks associated Taurus with the abduction of the nymph Europa by Zeus, who assumed the form of a bull to seduce her; and with the horrendous tale of the Cretan Minotaur, the monster born to a queen who was infatuated with a bull. There are symbolic indications here regarding the possible pitfalls of excessive and possessive sensuality in the Taurean consciousness.

It should be noted that not all Taurus personalities are sensual, by any means; many overcompensate and deny that aspect of their nature. Comparing Taurus with its polar opposite Scorpio, we may say that whereas Scorpio, ruled by fierce Mars in a water element, is more involved in emotional depth and passion, Taurus, with its Venus and earth connotations, is more interested in beauty of form and sensory pleasure. Both being fixed signs, both are slow to learn the lessons of possessiveness.

If the Moon is in Taurus, it is said to be exalted because here the lunar, feminine principle of form is combined with the Venusian principle of beauty. In women this can produce the extremely magnetic, serenely sensual Earth-goddess type (in men, an attraction for that type of woman). More generally, the Moon in Taurus indicates a magnetic capacity to attract abundance, the love of form expressed in the collecting of articles of beauty, fondness for good food and earthly luxury, and a decided "green thumb" for relating with the plant kingdom.

When Taurus is on the Ascendant, there may be either the graceful, willowy Venusian kind of form, or else the classic, stocky, round-headed, bull-necked structure. There is a preference for earth materials (wood, leather, stones), natural clothes and surroundings, beautiful jewelry, and blue-green or turquoise color tones.

Taurus rules the throat and is related in the Tarot to The Hierophant, also called The Speaker. It has long been assumed therefore that this type is attracted to singing and other professions in which the voice is used. We recall the association with the creative principle in the Egyptian myth of Apis-Ptah, and in the Greek myth of the maze built by the creative genius of Daedalus to house the monstrous Minotaur. The Taurus consciousness is basically concerned with discovering and building the right relationship between the procreative force and the creative force, between the desires of the sensual nature and the purposes of the soul nature. As these are brought into focus and integrated, we no longer have the earth bull charging wildly and blindly, but the open-eyed bull of light, moving steadily toward his/her evolutionary objective.

Virgo. The symbolism of Virgo is a multifaceted jewel. She is Demeter-Ceres, the guardian of earth's fruitfulness, holding a sheaf of corn. In the constellation Virgo, this sheaf of corn is crowned by the brilliant white star Spica, considered one of the most beneficent and abundant in its influence. Virgo also represents Isis, the wise teacher-goddess, and the Sphinx, half woman and half lion, which marked the transition from the Virgo to the Leo precessional age. And Virgo is the Christian Virgin Mother and Madonna, polarized counterpart to the Ichthys-Pisces Jesus figure during the Pisces-Virgo age.

In the solar year, Virgo is the time for the gathering and handling of resources, bringing earthly fruits to harvest, and sorting the grain from the chaff. In the body, Virgo rules the pancreas, the spleen, and small intestines—organs of assimilation, metabolic sifting, and discrimination. Thus qualities of purity, discernment, and criticalness have always been associated with this sign.

The Virgo type is basically extremely fastidious and perfectionist in his attitudes and behavior, though it is not uncommon to find the critical orderliness limited to one area, with compensating carelessness in other departments of life (the "closet slob" phenomenon). Their emphasis on the exactness of detail and the precision of technique can cause them to lose the perspective of the detached, long-range view. And yet no other sign has such a gift for craftsmanship and technical processes, whether in medicine, scientific research, or any other kind of human endeavor.

The contrast with the preceding sign in the zodiac circle could hardly be greater: Where Leo assumes regal splendor, Virgo cares nothing for the limelight, and wants only to get the job done, precisely and efficiently. Instead of the noble King, we have the humble servant and dedicated worker. These people derive their sense of identity and self-acceptance from work accomplished efficiently and well. Though they are helpful to others, they seem to relate less to people than to technical processes and systems that indirectly serve and nourish people, as in nutrition, nursing, healing, and accounting.

When the Moon is in Virgo, the sharp exactingness is extended to the personal realm of home and family relationships. Women with this sign may be meticulous housekeepers, but somewhat cold and fussy mothers. They seem to emanate an aura of virginal untouchability. Men with this sign like their mate to be hard-working, sensible, and unglamorous. Both sexes tend to be very attentive to nutrition and diet.

The appearance of one with Virgo on the Ascendant is often remarkable for the narrow, elongated face, with domed head and pointed chin. Rust brown and earth colors are preferred, and their demeanor is self-effacing, fastidious, and highly analytical. They always want to know the detailed whys and wherefores. With Virgo rising they tend to attract warm, emotional Piscean partners who are less efficient and organized than they are.

In the Tarot, Virgo corresponds to the Hermit, and there is something of the celibate monk or recluse in the Virgo consciousness. In personal relationships they tend to be reclusive, and they usually devote themselves to service and hard work. They may become "workaholics." Their loving care for material structures and detail makes them liable to perfectionism, but it also brings them probably as close to perfecting their chosen task and mission as is humanly possible.

TABLE 6
Symbolic Associations with Zodiac Signs

SIGN	NATURE SYMBOL	TAROT	RULING DEITY ACCORDING TO PLATO
Aries	volcano	Emperor	Athena or Ares
Taurus	plain or meadow	Hierophant	Aphrodite (Venus)
Gemini	wind	Lovers	Apollo
Cancer	rain or river	Chariot	Hermes (Mercury)
Leo	sunlight	Strength	Zeus (Jupiter)
Virgo	valley or field	Hermit	Demeter (Ceres)
Libra	rainbow	Justice	Hephaistos (Vulcan)
Scorpio	deep pool or lake	Death	Ares (Mars)
Sagittarius	lightning	Temperance	Artemis (Diana)
Capricorn	mountain or rocks	Devil	Vesta or Pan
Aquarius	high clouds	Star	Hera (Juno)
Pisces	ocean	Moon	Poseidon (Neptune)

Solar Progressions and Personal Growth

It is possible to obtain a quick overview of the major developmental phases of one's life by examining the "secondary progressions" of the Sun. These are based on the formula of "a day for a year"—that is, one day's progression of the natal horoscope indicates one year's development in the life. For example, if a person is born with the Sun at 15° Taurus, at the age of 10 his progressed Sun would be at 25° Taurus, and at the age of 15 it would progress into Gemini. Generally, people born within the last five degrees of any sign will come across more with the qualities of the progressed Sun that they have been living with for most of their formative childhood period.

The simplified table of solar progressions in the Appendix to this chapter allows one to quickly calculate the current progressed Sun. Simply start at the birthday and count down the number of days (and degrees) equal to the years of your age. The Sun's position at that point is your progressed Sun for your current year. If you are forty years of age, this is equivalent to the Sun's position forty days after your birth.

Note especially at what age the Sun progresses from one sign to another. Such changes will be experienced in the life as a shift of emphasis from one level of consciousness to another. For example, the transition from an air sign to a water sign would likely be accompanied by a gradual shift from head dominance to greater emotionality. A progression from water to fire would imply more vitality and movement, with perhaps less emotional turmoil. Fire to earth suggests more emphasis on the practical application of visions and ideas, less pure speculation, and fewer flights of fancy. Earth to air would indicate renewed intellectual interests and expanded mental horizons. These changes are slow and pervasive; we stay in one sign for thirty years.

TABLE 7
The Sun's Progressions

Jan.1	♑ 10	Mar.1	♓ 10	May.1	♉ 10	Jul.1	♋ 8	Sep.1	♍ 8	Nov.1	♏ 8
2	11	2	11	2	11	2	9	2	9	2	9
3	12	3	12	3	12	3	10	3	10	3	10
4	13	4	13	4	13	4	11	4	11	4	11
5	14	5	14	5	14	5	12	5	12	5	12
6	15	6	15	6	15	6	13	6	13	6	13
7	16	7	16	7	16	7	14	7	14	7	14
8	17	8	17	8	17	8	15	8	15	8	15
9	18	9	18	9	18	9	16	9	15	9	16
10	19	10	19	10	19	10	17	10	16	10	17
11	20	11	20	11	19	11	18	11	17	11	18
12	21	12	21	12	20	12	19	12	18	12	19
13	22	13	22	13	21	13	20	13	19	13	20
14	23	14	23	14	22	14	21	14	20	14	21
15	24	15	24	15	23	15	22	15	21	15	22
16	25	16	25	16	24	16	23	16	22	16	23
17	26	17	26	17	25	17	24	17	23	17	24
18	27	18	27	18	26	18	25	18	24	18	25
19	28	19	28	19	27	19	26	19	25	19	26
20	29	20	29	20	28	20	26	20	26	20	27
21	♒ 0	21	♈ 0	21	29	21	27	21	27	21	28
22	1	22	1	22	♊ 0	22	28	22	28	22	29
23	2	23	2	23	1	23	29	23	29	23	♐ 0
24	3	24	3	24	2	24	♌ 0	24	♎ 0	24	1
25	4	25	4	25	3	25	1	25	1	25	2
26	5	26	5	26	4	26	2	26	2	26	3
27	6	27	6	27	5	27	3	27	3	27	4
28	7	28	6	28	6	28	4	28	4	28	5
29	8	29	7	29	7	29	5	29	5	29	6
30	9	30	8	30	8	30	6	30	6	30	7
31	10	31	9	31	9	31	7	Oct.1	7	Dec.1	8
Feb.1	11	Apr.1	10	Jun.1	10	Aug.1	8	2	8	2	9
2	12	2	11	2	11	2	9	3	9	3	10
3	13	3	12	3	12	3	10	4	10	4	11
4	14	4	13	4	13	4	11	5	11	5	12
5	15	5	14	5	14	5	12	6	12	6	13
6	16	6	15	6	15	6	13	7	13	7	14
7	17	7	16	7	16	7	14	8	14	8	15
8	18	8	17	8	16	8	15	9	15	9	16
9	19	9	18	9	17	9	16	10	16	10	17
10	20	10	19	10	18	10	17	11	17	11	18
11	21	11	20	11	19	11	18	12	18	12	19
12	22	12	21	12	20	12	18	13	19	13	20
13	23	13	22	13	21	13	19	14	20	14	21
14	24	14	23	14	22	14	20	15	21	15	22
15	25	15	24	15	23	15	21	16	22	16	23
16	27	16	25	16	24	16	22	17	23	17	24
17	28	17	26	17	25	17	23	18	24	18	25
18	29	18	27	18	26	18	24	19	25	19	26
19	♓ 0	19	28	19	27	19	25	20	26	20	27
20	1	20	29	20	28	20	26	21	27	21	28
21	2	21	♉ 0	21	29	21	27	22	28	22	29
22	3	22	1	22	♋ 0	22	28	23	29	23	♑ 0
23	4	23	2	23	1	23	29	24	♏ 0	24	1
24	5	24	3	24	2	24	♍ 0	25	1	25	2
25	6	25	4	25	3	25	1	26	2	26	3
26	7	26	5	26	4	26	2	27	3	27	4
27	8	27	6	27	5	27	3	28	4	28	5
28	9	28	7	28	5	28	4	29	5	29	6
		29	8	29	6	29	5	30	6	30	7
		30	9	30	7	30	6	31	7	31	8
						31	7				

Notes to Table 7, Solar Progressions

For example, a person born on May 10 wishes to know where his progressed Sun is at the age of 55. Looking in the third column, we find May 10 is opposite Taurus 19°. Counting down, the Sun progressing at the rate of 1 day=1 degree=1 year of life, at the age of 11/12 his Sun progressed into Gemini. Continuing on down, at the age 31/32 his Sun progressed into Cancer. At 55 his progressed Sun is at 22° Cancer. In another 8 years or so, it will progress into Leo. The apparent doubling of some degrees for 1 day (date) is due to the discrepancy between the 365 days in the year and the 360 degrees in the zodiac circle. The actual motion of the Sun in one day is 59 minutes and 8 seconds of arc. The table is approximate; one should allow an error factor of plus or minus 1 degree (day, year).

5

---◆---

Planetary Types

Besides the well-known typology of the zodiac, there are several other type systems that are based on astrology. One of these is derived, not from the sign positions of the Sun and Moon, but from the angular relationship between them—that is, the phases of the Moon. Another type system is based on the idea that each person is ruled by, or expresses strongly, the influence of a particular planet. From this idea, which was widely believed throughout antiquity and the Middle Ages, we still retain everyday-language adjectives such as mercurial, venial (and venereal), martial, jovial, saturnine, sunny, and lunatic.

Typology of the Lunation Cycle

The cycle of the Moon's constantly changing angular relationship with the Sun has been made the basis of an eightfold-type system by the astrologer Dane Rudhyar (1971). The primary importance of the Sun, indicative of the inner essence Self, and the Moon, symbolic of instinctual personality reaction patterns, have been described before. Here we are not concerned with the position of the Sun and the Moon in the signs of the zodiac, but purely with the angular or phase relationship between them.

This lunation cycle, as it is called, goes from conjunction

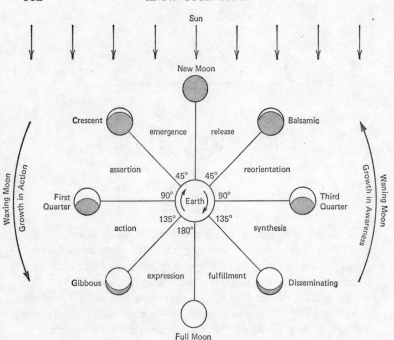

(New Moon) to opposition (Full Moon), and back again to conjunction, in a period of about twenty-nine days. The cycle can be divided and analyzed in several ways. First, we can compare the two hemicycles: the waxing Moon hemicycle, when the Moon's light is increasing, and the waning hemicycle, from Full Moon decreasing back to New Moon. The former is said to be more subjective and spontaneous in its consciousness, concerned with action and the beginnings of things. The latter is said to be more objective and aware, concerned with meaning and the endings of things. These two hemicycles can in turn be divided into four quadricycles, as follows:

New Moon to First Quarter: instinctual, unconscious activity, search for self.

First Quarter to Full Moon: development of personality, setting goals.

Full Moon to Third Quarter: repolarization, finding meanings, expanding awareness.

Third Quarter to New Moon: breaking down old habit patterns, assimilation of experiences.

When the four phases are further subdivided by two, we obtain the eight soli-lunar types delineated in the following table.
It is a simple matter to determine one's type by finding the
Sun's and the Moon's positions in the horoscope and calculating the angular difference between them, proceeding counterclockwise in the direction of the zodiac. For more detailed
descriptions of the types, the reader may wish to refer to
Rudhyar's book *The Lunation Cycle*.

TABLE 8
The Eight Lunation Types

1. *New Moon type*   (Moon 0° to 45° ahead of Sun)
                      Emergence. Subjective, impulsive, in-
                      stinctive.

2. *Crescent Moon type*   (Moon 45° to 90° ahead of Sun)
                      Assertion. Confident, challenging, grow-
                      ing.

3. *First Quarter type*   (Moon 90° to 135° ahead of Sun)
                      Action. Constructive, purposeful, ener-
                      getic.

4. *Gibbous Moon type*   (Moon 135° to 180° ahead of Sun)
                      Expression. Creating, searching, devel-
                      oping.

5. *Full Moon type*   (Moon 180° to 135° behind Sun)
                      Fulfillment. Objective, functioning, re-
                      lating.

6. *Disseminating type*   (Moon 135° to 90° behind Sun)
                      Synthesis. Assimilating, evaluating, dis-
                      seminating.

7. *Third Quarter type*   (Moon 90° to 45° behind Sun)
                      Reorientation. Planning, applying, in-
                      venting.

8. *Balsamic Moon type*   (Moon 45° to 0° behind Sun)
                      Release. Prophetic, inspiring, intuitive.

A more elaborate typology based on lunar phases was proposed by the poet W. B. Yeats in a remarkable work, first published in 1925, entitled *A Vision*. In it, Yeats summarized and synthesized the results of seven years of communications that had been mediumistically received by his wife and recorded through automatic writing and sleeptalking. It is a complex and difficult system of symbols and metaphors based on the phases of the Moon that was applied by his "communicators," as he called them, to both human temperament and history. These symbols and images form the occult basis of much of Yeats' poetry.

Yeats begins with the symbol of two cones (or "gyres"), interacting and whirling in opposite directions, which represent subjectivity and objectivity. This double cone forms the framework of the lunar phase cycle. He divides this cycle into two alchemical "tinctures": "primary," when the Moon is less than half full, and "antithetical," when it is greater than half full. The four main phases are then described as:

First quarter (0° to 90°): primary and waxing—instinct
Second quarter (90° to 180°): antithetical and waxing —emotion
Third quarter (180° to 270°): antithetical and waning—intellect
Fourth quarter (270° to 360°): primary and waning—perception

Yeats then goes on to present a system of twenty-eight "incarnations," each approximately equivalent to one day of the lunar cycle. He categorized these as character types formed by the interaction of four faculties of man: the will, the mask, the creative mind, and the body of fate.

To give a flavor of the Yeats symbology, Table 9 simply lists the names for the "will" of each of these lunar types. Each of these characters will manifest positive or negative traits, depending on whether he is "in phase" or "out of phase." The traits are produced by the interaction of the primary and antithetical tinctures, which are subtle but pervasive qualities in

TABLE 9
The Twenty-eight Lunar Incarnations
(according to W. B. Yeats)

1. Plasticity	15. Beauty
2. Beginning of energy	16. The positive man
3. Beginning of ambition	17. The daimonic man
4. Desire for primary objects	18. The emotional man
5. Separation from innocence	19. The assertive man
6. Artificial individuality	20. The concrete man
7. Assertion of individuality	21. The acquisitive man
8. War between individuality and race	22. Balance between ambition and contemplation
9. Belief takes place of individuality	23. The receptive man
10. The image-breaker	24. The end of ambition
11. The consumer	25. The conditional man
12. The forerunner	26. The multiple man
13. The sensuous man	27. The saint
14. The obsessed man	28. The fool

that person's being; the reader is encouraged to investigate the details of Yeats' system in *A Vision*.

Elaborating on the Yeats symbolism, three contemporary astrologers—Busteed, Tiffany, and Wergin—have produced a more detailed and comprehensive schema of lunar phase typology, correlated more closely with the modern symbolism of the solar zodiac. Readers interested in this system are referred to their excellent and lucid book *Phases of the Moon* (Busteed et al., 1974).

Astrological Indicators of Planetary Prominence

Several factors are used in astrological horoscope reading to determine the dominance or prominence of a given planet in the chart. First, there is *angularity,* the proximity of the planet to one of the four main angles: the Ascendant, the Midheaven, the Descendant, and the Nadir. The closer the orb, the stronger the effect, but 5° on either side of the angle would generally be considered strong. Some astrologers think of angular planets as constituting the foreground or *gestalt,* against the background or field of the rest of the horoscope.

To describe the symbolism of the angles briefly: The Ascendant indicates personal identity and self-projection; the Nadir indicates the inner, private sphere, the home and roots of the self; the Descendant symbolizes relationships, the qualities of others that we attract toward us; and the Midheaven symbolizes the public, outer self-expression, the professional and social environment.

Another factor contributing to the prominence of a planet's position in the horoscope would be the *number* and *closeness* of *aspects*—that is, how many other planets are in strong phase relationships to it. The planet then appears almost like a kingpin factor in the personality, around which other traits and qualities cluster. The reverse also applies: A planet with no aspects at all, or only minor ones, can assume unusual importance by indicating an area of lack, or a conspicuous absence, in the personal constitution.

Yet another indicator of important planetary influence would be what is called *singularity:* the phenomenon of a given planet occupying an entire side or half of the chart by itself, with all others clustered on the opposite side. These three factors—angularity, aspect strength, and singularity—indicate to the astrologer which planet is most crucially important in a chart, and the extent to which the person's makeup is "dominated" by that planet.

Statistical Research of Michel Gauquelin

The French statistician Michel Gauquelin, who initially set out to disprove astrological assumptions, has accumulated an incredibly huge body of data on the relationship between birth time and professional success. He calculated the positions of the planets with respect to the diurnal cycle (including the four angles and the houses) in the horoscopes of thousands of professionals, chosen for their success or eminence from public listings and directories. The details of his research are described in several of his books, but they essentially confirm certain aspects of the astrological hypothesis just discussed—that prominence is indicated by angular position of the planets (at least for two of the angles, the Ascendant and Midheaven).

The main findings were that (1) Saturn or Mars were either rising (near the Ascendant) or culminating (near the Midheaven) in the nativities of successful physicians and scientists; (2) Mars was rising or culminating at the births of successful athletes and soldiers; (3) Jupiter was rising or culminating at the births of politicians, journalists, and actors; (4) The Moon was rising or culminating at the births of successful writers. Readers are referred to Gauquelin's books for details of his findings.

The Planetary Ruler

It is common practice in astrology to assign as "ruler" of the chart, the planet that traditionally rules the sign of the Ascendant (even although that planet may actually be nowhere near the Ascendant or any other of the four angles). Some astrologers feel that this planet is automatically important; others do not. There is also some disagreement about which planet does

TABLE 10
Planetary Rulerships and Exaltations

PLANET	TRADITIONAL RULERSHIP	ESOTERIC RULERSHIP	EXALTATION
Sun	Leo	Leo	Aries
Moon	Cancer	Virgo	Taurus
Mercury	Gemini/Virgo	Aries	Aquarius
Venus	Taurus/Libra	Gemini	Pisces
Mars	Aries/Scorpio	Scorpio	Capricorn
Jupiter	Sagittarius	Aquarius	Cancer
Saturn	Capricorn	Capricorn	Libra
Uranus	Aquarius	Libra	Scorpio
Neptune	Pisces	Cancer	Cancer
Pluto	Scorpio	Pisces	Leo

rule which sign. Alice Bailey has presented an alternative list of "esoteric" rulers, different from the orthodox set (see Table 10). Generally, a rulership suggests that the symbolism of the planet is congruent with or similar to the symbolism of the sign it rules. In addition, a planet may be "exalted" in a given sign. If the planet is found in the sign of its exaltation, this indicates that the qualities of that planet have a "higher octave," or more spiritually elevated expression, in that person's chart.

In antiquity, the rulers of the signs were not planets, but gods and goddesses. According to Plato, a person born under a certain sign, had chosen to model himself after that particular deity—he became a "follower" of Zeus, or Venus, or Neptune. These mythic god-rulers of the signs were shown in Table 6 at the end of Chapter 4.

Edgar Cayce on Astrology

An interestingly different perspective on astrological influence emerges out of the readings given by the extraordinary psychic Edgar Cayce (Gammon, 1967). In the course of his many thousands of health and life readings, Cayce would frequently refer to planetary factors as being important in the particular individual. He stated that the influence stemmed from the period between incarnations on Earth, when the individual would tend to go to the sphere of influence of another planet.

> Thus we find that the sojourns about the earth, during the interim between earthly sojourns, are called the astrological aspects. Not that the entity may have manifested physically on such planets; but in the consciousness of that environ. And these [consciousnesses] have been accredited with certain potential influences in the mental aspect of an entity [Reading No. 2144–1].

In another reading Cayce states that prior earth incarnations, or "sojourns," as he called them, bring about certain emotional inclinations, whereas the sojourns in the spheres of other planets bring about mental urges.

The Glandular Hypothesis

In several of the readings, Edgar Cayce also offers the idea that planetary influences bring about a special attunement or development of the endocrine glands, or "glandular centers." This intriguing hypothesis was also espoused by the Theosophists, the Rosicrucians, and other writers on occult astrology. It finds its strongest expression in the remarkable book by Rodney Collin *The Theory of Celestial Influence,* in which he interrelates nerve plexuses, glands, and planets.

> . . . the intricate antennae of the great nervous plexuses—the cervical, the cardiac, the solar, lumbar and sacral—constitute the apparatus sensitive to . . . planetary transmission, while the endocrine glands through which they take effect, like loudspeaker or television screen, provide the mechanism by which such invisible impulses manifest as physical motion and action [p. 142].

Collin, who was a student of the Gurdjieff-Ouspensky teachings, suggested that the glands, and their associated nerve plexuses, are "set" at a particular vibratory rate at the moment of birth, according to the positions of the planets, and that this setting is the primary determinant of endocrine and planetary type.

The hypothesis of a planetary-glandular correspondence has not so far undergone any empirical testing, and the endocrine typology has itself fallen into disfavor, although some physicians still use it (see, for example, Henry Bieler's book *Food Is Your Best Medicine* for a description of adrenal, thyroid, and pituitary types). A further complication is that there exists considerable disagreement among the different writers as to which gland corresponds to which planet. In spite of these shortcomings, the theory is an interesting one and deserves to be more closely investigated. We shall examine some of the correspondences when we discuss the individual planetary types.

The Planetary Visions of Emanuel Swedenborg

In the voluminous writings of the great eighteenth-century scientist-clairvoyant-mystic Emanuel Swedenborg, there appear to be no references to astrology or typology. Nevertheless, one series of his writings contains passages very relevant to the symbolism and consciousness associated with the planets. Swedenborg wrote thousands and thousands of pages on his clairvoyant observations of beings—angels or spirits—in other dimensions or planes of consciousness. He recorded "conversations" that he held with these beings. These observations and records are, like those of Edgar Cayce, remarkably consistent and coherent.

The observations and conversations Swedenborg recorded regarding other planets and the beings on them are collected in a volume called *Earths in the Universe,* which is generally dismissed as the most farfetched and unbelievable of his writings. Yet it contains passages that are remarkably congruent with astrology. The characteristics he finds in the spirits of a planet are often similar to the characteristics ascribed to those people on Earth who are influenced astrologically by that planet. Thus, between totally different sources there is an unexpected convergence in the understanding of the consciousness of planetary types.

Solar and Lunar Types

The typology based on the twelvefold zodiacal division of the ecliptic has already been described in the previous chapter, where sign positions of Sun and Moon were discussed. We have also discussed the typology of Sun-Moon phase relationships. It remains for us to consider whether a recognizable type exists that can be described as solar or lunar, based on prominence or eminence of these bodies in the natal chart.

The Sun is generally considered to represent the basic inner light of the individual, as the outer Sun is the light of the solar system. The Sun represents the source of life and vitality, related in the body to the heart and circulation, and perhaps also to the *solar* plexus, as a main center for nervous vitality. Collin relates the Sun to the thymus gland, because of its connection with growth. However, the qualities of delicate, childlike beauty, associated in the traditional endocrine typology with the thymus type, do not fit the usual conception of a solar character. (Cayce and others relate the thymus to Venus.)

When the Sun is on or near one of the four angles, the personality expresses itself with extraverted warmth and generous nobility. Health, energy, self-awareness, and creativity are all strong, and the person is a dynamic force to all those with whom he or she relates. In Jungian terms, it relates to a strong *animus* factor in women. Egotism and arrogance are possibilities when the Sun is emphasized in this way. When the Sun is in a weak position in the horoscope, the person often gives the impression of being uncentered or scattered. If the Sun is unaspected, the person may be constantly searching for his own identity. The Sun rules Leo, and is exalted to its highest expression in the outpouring, fiery vitality of Aries.

The Moon represents the magnetic or feminine element in the psyche, the maternal influence, domesticity, adaptiveness, the *anima* in men; and also the reactive instincts, the "evolutionary tail," as it is often called in esoteric literature. The Tarot card "Moon" shows an amphibious and a mammalian creature climbing out of the water, symbolizing man's evolutionary ancestry. In one new version of the cards, the "Moon" card is called the "Reacter," whereas the former "Sun" card is called the "Doer." In other words, the Sun shows how *we* function, the Moon shows how *our bodies* react.

Traditionally, the Moon is associated with the lymphatic system of the body, and the fluctuating, watery component of tissues, subject to tidal-lunar magnetism. People with the Moon close to the Ascendant often have a round, fleshy, "moon-faced" appearance. They are also moody, shy, vacillating, emotionally vulnerable, and strongly attracted by sensory experience and physical desires. They are extremely reactive to the feelings and expectations of others, and tend to have a strong identification with the mother, or with a mother figure. In some respects, though not all, this type corresponds to the phlegmatic temperament of the alchemists.

The Moon traditionally rules Cancer, with its nurturant domesticity. It is said to be exalted in Taurus, where form is highly prized and beautified; and is, according to Alice Bailey, the esoteric ruler of Virgo, as Cosmic Virgin-Mother.

The lunar type is not necessarily related to the *lunatic*. The latter idea is derived from the old folklore, that connects the Full Moon with unusually high incidence of emotional disturbance, insanity, crime, accidents, and violence. For a summary of recent scientific evidence regarding this relationship, the reader is referred to *The Lunar Effect* by Arnold L. Lieber and Jerome Agel. In this work, it is suggested that a person's sensitivity to the "biological tides," triggered by the Moon, might be a function of the lunar phase angle that existed at the time of birth.

The Mercurial Type

Mercury in astrology relates to the mind, the senses, memory, communication, perception, verbal expression, education—the acquisition and dissemination of knowledge. Because the planet Mercury has always been recognized as the fastest moving of the planets, and associated with Hermes-Mercury, the fleet-footed messenger of the gods, "mercurial" has come to denote a quick, changeable mentality. Eloquence, shrewdness, wit, curiosity, and perceptiveness are all attributes of the Mercury-dominated individual. When Mercury is conjunct one of the angles, the person is likely to work in a mental capacity, whether in education, publishing, the media, writing or lecturing, journalism, or academic research. The conceptual mind is highly developed and valued; labels, words, and names are regarded as keys to effective living and relating.

Mercury is traditionally the ruler of two signs: Gemini,

where it functions as associative and logical thinking, and Virgo, where its influence emerges as applied thought and analytic discrimination. It is exalted in Aquarius, where the personal mind is attuned to the more spiritual intuitions of the higher mind. According to Alice Bailey, Mercury is the esoteric ruler of Aries, where the mind functions with the fiery power of creative inspiration.

In traditional astrology the brain and central nervous systems are the domain of Mercury in the body. Rodney Collin and the Rosicrucian teachings ascribe the thyroid function, and the thyroid type, to Mercury. Hyperfunction of the thyroid gland produces high metabolic rate, restlessness, and insomnia: the thyroid type is nervous, bright-eyed, fast-thinking, and volatile. An underactive thyroid is associated with fatigue, depression, and melancholy. Edgar Cayce, however, relates Mercury to the pineal gland.

Most interesting sidelights on the Mercury consciousness are provided by Swedenborg's extensive descriptions of the "spirits of Mercury," who are similar to Mercury-dominated individuals in their perceptiveness:

> Some spirits came to me, and it was stated from heaven that they were from the earth nearest to the Sun, which on our Earth is called Mercury. Immediately on their coming they sifted out of my memory the things that I knew. This, spirits can do most skillfully, for when they come to a man they see in his memory all the particulars it contains. . . . The spirits of Mercury have an exquisite perception, in consequence of their continually exploring, by means of perception, what others know [Swedenborg, op. cit., p. 5].
>
> The spirits of Mercury, more than other spirits, possess the knowledges of things, both of those which are within the solar system, and those which are beyond it in the starry heavens; and whatever they have once acquired they retain, and recollect them as often as similar ones occur [op. cit., p. 7].

According to traditional astrology, Mercury-Gemini relates to travel, particularly travel for the purposes of communication and education. And, according to Swedenborg,

> The spirits of Mercury do not tarry in one place . . . but wander through the universe. The reason is that they have reference to memory of things, which requires to be continually enriched; therefore it is granted to them to wander about, and everywhere acquire knowledges [op. cit., p. 10].

Swedenborg describes these spirits as often responding to questions with opposites, rather than answer: "for when they present opposite things, and conceal things in a certain manner, the desire of knowing is excited, and thus from the zeal of exploring those things, the memory is perfected." (op. cit., p. 14)

Thus memory, perception, travel, curiosity, and dualistic thinking are all attributes of the "spirits" of the planet Mercury, if we are to credit the observations of that extraordinary scientist of the interior. Swedenborg's spirits differ from the astrological conception of Mercury consciousness only in that they are not verbal, but dislike words as being too gross and material; and in that they communicate purely by mental telepathy.

Four Mental Types of the Mercury-Sun Cycle

Like the lunar-phase typology described above, the phase relationship of Mercury with the Sun has also been made the basis for a typology of mental attitudes by astrologer Dane Rudhyar. If Mercury is ahead of the Sun in terms of the diurnal cycle (proceeding clockwise in the chart)—that is, rising before the Sun—Mercury is said to be "Promethean." The mentality is progressive and functions with forethought. When Mercury rises after or later than the sun, Mercury is said to be "Epimethean," and the mentality is conservative, functioning more with afterthought.

Each of these two phases can in turn be divided according to whether Mercury's motion in the sky is direct or retrograde, which indicate objective or subjective mental attitudes. Thus we have four types:

1. Promethean direct: Progressive (forward-looking), thought (Mercury) precedes inner direction (Sun). *Projective thinking*.

2. Promethean retrograde: Progressive, but inwardly oriented. *Subjective thinking*.

3. Epimethean direct: Conservative (backward-looking), thought (Mercury) follows inner direction (Sun). *Objective thinking*.

4. Epimethean retrograde: Conservative, inwardly oriented, philosophical, introspective. *Reflective thinking*.

The Venusian Type

Venus is traditionally the planet of love, beauty, harmony, refinement, and aesthetic appreciation. When Venus is angular or otherwise prominent in the horoscope, romance, friendship, and conviviality are prime interests of the individual. Aesthetic and artistic appreciation are also highly developed, though not necessarily creative activity. Pleasure, creature comforts, sensory delights, and erotic values are highlighted. Relationships between the sexes are emphasized, but not necessarily physical sexuality, which is ruled by Mars. Venusian love can expand to be large and inclusive, or can contract to lazy, narcissistic possessiveness.

Venus is the traditional ruler of Taurus, where it is expressed as tactile sensuality and love of form; and of Libra, where it harmonizes and balances interpersonal relationships. The cosmic and mystical power of love is expressed through Venus in Pisces, the sign of its exaltation. The sign that Venus rules esoterically is Gemini; here it is said to have a particularly positive influence on the evolutionary advancement of the human kingdom. Interestingly enough, the "Lovers" card of the Tarot is usually related to Gemini.

According to Edgar Cayce's readings and the Rosicrucians,

Venus relates to the thymus gland in the body. (Collin, however, relates Venus to the parathyroids.) The thymus is believed to be involved in the growth processes of children, in the body's immune-defense system and also in regenerative functions. The thymus type is said to be youthful, delicate, and elfin, with childlike eyes, thin hair, and transparent skin. The existence of a distinct thymus type must be considered a matter of conjecture. However, the Venusian qualities of beauty, harmony, and sensual orientation are unmistakable in those individuals ruled by the planet Venus. This type has many of the characteristics of the old sanguine temperament.

There is also a twofold typology based on the Venus-Sun cycle. When Venus rises ahead of the Sun, as the morning star, it is called *Venus Lucifer* (the "light-bringer"), and is associated with spontaneous and responsive affections, with emotions expressed freely and directly. When Venus rises after the Sun and appears in the sky as the evening star, it is called *Venus Hesperus,* and is associated with a more structured, evaluative, emotional nature.

The Martial Type

The Mars consciousness is that of the fighter: Energy, assertion, aggression, and activity of all kinds, including sexual, predominate. Martial energy can be expressed constructively as courage, power, and initiative; we recall Gauquelin's findings of angular Mars in the nativities of successful soldiers and athletes. But this energy can also be expressed destructively as violence, rage, jealousy, and impatience. Astrological observation has implicated Mars aspects in the victims of heart disease and violent accidents.

People with a prominent Mars in their horoscope tend to view life as a battlefield, a continuing and invigorating power struggle. Even sexual relationships are thought of as "conquests." The desire for competitive struggle and mastery may be exhibited in sports, engineering, or military activities; or in active forms of healing (for example, surgery), or the arts (for example, dance). This is decidedly a masculine consciousness, marked by dynamic vitality and vigorous struggle for survival.

In terms of the zodiacal signs, Mars rules both Aries (the fighter-pioneer) and Scorpio (the warrior-healer). Mars is said to be exalted in Capricorn, where its qualities of energy and initiative are structured and disciplined to practical and realistic objectives.

In relationship to the glandular hypothesis, there is general agreement (for once) that Mars rules the adrenal glands, the power glands of the body. They are known to regulate and stimulate energy expenditure in fight-flight stress situations; to trigger the body's defense reactions against infection or inflammation; and to contribute hormones that activate gonadal responses. Thus *energy*—aggressive, healing/defensive, and sexual—is the prime focus of the adrenal consciousness. The evidence suggests that the *choleric,* the *adrenal,* and the *martial* are one and the same type.

Swedenborg's descriptions of the spirits of Mars are provocative in that he describes them as having a total unity between inner thoughts and feelings, and their outer expression through speech or the eyes:

> Among them the very affection of the speech is also represented in the face, and its thought in the eyes; for with them thought and speech, and affection and the face act in unity. . . . They know not what hypocrisy is, nor fraudulent simulation and deceit [Swedenborg, op. cit., p. 45].

This absence of deceit and hypocrisy is one of the characteristics of the martial character, who is generally too spontaneous and impulsive to be good at fraud or cover-up.

Swedenborg described a vision supposedly symbolic of the character of the Martian spirits. In the vision, a flaming object, glowing with several colors, mostly ruby and crimson, changed into a vigorous, fiery, multi-hued bird. The vision is reminiscent of the phoenix symbolism associated with Mars in Scorpio, the uplifting and transmuting power of life-fire.

The Jupiter Type

Jupiter represents the principle of expansion and abundance. Significantly, it is by far the largest planet in our solar system. When Jupiter is near the Ascendant in a chart, the character is optimistic, extraverted, full of good will and confidence. When it is on the Descendant, relationships are fortunate and prosperous; on the Midheaven, the profession or occupation brings abundance and social recognition; on the Nadir, the home and family are large and benevolent. Of course, even expansion can become excessive, in which case we get over-idealized, inflated self-images and pompous self-righteousness.

A strong sense of humor is usually found in the jovial character. Philosophic, broad-minded perspectives are cultivated, and there is interest and faith in universal principles of religion and higher mind. As Jupiter rules Sagittarius, the mind soars with lofty spiritual aspirations; and as it is exalted in Cancer, it brings emotional expansiveness into the close personal-relationship nexus of the family. Piscean mysticism and Aquarian idealism are also part of Jupiter's personality. "Ennoblement" is the term used in the Cayce readings to describe the Jupiter influence. Whatever sign, house, or planet it touches, Jupiter expands and spiritualizes those aspects of the personality.

In the body, Jupiter is usually associated with the liver, one of the largest organs, and one through which emotional life is dynamically expressed (as opposed to the heart, which represents the receptive, feminine side of emotional response). The French word for liver (*le foie*) is almost identical with the word for faith (*la foi*). Edgar Cayce, however, relates Jupiter to the pituitary.

The planet Jupiter is described by Swedenborg as one of peace and abundance, and its spirits "better disposed than the spirits of many other earths":

> I could distinguish the presence of the spirits of
> Jupiter, not only by the gentleness and sweetness of

their approach and influx . . . but that their influx was for the most part into the face, which they rendered cheerful and smiling, and this continually, as long as they were present [Swedenborg, op. cit., p. 24].

Swedenborg describes the Jupiter spirits as having faces much larger than the spirits of Earth because the Jupiter spirits express their thoughts by means of the face—"they have an idea of the face as the mind in form." He describes their faces as being warm, cheerful, turned toward Heaven, and completely expressive of their interior thoughts. "They never show a face at variance with the mind, nor have they the power to do so."

Thus optimism, benevolence, nobility, and faith are all characteristics of the jovial type, confirmed in a most unusual way through the observations of Swedenborg.

The Saturnian Type

This is the type that corresponds to the melancholic of the old alchemical classification of temperaments. Astrologically, Saturn is the great taskmaster and teacher, the one who sets the limits and tests that must be mastered for growth and evolution to take place. When Saturn is angular or otherwise prominent, we find that qualities of discipline, perseverance, patience, and orderliness are usually developed to a high degree. These are people who submit themselves to the demand of difficult situations in order to learn from them, and temper their will through adversity. However, they are also the people who at times succumb to pressures and limitations, and seem to get caught in feelings of anxiety, depression, failure, and helplessness.

Edgar Cayce described Saturn as a catalyst for change—"all insufficient matter is cast unto Saturn . . . to work out his own salvation. The entity or individual banishes itself" (Gammon, op. cit., p. 35). A sense of isolation and reclusive determination, as in a monk or solitary research worker, is characteristic of the Saturnian type. We recall Gauquelin's research, which showed Saturn near the Ascendant or Midheaven in the chart of prominent scientists and physicians; and also the strong association between Saturn on those two angles and introversion. Saturn near the Descendant indicates serious working partnerships, and sometimes restriction and limitation in relationships. Saturn on the Nadir often indicates that home and family life was or is marked by austerity, isolation, and deprivation.

Saturn traditionally *and* esoterically rules Capricorn, and thus the organizing capabilities and functions. Saturn is exalted in Libra, where the principles of justice and balance, of reaping what one has sown, have their strongest expression. In terms of the glandular hypothesis, Saturn has been variously related to the gonads (by Cayce), or to the anterior pituitary (by Collin). The Saturnian character is oriented toward the attainment and maintenance of authority and power and yet often accepts powerlessness and a lesser role with humility.

According to Swedenborg, the Saturn spirits are well disposed, modest, and extremely humble in their worship of God. He saw them as relating to the knees in the macrocosmic "Grand Man"—an interesting observation in light of the traditional Saturn association with the knees and bones.

The Uranian Type

The characteristics of personality associated with the three outer planets were not described in the traditional literature of astrology. As they have emerged in the past hundred years or so, however, it has become evident that they relate primarily to the transpersonal dimensions of man's nature, to the higher and lower levels of consciousness. For each of them there is a type of higher sensitivity, and also a type of disturbance or madness if that sensitivity is not adequately grounded, or integrated with the overall organization of the personality.

Cayce described the Uranian influence as one of extremism. There are exceptional abilities, extreme mood swings, spectacular mistakes, outstanding insights, and unusual intuitions. Sudden, unexpected events that highlight individuality are the marks of Uranus on the angles. People with Uranus on the Ascendant emerge as unusual, gifted, or eccentric characters. They may be psychic or clairvoyant. They tend to be extremely high-strung and possess an exceptional degree of nervous energy, which can cause the nervous system to break down if they don't learn to handle it. They may have exceptional intuitive understanding in scientific or occult study or be able to produce lightninglike breakthroughs, inventions, and discoveries. Their personal affairs, financial and romantic, may fluctuate wildly and erratically, especially if Uranus is on the Descendant; or their partners may be peculiar, eccentric personalities. If Uranus is on the Midheaven, there is potential for high professional originality; if on the Nadir, there are often strange or unusual factors connected to early home and family conditions.

Uranus is the traditional ruler of Aquarius, with its independence and originality; and the esoteric ruler of Libra, where the balance of the spiritual and material is worked out. Uranus is said to be exalted in Scorpio, where its electrifying dynamic energy plumbs the emotional depths for regeneration. In terms of the glandular hypothesis, there is little agreement as to Uranus' correspondence; some relate it to the thyroid, some to the pituitary, and some to the gonads.

The Neptunian Type

The Neptune influence is more emotional and mystical than the Uranian. There is interest in higher realities and worlds, but these worlds are more likely to be entered through dreams, visions, fantasies, mystic raptures, or even drugs, rather than through the kind of inventive breakthrough associated with Uranus. There is the strong possibility of delusion and self-deception, of becoming a victim of one's fantasies, or the slavish follower of a false teacher. But there is also the potential for a high degree of poetic or musical inspiration, and a kind of spiritual magnetism, especially if Neptune is on the Ascendant.

If Neptune is on the Descendant, there may be a mystical kind of love relationship; if on the Midheaven, professional work is often involved with collective fantasies in some way (the person may be a rock musician). With Neptune on the Nadir, there can be mystical attunement to the home, to personal roots and ancestral traditions, or to the magnetic vibrations of earth and sea.

With Neptune strong in the chart, there is usually a vivid imagination, and sensitivity to the subtle world of astral images. There is a love of the mysterious, and a fascination with the unknown, whether it be in outer space, man's past, the depths of the ocean, or microscopic matter. Neptune is the exoteric ruler of Pisces and the esoteric ruler of Cancer, where it is also exalted. Cayce relates Neptune to the Leydig cells inside the gonads; others relate it to the pineal gland.

The Plutonian Type

Studied only since its discovery in the 1930s, Pluto emerges as a planet of power, particularly in relationship to mass-consciousness factors. Individuals with Pluto angular seem to find themselves in the hub of a vortex of changing power structures. This can be manifested in psychic or healing abilities; or, if the personality structure is weak and poorly organized, in criminal and psychopathic tendencies.

There is a sense of depth, of isolation, and relentless confrontation with greater realities; sometimes a feeling of being at the mercy of uncontrollable social or political forces. A kind of do-or-die attitude is not uncommon. The individual feels almost compelled or driven to bring about change; and as he changes himself, the world around him also changes.

If Pluto is on the Midheaven, there can be fame and power, or notoriety and infamy. If on the Ascendant, there is an almost desperate need for self-transformation that can make others uncomfortable in its intensity. With Pluto on the Descendant, relationships become a battleground of vast social forces that transcend personal concerns. On the Nadir, there are struggles focused around the family and traditional value systems.

With Pluto nothing is left unchanged or unchallenged. The planet rules Scorpio, as the regenerative warrior-healer; and is exalted in Leo, where it expresses as the transmutational power of creativity. Its chief characteristics are intensity, power, and drastic, in-depth transformation.

Table 11 summarizes those features of the planetary typology that seem to have attained a degree of consensual agreement.

TABLE 11
Summary of Planetary Associations

PLANET	KEY QUALITIES	ORGAN/ GLAND	HUMOR	PROFESSIONS
Sun	creative, dynamic	heart, solar plexus	————	————
Moon	receptive, magnetic	lymph, fluids	phlegmatic	writers
Mercury	perceptive, communicative	nerves, thyroid	————	————
Venus	loving, harmonious	heart, thymus	sanguine	————
Mars	active, aggressive	adrenals	choleric	athletes, soldiers
Jupiter	expansive, benevolent	liver	sanguine	actors, politicians
Saturn	disciplined, introverted	bones	melancholic	doctors, scientists
Uranus	intuitive, independent			
Neptune	mystical, imaginative			
Pluto	radical, challenging			

6

Styles of Thinking

In previous chapters, we have examined and discussed several approaches to human typology that divide humanity into thinking types, feeling types, sensory types, and so forth. In the chapter on the four humors, a classification of emotional attitudes was described, with its correlated system of psychophysical diagnosis. In this chapter we consider some of the systems that have been devised to categorize different mental attitudes and styles. The Bible says, "as a man thinketh in his heart, so is he"; and for as long as men have recognized the crucial role of thinking in the shaping of character and the patterning of destiny, attempts have been made to classify and describe different types of thinkers.

Visual vs. Nonvisual Thinking

Interest in this line of research goes back to the work of Francis Galton, who in 1880 published his *Inquiry into Human Faculty,* one of the first large-scale psychological questionnaire studies. Galton asked a large number of people questions concerning mental images, their brightness, definition, and coloring, assuming that everyone had them. He wrote:

To my astonishment, I found that the great majority
of men of science, to whom I first applied, protested
that mental imagery was unknown to them. . . . They
had no more notion of its true nature than a color-
blind man, who has not discovered his defect, has of
colors [cited in James, 1891].

Thus scientific thinkers, according to both Galton, and the
later work of William James, are poor visualizers. Galton also
found, however, that they are quite proficient at giving life-life
descriptions from memory of what is seen. Women and children, on the other hand, appeared to be stronger than average
at visualizing. Later research by Anne Roe revealed that social
scientists (psychologists and anthropologists) are more likely
to be visual thinkers than natural scientists.

William James also described individuals in whom the predominant type of imagination was auditory rather than visual;
some in whom it was tactile; and some very rare cases who had
strongly articulated motor images and movement memories. He
proposed, but apparently did not develop, a classification of
people according to their preferred mode of imagery and perception—that is, "visile," "audile," "tactile," and "motile"
types. The possibility that individuals may differ characteristically according to inherent differences in preferred sense
modality is also indicated by the existence of specialists in sense
discrimination, such as professional tea tasters or perfume
sniffers.

Later research into the difference between visual and nonvisual thinking has extended some of these early observations.
It is found that, characteristically, visualizers are surprised to
learn that not everybody thinks as they do; and, conversely,
nonvisualizers—for example, many scientists—are often
frankly disbelieving of the imagery claims of their opposites.
There are two simple tests to determine whether someone is
primarily a visual or a nonvisual thinker. One test is to ask the
person if, when he does a calculation in his head, he imagines a
piece of paper or a blackboard, with the numbers on it, and
goes through the steps of the computation in his *mind's eye,* or

if he just computes, abstractly and directly. Another test is to swing a pendulum, or any object on a string or chain, back and forth in front of the person's eyes. After doing this for a minute or two, and his eyes are tracking the moving object, you ask him to close his eyes and *imagine* the continuing swings of the pendulum. With some people, you will notice a marked horizontal movement of the eyeballs under the closed lids; these are the visualizers. With others, there will be no such movement.

Using these tests, the research of Barbara Brown has shown differences in alpha production between the two groups. The alpha frequencies of the brain, eight to twelve cycles per second, are normally present when the brain is in a relaxed, nonthinking state, and the eyes are closed. There is no difference in alpha between the two groups under resting conditions. But the visualizers produce less alpha when asked to visualize a scene, or do a mental computation; the nonvisualizers show no such reduction. This suggests that nonvisualizers use a different process for thinking (or perhaps a different part of the brain) than the visualizers.

Under LSD, visualizers have greatly enhanced sensory perception, whereas nonvisualizers usually report accelerated and expanded conceptual and philosophical thinking. Scalp muscle tension, which is normally higher among visualizers than among nonvisualizers, rises dramatically in the visualizers after ingestion of LSD. Several studies have shown that verbalizers have more irregular breathing patterns than visualizers, under both resting and working conditions. It is assumed that this is due to subvocal movements of the laryngeal muscles—that is, implicit speech—in the verbalizers. The two types also use different kinds of memory process, according to research by Frederic Bartlett. Verbalizers rely more on general cognitive categories in remembering something; while visualizers remember through pictorial similarities to personal visual experiences (Richardson, 1977).

In most of these studies, the evidence indicates that people can and do switch mode of thinking according to the nature of the situation, but there are also consistent individual preferences for one style or the other.

The distinction between visual and conceptual thinking has many parallels with the difference, described later in this chapter, between right-brain and left-brain thinking. It has not been determined whether it corresponds or correlates with Jung's distinction between "thinking" and "intuition," although this would seem to be a fruitful avenue of investigation. There is some evidence indicating that introverts generally have more vivid visual imagery than extraverts, as measured by the Eysenck scales of extraversion-introversion.

Reflectivity-Impulsivity

When a child or an adult is presented with a task in which one can measure how fast he or she responds as well as how many errors are made, there is generally a negative correlation between these two measures. Those who are fast in responding make more errors—they are *impulsive;* those who respond more slowly make fewer errors—they are *reflective.* This appears to be a stable trait or conceptual style: The impulsive ones take quick action, and use repeated, random, trial-and-error strategies to solve problems; the reflective ones use orderly, systematic strategies, evaluating alternatives, censoring their ideas, and weighing the consequences of their choices. This polarity of cognitive style, first formulated in research by Jerome Kagan, probably relates to the basic extraversion-introversion polarity.

Leveling-Sharpening

Some individuals tend to see similarities in things and make them more alike when they recall them—they are *levelers.* Others tend to see differences in things and emphasize their uniqueness when they recall them—they are *sharpeners.* This appears to be a general style or strategy also, applicable in many different cognitive situations. Sharpeners tend to recall more details in things heard; levelers tend to simplify the structure of things they remember. Again, there is some evidence suggesting that extraverts tend to be sharpeners: They notice more details and emphasize differences.

Field Dependence and Field Independence

This dimension of cognitive style, originally described by Witkin, is defined by a person's performance in the "rod and frame" test: Sitting in a dark room confronted by a luminous rod surrounded by a luminous frame, one is told to make the rod vertical. Some people consistently make the rod vertical with respect to the frame, even if the frame itself is tilted: they are called "field dependent." Others ignore the frame, and make the rod vertical using their own body for alignment: they are called "field independent." One could say that the former rely more on visual perception, and the latter more on their sense of gravity.

This cognitive or perceptual style is related to a number of personality and other variables. Women and younger children are generally more field dependent than men or older children. Field dependent people are more likely to change their opinions to conform to those of an authority. They are more people-oriented than the independents: field dependent people remember faces better and prefer occupations involving human contact, the field independents are generally more assertive and more oriented toward intellectual performance. Cognitive or perceptual field dependence also seems to be related to emotional dependence as a personality trait. Again, an extravert-introvert, masculine-feminine polarity appears to be involved here.

Convergent and Divergent Thinking

This is a distinction of conceptual style considered by many psychologists to be extremely relevant to the understanding of creativity. Convergent thinking is involved when you find the one correct answer to a given question. Divergent thinking, or fluency of ideas, is involved in tasks such as creating as many words as possible from a given set of letters, or in thinking of as many unusual uses as possible for a common object, such as a brick or a stick.

Divergent, creative thinking of this kind is generally found to be independent of scores on standard intelligence tests. In other words, creativity and IQ are two different things. Research indicated that the creative thinkers seem to be able to switch from an open, free-associative, divergent mode of thinking, to a more highly directed, structured, and convergent mode. Divergence, or fluency of ideas is more common in the less inhibited, more spontaneous, extraverted type of personality. By contrast, high levels of anxiety and nervous tension are associated with perceptual rigidity, and low levels of divergent fluency. Creative thinkers are generally found to be more open to novel situations and more willing to take risks (Barron, 1968).

The precise nature of all the interrelationships between these different variables of cognitive style or conceptual strategy, and personality and creative expression, is still very much under investigation.

Left-brain and Right-brain Thinking

The subject of different modes of thinking entered a new era in the past ten years with the discovery of the dualistic nature of brain function. While it had been known for years that one hemisphere (the left, in most people) was largely responsible for language and verbal recognition, the true nature of the "nondominant" hemisphere did not become clear until experiments were carried out with individuals who, for medical reasons, had to have the two hemispheres disconnected. The results of these and related researches carried out by Roger Sperry, Joseph Bogen, Michael Gazzaniga, Josephine Semmes, David Galin, Robert Ornstein, Paul Bakan, and others are summarized in the following overview (see Bakan, 1975; Ornstein, 1972; Lee et al., 1976).

1. If people with split-brain hemispheres are given a shape to feel with their right hand and are not allowed to see it, they can describe it, as one would normally. However, if the shape is placed in their left hand, they cannot. Since the left hand connects to the right hemisphere, which is no longer connected to the left, verbal hemisphere, the speech system literally does not know what is in the left hand. However, these people are perfectly capable of identifying the object in their left hand if they are asked to indicate it nonverbally or choose the given object out of several alternatives. The left brain functions verbally, the right brain spatially.

2. In split-brain patients, the right hand loses the ability to work in a relational, spatial manner—since it is now governed solely by the nonspatial left hemisphere. By contrast, the left hand loses the ability to write words, since it is now connected solely to the nonverbal right hemisphere.

3. People with their hemispheres disconnected seem to be able to function, and solve problems, with each of their two separated hemispheres simultaneously. According to Roger Sperry, "The surgery has left each of these people with two separate minds, with two separate spheres of consciousness." Similar results are found in normal people with their brains intact if information is carefully presented to each of the two hemispheres separately. The difference between the two halves seems to be not so much one of content as of modes of processing information; they have different cognitive styles.

4. When information is flashed only to the right hemisphere, it takes the person longer to respond verbally than nonverbally. The reason for this is presumably that it takes time to transmit the verbal response across the corpus callosum (the "bridge" between two hemispheres) to the left, verbal hemisphere. It has been suggested that this crossing is a possible basis for the *déjà vu* phenomenon: Perhaps the left brain is recognizing, a split second later, a scene that the right brain has already recognized.

5. During a verbal task, alpha-wave activity increases more in the right brain than in the left. The alpha rhythm is generally thought to be an indicator of a relaxed, "idling" state of brain

activity. Thus, during a verbal task, the left brain is active, and the right brain is relatively de-activated, producing more alpha. Conversely, alpha-wave activity increases in the left brain during a spatial task.

6. In people who are trained in predominantly analytic, verbal functions (for example, lawyers), there are more EEG activity changes in the left hemisphere than in people who work primarily with shapes and forms (for example, sculptors or potters).

7. The right brain appears to be more responsive to music than the left. Split-brain patients can sometimes sing sentences they can't pronounce! In normal people, there is more electrical activity on the right brain than the left when they are listening to music. However, this is not true in trained musicians, which suggests that with training the analytical, discriminative left-brain modality also enters into musical perception. The right brain also has greater depth perception, and is more adept at recognizing faces (patterns).

8. If people are asked a verbal-analytical question, such as the spelling of a long word, as they are thinking about it, their eyes will tend to move to the right (right movements are controlled by the left hemisphere). However, when thinking about questions that involve spatial orientation, such as which way Lincoln faces on a penny, people tend to make more movements to the left with their eyes (right hemisphere function).

9. Although the direction of eye movements varies according to the nature of the task, the eye-movement effect can be used to differentiate people according to consistent personality-type preference for right- or left-brain thinking styles. People with more vivid visual imagery tend to move their eyes to the left. To give the test, ask the person a series of questions, and note the direction of their eye movements as they are figuring out the answer. Many people tend to move their eyes consistently to one side or the other. Right movement indicates left-brain dominance, and left movement indicates right-brain dominance. The questions should include both verbal and mathematical problems. Observation of eye movements and inferences to the person's preferred conceptual or representational style are an important feature of the new meta-therapy known

as "neuro-linguistic programming" (Bandler and Grinder, 1977).

Studies on differences between right movers and left movers closely parallel the findings on left-brain vs. right-brain specialization. Left movers (right-brain dominant) are more susceptible to hypnosis, produce more alpha waves, prefer the humanities to the sciences, and are generally more oriented toward imagery, symbolism, people, music, and religious experience than are their left-brain peers. Thus, since eye movements are indicators of visual thinking as discussed earlier, the distinction between left movers and right movers probably coincides with the polarity of visual vs. nonvisual thinking described by Francis Galton and William James.

10. There is evidence from EEG studies that the right hemisphere is more active during REM (rapid eye-movement) sleep, when most dreaming is believed to occur. This finding is congruent with the observation that the nonlogical, fantastic, emotional, and symbolic nature of dreams has many parallels to the nature of right-brain function. Patients with disconnected hemispheres typically report loss of dreaming. However, this may simply be the loss of the ability to verbally report their dreams, since the connection to the verbal hemisphere has been severed.

11. Studies of cyclical brain activity have shown that REM sleep, correlated with dreaming, and dreamless, non-REM sleep generally alternate over a ninety-minute cycle during the night. Some investigators have proposed that a similar cycle continues throughout the day. When people are asked to write their thoughts on cards every five minutes throughout the day, a cycle was found in which fantasy thinking increased every ninety minutes or so. It may be, as suggested by Paul Bakan, that this reflects a general brain cycle that switches between the two hemispheres every ninety minutes throughout a twenty-four-hour day. However, the existence of personality differences and preferences must also be taken into account here.

12. There is some indication that schizophrenia may in part involve excessive and uncontrollable spillover between the two hemispheres. Careful anatomical comparisons between the brains of schizophrenics and those of normals revealed only

one significant difference: The corpus callosum connecting the
two sides was an average of 20 per cent thicker in the schizophrenics' brains, suggesting increased brain crossover. Some
psychiatrists have also speculated that the phenomenon of
repression, in which certain mental perceptions are blocked out
of reality awareness but continue to function in an autonomous
way, erupting into consciousness through dreams, fantasies, or
slips of the tongue, may represent a left-brain inhibition of
right-brain perception.

13. It has been further suggested that the lateralization
of cerebral function may extend downward to the autonomic
nervous system. For example, penile erection and other elements of sexual arousal are generally found to be associated
with REM dreaming sleep, and therefore with right-brain ac-
tivation. Hence, the parasympathetic system may be linked
more with the right brain, and the sympathetic more with the
left brain. Left-right specialization of autonomic responsiveness
is a current frontier area of psychosomatic research.

14. Anthropologists have shown that different cultures, and
even subcultures within the United States, differ in their predominant cognitive mode. For example, the middle class uses
primarily the verbal-analytic mode, whereas the urban poor
operate more often in the spatial-synthetic style. This has obvious implications for education and the resolution of inter-
cultural conflicts.

To summarize these relationships, Table 12 lists the different
polarities that have been associated with the left-brain, right-
brain distinction. It should be noted that the findings described
here apply mostly to right-handed males. The differences between the two modes of thinking seem to be less pronounced
for females. And in left-handed individuals, cerebral specialization may be the opposite of that for right-handers, or it may be
mixed.

The well-established linkage between the brain hemispheres
and the opposite sides of the body also has many implications
and applications in therapy and perceptual education. In various forms of body therapy such as those developed by Rolf,
Alexander, or Feldenkrais, differences in muscle-tension pat-

TABLE 12

Summary of Differences in Hemisphere Function

	LEFT BRAIN	RIGHT BRAIN
Information Processing	analytic (taking apart)	synthetic (putting together)
Recognition and expression of	words	shapes, images
Discrimination of	temporal sequences	spatial patterns
Category boundaries	discrete, precise	diffuse, fluid
Perception of complex stimuli	sequential	simultaneous
Reasoning	logical, causal	alogical, synchronistic
Cognitive styles	convergent sharpening nonvisual field independent	divergent leveling visual field dependent
Interests	realistic	symbolic
Attitudes	objective	subjective
Computer modality	digital	analog
Indian philosophy	*nama* (names)	*rupa* (forms)
Body sensation and movement	right side	left side
Eye movements when thinking	to the right	to the left
Auditory perception	right ear	left ear
Visual perception (both eyes)	right half of field	left half of field
Jungian functional typology	thinking	intuition
Freudian theory	secondary process (realistic)	primary process (fantastic)
Sleep patterns	non-REM	REM sleep, dreams
Autonomic system link	sympathetic	parasympathetic

terns between the left and the right sides of the body are often noticed and worked on. Presumably this indirectly affects the sensory-motor nerve systems of the opposite brain hemisphere, bringing about a closer integration of the two hemispheres. In the Doman-Delacato system of sensory-motor "patterning" for brain-damaged and retarded children, there is deliberate and repetitive stimulation of the crossover connections—for example, with techniques such as cross-crawling, in which the left arm and right leg move together, alternating with the right arm and left leg. Such procedures have had demonstrably beneficial effects on cognitive and perceptual learning (Delacato, 1963).

There are essentially *three hypotheses* regarding the nature of brain hemispheric specialization, and all three have some evidence supporting them. The first is that the functioning of the hemispheres is *situational:* One side or the other, the verbal or the spatial mode, is turned on by the nature of the external environmental situation or cognitive task. The second hypothesis is that the alternation of function is *cyclical:* Everyone goes through a more or less regular cycle of activity predominantly in the left or right hemisphere, perhaps every ninety minutes. The third hypothesis is *temperamental:* Over and above situational and cyclical factors, there are consistent individual preferences for one cognitive style or the other. If this is so, then lateral eye movements in response to questions are good indicators of such type differences, as discussed in point 9 above.

One needs to avoid making value judgments as to the superiority of one mode over the other. Clearly, they have different purposes and functions, each appropriate and necessary in its sphere of operations. As was mentioned earlier, uncontrolled, excessive bleed-through between the two brain systems may be one of the factors in psychopathology such as schizophrenia. If it is true that dreaming is primarily associated with activity in the right brain, then it may be, as Paul Bakan suggests, that dreaming allows everyone a safe way to regularly go crazy.

Exceptionally creative individuals appear to be able to allow the fantastic, dreamlike imagery of the right brain to come into awareness and be structured in socially acceptable forms of artistic expression by left-brain activity. The striking and vivid images of the surrealist painters come to mind particularly as examples. Thus high creativity may involve the ability to synthesize and integrate the processes and functions of the two hemispheres.

Another way in which the visual imagery of the right brain may assume the socially acceptable—that is, "realistic"—forms in which the left brain specializes is in a religious context. Historically, the visionary outpourings of many saints or "God-intoxicated" people would have been sufficient to brand them as insane were they not able to structure the expression of these visions in the symbols and allegories of religious belief systems.

Thus, creativity, religious visionary inspiration, psychic integration, and androgynous balance of left and right sides of the body all involve a sustained and harmonious communication between these two apparently opposite types of mentation. As individuals, we can pay attention to our thoughts and imagery processes to note which of the two modes appears to be operative at given times during the day. Observing our own eye movements or directional gaze can also be a useful clue in such self-study.

As an additional awareness exercise, in meditation, dreams, or visions we can observe how our body image is structured in regard to left and right. One may notice that one side is, or feels, larger, brighter, more expanded than the other. One side may be symbolically dressed differently than the other, or of a different color. There may be more pain and tension in one side, indicating more blockage of energy flow through that aspect of one's nature. Though they often go unnoticed, functional and structural left-right body differences are so common that they should be considered the general rule rather than the exception.

The Left-right Polarity in Yoga, Mythology, and Folklore

The lateralization of function between the two hemispheres has its underpinning in a much more far-reaching polarization of consciousness found in almost every culture of the world. Ori-

ental systems of yoga and the mythology of many cultures believe that the left side of the body (which we know to be related to the right brain) is feminine and receptive, and that the
right side is masculine and expressive. Some Indian sculptures
of Siva show the deity as a hermaphrodite, female on the left
and male on the right. In alchemical symbolism the Moon, the
feminine symbol, is always shown on the left of the human
figure, whereas the masculine Sun is on the right. The Hopi Indians distinguish the functions of the two hands—the right for
writing, the left for making music. Some cultures believe that
male-producing germ cells come from the right testicle and/or
right ovary, and female-producing germ cells from the left testicle and/or left ovary.

In tantric yoga, breathing through the right nostril is said to
stimulate the masculine nerve-energy system (*ida*), whereas
breathing through the left nostril stimulates the feminine nerve-
energy system (*pingala*). The cyclic hypothesis is part of tantric doctrine, which teaches that we normally alternate the two
breaths, also called Sun breath and Moon breath, throughout
the day and night.

One could make a symbolic-conceptual connection between
the twentieth-century research on brain lateralization and the
age-old yogic-mythic tradition of the masculine right and feminine left. In doing so, we would call the left hemisphere the
sun brain, and the right hemisphere the *moon brain.* The solar
brain functions with analysis, discrimination, and logic, and
mediates expressiveness, initiative, and activity. The lunar brain
functions with images, symbols, and metaphors and mediates
receptivity, assimilation, and rest.

Speculations aside, we can look to the traditional Western
marriage ceremony to provide an example where seating ar-
rangements reflect gender polarity: the groom's family and
friends sit on the right of the church, the bride's on the left.

In patriarchal, male-dominated cultures, including the Western, in which the feminine has long been considered inferior to
the masculine, the male-female, right-left dichotomy has become overlaid and confused with a good-bad, or strong-weak
dichotomy. Anthropologists have collected abundant data on

the association of taboo, illicit, and inferior functions with the left side of the body. For example, the Hindus and several other cultures use only the left hand for toilet functions, and only the right hand for eating. In medieval times, one of the signs of a witch was said to be left-handedness. The left-right value differentiation is deeply embedded in our very language. For example, in both French and German the word for "law" is the same as the word for "right" (*droit* and *Recht,* respectively). We have "rights" and privileges. On the other hand, (!) the English words "gauche" and "sinister" are derived from the French and Latin words for "left." Right/left and right/wrong are indelibly associated (and confused) in the cultural-linguistic matrix of our thought.

Studies of associative meaning using the "semantic differential" technique developed by Charles Osgood, have shown that, in American culture, the concept "left" is usually associated with the dark, bad, profane, unclean, female, limp, weak, mysterious, low, ugly, incorrect, and so forth; whereas the concept "right" was associated with the opposite of these polarized concepts—that is, the light, good, sacred, clean, male, erect, strong, commonplace, high, beautiful, correct, and so on (Domhoff, 1969). Generally, the left does not become strongly associated with bad until about age ten to twelve. However, even in three-year-olds the beginnings of a value distinction can be observed, the right hand being more often used for acceptable activities, the left hand more for socially unacceptable activities, including hitting another, or touching one's own body.

The psychologist Sylvan Tomkins has shown that a left-right dichotomy pervades many age-old ideological disputes and distinctions. In philosophy and metaphysics we have realism on the right and idealism on the left. In art and aesthetics, classicism and tradition veer toward the right; romanticism and experimentation lean leftward. In educational theory, there is the right-wing authoritative emphasis on achievement and structure, and the left-wing progressive demand for student-determined programs of learning. In politics, of course, there is the well-known dimension of right-wing conservatism vs. left-wing radicalism.

The psychoanalyst William Domhoff, in a paper entitled "But Why Did They Sit on the King's Right in the First Place?" addresses himself to the question of the origin of the political left-right ideological dichotomy. This is usually traced back to the seating arrangement of the eighteenth-century French National Assembly, where the nobles, the upholders of tradition, sat on the right of the chamber, and the bourgeoisie, then growing and expanding, sat on the left. After surveying the anthropological and psychological evidence previously cited, Domhoff concludes that the political left-right dichotomy is actually another expression of the more basic and pervasive polarity in consciousness.

> They [the nobles] were identified with the King-Father and his rightist values. They were part of the fatherhood—the ruling class. On the other hand, the capitalists and dissident intellectuals were on the left —a brotherly grouping espousing brotherhood and mother-derived values—because they were at that time the rebellious young upstarts who had not developed an identification with the patriarchal trappings of the French monarchy.

In other words, those who identified with the patriarchal male value system naturally gravitated toward the right. They were the King's "right-hand men," so to speak; they wanted to maintain and *conserve* the established monarchic-patriarchal power structure. Those who gravitated to the left were more feminine, matriarchal; they were, and are to this day, more receptive to new ideas, new solutions, *radical* new approaches, and thus they were polarized in opposition to the conservative rightist establishment.

7

Political, Occupational, and Aesthetic Typologies

If, as has been suggested throughout this book, personality types are basic organizing patterns of human consciousness, then we would expect type considerations to arise in many areas of human experience and behavior. A person's attitudes in politics, their vocational choices, and their aesthetic tastes would all be expected to be related to their basic personality type or character style. Their choices in these and other areas are presumed to be expressions, at least in part, of underlying temperamental predispositions.

Many people immediately take exception to such an idea. Especially in the area of political behavior, psychological type considerations are rather unpopular. Political people would prefer to think that people make choices, vote, etc., on the basis of rational evaluation of the issues or of the candidates. Yet studies have shown that even such external trappings as the kinds of clothes a person wears or the kind of car he drives can be reliable indicators of political attitudes. Thus it should not be surprising that political behavior, as well as vocational choices and aesthetic preferences, are related to personality factors.

The oldest historical type system in Western culture, that of Plato, is in fact a political-psychological typology. In the eighth book of *The Republic,* Plato writes: "Governments vary as the dispositions of men vary and there must be as many of one as there are of the other." He proceeds to describe at length five different systems of government and the kinds of men they are suited for, implying indeed that the form of government in some way brings about different characteristic attitudes and behavior in men.

Aristocracy, government by an elite of the "best philosophers and the bravest warriors" (not a hereditary aristocracy), he considers the best form. The next best is *timocracy,* a government based on fear of the power of the ruling warrior class. This form of state is marked by contention and ambition. Next in descending order is *oligarchy,* government by the wealthy, the property holders. This, according to Plato, inevitably leads to a split between the haves and the have-nots, and thence to dissatisfaction and eventually revolution. Then we have *democracy,* government by the mass of the people. This allows for the greatest variety of human expression, "like an embroidered robe spangled with every sort of flower." However, it tends toward waste, neglect, and anarchic disorder. In reaction to this we then get *tyranny,* the worst kind, in which the tyrant first appears as a protector of the people. In time, however, this form of constitution is "dominated by madness, evil lusts, false accusations, drunkenness, fear, and misery."

The detailed and subtle discussions of how each of the governmental systems, through the kinds of education it provides to young people, shapes and molds certain basic attitudes that in turn lead to a progression to other forms of government still has much relevant and thought-provoking material to recommend it after twenty-five hundred years.

Personality Types and Political Attitudes

Do people with different ideological beliefs, such as radicals and conservatives, differ in personality type? This is a question that has stimulated much thinking among political writers and a considerable amount of research among social psychologists. A major portion of the research originally centered on the concept of the "authoritarian character." This was first delineated by the psychoanalyst Erich Fromm, with particular reference to the Nazi political movement. In the 1940s, a team of social psychologists at the University of California in Berkeley carried out an in-depth study of this personality type, which was reported in the book by Adorno et al., *The Authoritarian Personality*. This work was of particular interest to many people because of the key elements of power and authority in the authoritarian syndrome, and because of its obvious relevance to the rise of nondemocratic political systems.

The Berkeley researchers described a personality type with anti-Semitic and other ethnocentric political attitudes, who had a high degree of respectful submission to authority in general, a conventional and conformist value system, a general denial of psychological or motivational views of oneself and others, and a strong tendency to imagine dangerous and destructive forces at work, "out there," in the world. Compared to nonauthoritarian individuals, these people tended to be more interested in power and material success, and less interested in aesthetic, sensuous, and emotional experiences. In-depth clinical interviews showed that while both groups had equal amounts of hostility, sexuality, and dependency, the prejudiced group tended to have a more rigid and repressive defense system, whereas the tolerant group had these qualities more integrated into their total personality.

The original research on authoritarianism, with the famous F-scale (for fascism), focused on this personality type, as found on the extreme right of the political spectrum, the fascist end of the continuum. Later studies indicated that individuals with less extreme right-wing ideologies, such as conservatives, also had authoritarian personality traits, though to a lesser degree. Other researchers argued that authoritarianism could be found equally on the right or the left pole of the political continuum. In other words, the authoritarian personality would tend toward political *extremism* of either the left or the right.

One such analysis of political attitudes was developed by H. J. Eysenck, who, on the basis of research in England, described ideologies as varying on two independent dimensions: tough-mindedness vs. tender-mindedness, and radicalism vs. conservatism. Tough-mindedness involves beliefs that are worldly, realistic, strong, and aggressive. Tender-mindedness is characterized by beliefs that are ethical, gentle, humane, and sympathetic. This dimension correlates moderately with extraversion-introversion and with masculinity-femininity.

According to this theory, there is a vertical dimension, as well as the familiar horizontal, left-right dimension of political attitudes, as summarized in the figure below. In this scheme, the

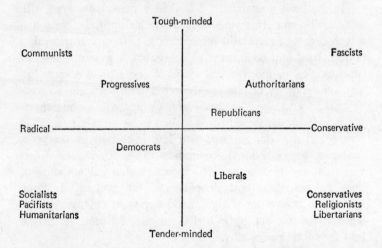

radicalism-conservatism continuum distinguishes political groups from communists on the left to fascists on the right. But both communists *and* fascists are more tough-minded than socialists, liberals, or conservatives.

Generally, the working classes were found to be more tough-minded than the liberal middle classes. This provides an interesting sidelight on the familiar American stereotypes of the "hard hat" workingmen and the "bleeding heart" middle-class liberals. Labourites and Conservatives in England, or Democrats and Republicans in America, would differ consistently on the left-right dimension, but could be anywhere on the vertical axis.

Individuals in the upper-right or *tough-minded conservative* quadrant tend to espouse predominantly economic and political values; they are likely to be pro-draft and pro-death penalty, nationalistic, and ethnocentric. Those in the upper left, or *tough-minded radical* quadrant, tend to pursue theoretical and scientific values, to favor euthanasia, eugenics, easier divorce, and easier abortion laws. They seem generally to favor scientific or engineering solutions to social problems.

The lower left, *tender-minded radicals,* pursue social and aesthetic values; they believe in a rehabilitation approach to crime, and generally favor transnationalist and pacifist movements. The lower right, *tender-minded conservatives,* have strong religious and traditional values; they tend to favor decentralizing government, religious education, and individual liberties. Although the English research did not evaluate this, they would, in current terms, probably also be environmentalists. Generally, the tough-minded types are more externally oriented than the tender-minded. The tough-minded types look to economic and material causes of human behavior and human happiness rather than to psychological states or attitudes.[1]

Vocational and Occupational Types

Several type systems have been developed in Western psychology and social science to describe and categorize vocational and professional values, attitudes, and behavior. One of the best known is that of Eduard Spranger, published in Germany in the 1920s. This later became the basis of the Allport-Vernon values study. In this system six values are described: religious,

[1] The Eysenck tests of social-political attitudes, as well as the personality dimensions such as extraversion-introversion, are given in detail, in a self-testing format, in the book *Know Your Own Personality* by H. J. Eysenck and Glenn Wilson. Readers interested in assessing their own attitudes and traits are referred to that source.

social, aesthetic, political, scientific, and economic. We noted, in the chapter on body types, that the last three of these values are found more often in men than in women, and in mesomorphs than in other body types. In the last section, we saw how people with different political attitudes differ in the degree to which they espouse these different value systems.

The Strong Vocational Interest Test is a test that measures a person's vocational interests and compares them to those of people engaged in a very large variety of different occupations. When this test is factor-analyzed into its component elements, four primary factors have usually been found to account for most of the variability. They are called interest in science, interest in language, interest in people, and interest in business. The Spranger and Allport-Vernon values system can be related to these four factors, as shown in Table 13, which also indicates a possible correlation to the Jungian typology of functions.

TABLE 13
Vocational Interests, Values, and Personality

VOCATIONAL INTERESTS	VALUES	PERSONALITY FUNCTIONS
Interest in science	theoretical	mental (thinking)
Interest in language	aesthetic	perceptual (intuition)
Interest in people	religious/social	emotional (feeling)
Interest in business	economic/political	physical (sensing)

A very extensive body of research, involving many years of testing and thousands of cases, underlies a theory of careers and occupational types developed by Dr. John Holland of Johns Hopkins University. In this theory, six personality types and the occupations preferred by each are described.

1. The *realistic* types are interested in activities involving objects, tools, and machines. They value mechanical and physical abilities, and tangible, material objects. They are likely to become involved in engineering, mechanics, agriculture, and technical occupations.

2. The *investigative* types are interested in activities that in-

volve the probing and analyzing of physical, biological, and social phenomena. They are critical, cautious, methodical, and rational. They lean toward scientific and research occupations.

3. The *artistic* types prefer nonsystematic, nonorderly, spontaneous activities, and value aesthetic qualities and imaginative experiences. They are drawn toward occupations involving language, arts, music, drama, or writing.

4. The *social* types like to work with people, to inform, train, cure, teach, develop, or enlighten others. They typically tend to become physicians, counselors, or teachers.

5. The *enterprising* types seek activities that will enable them to accomplish certain physical or economic goals. They are people who become administrators, executives, salesmen, lawyers, or managers.

6. The *conventional* types prefer activities that follow along prescribed organizational plans and goals. They become involved in clerical, computational, and business systems occupations.

There is clearly considerable overlap between this typology and the six value systems described previously. The differences between them are probably due to the fact that one was derived from general studies of values and attitudes, the other from the specific area of occupational and vocational interests. Correlational studies reported in Holland's book *Making Vocational Choices* generally confirm the expected similarities.

It would be possible to correlate the Jungian type system with these occupational and value classifications, and some research has been done along those lines (Holland, 1973; Myers, 1962). Theoretical and investigative interests are found in mental types. Social and religious values and attitudes are correlated with the feeling function. The aesthetic and artistic predispositions are found in intuitive (perceptual) types. The economic and political value systems, and the realistic and conventional occupational types, all appear to be related to the sensing, practical function. The enterprising type has some of the qualities of the intuitive and some of the sensing. If we include a division by extraversion and introversion, we find that there may actually be eight rather than six types, as shown in Table 14.

TABLE 14
Values, Occupations, and Personality

VALUES	OCCUPATIONS	PERSONALITY FUNCTIONS
theoretical	————	introverted thinking
————	investigative	extraverted thinking
religious	————	introverted feeling
social	social	extraverted feeling
aesthetic	artistic	introverted intuitive
————	enterprising	extraverted intuitive
————	————	introverted sensing
economic/political	realistic/conventional	extraverted sensing

The strong emphasis on the physical-material orientation (two subtypes) and the preponderance of occupations related to extraverted functions are not surprising in view of the fact that occupational activities are those that relate us in an outgoing manner to the world of physical reality.[2] The relationships suggested between Jung's typology and that of Holland were studied and largely confirmed in a study by Hockert (1975).

Executive Types and Managerial Styles

A very interesting study of 250 top executives of high-technology American corporations was recently published by Michael Maccoby (1976), a social psychologist and psychoanalyst. Based on intensive questionnaires, Rorschach tests, and in-depth interviews, Maccoby and his associates evolved a system

[2] Holland's theory and research are described in his book *Making Vocational Choices: A Theory of Careers.* He also devised a test, based on this theory, that is self-administered and self-scored, and can be used as a guide for vocational and career planning. It is called "The Self-directed Search," and is available from the publishers.

of four main psychological types to describe corporate managers. His descriptions of these types bear an interesting and provocative resemblance to the four Jungian functional types and the elemental types of astrology, although Maccoby himself does not discuss either.

1. *The Craftsman.* This type is primarily oriented toward efficiency and excellence in work. He is dedicated to the process of building things and to the quality of the products. He is generally quiet, sincere, conscientious, and practical, although some members of this type become narcissistic and grandiose. They usually do not become the leaders of the organization, being too self-contained and perfectionistic. This type corresponds roughly to the sensing function, with its emphasis on detail and efficiency, and the elemental consciousness of "earth" (especially Virgo and Taurus).

2. *The Jungle Fighter.* This type is after power. He sees the corporate world as a jungle, ruled by the law of "eat or be eaten." He is fiercely competitive and defensive in his actions, and tends to manipulate his subordinates. This includes the classic type of the industrial robber baron, who builds and runs corporations single-handedly with autocratic verve; Maccoby calls this subtype the lions. The other subtype are the foxes, who operate within the corporate structure with cunning and subtle maneuvering. The jungle fighter corresponds to the "fiery" type in astrology (especially Leo and Aries), and, to a certain extent, to the intuitive function.

3. *The Company Man.* This type, also known as the "organization man," is a functional bureaucrat who operates within the protective structure of the company and identifies strongly with it. When creative, these people generate an atmosphere of cooperation and humane mutuality. When uncreative, they find a niche in the company in which they operate to their satisfaction. This corresponds in many ways to the functional style of the emotional or feeling type, whose element is "water" (including Cancer and Scorpio).

4. *The Gamesman.* This is the type whom Maccoby identifies as representing the emerging corporate leadership.

They are interested in the competitive challenge of the game. They take risks, analyze strategies, and respond enthusiastically to new ideas and techniques. They are quick, dynamic thinkers and talkers, and are constantly focused on winning. Actually, the most effective top executives have some of the qualities of both the gamesman and the company man. According to Maccoby, "he is a team player whose center is the corporation. He feels himself responsible for the functioning of a system, and in his mind, his career goals have merged with those of the corporation."

In terms of the Jungian and elemental typologies, the gamesman corresponds most closely to the thinking (air) types, although the interest in future potentials and developments also indicates a strong intuitive component. John F. Kennedy (a Gemini) is cited by Maccoby as an example of the gamesman type; Gerald Ford (a Cancer) and Dwight Eisenhower (a Libra) are examples of the company man. Lyndon Johnson (Virgo) and Richard Nixon (Capricorn) are seen as examples of jungle fighters.

Personality Types and Aesthetic Styles

Art critics and historians have devised numerous systems to describe and categorize different styles of art and aesthetic expression. English art historian Sir Herbert Read, in his book *Education Through Art* (1974), attempted to correlate various personality typologies to art styles in order to provide a rationale for the use of artistic expression in an educational context.

Read presents the results of experiments in the perception of single colors, carried out in 1906 by psychologist Edward Bullough. These experiments resulted in a classification of four perceptive types, differing consistently in their response to simple colors, and hence, presumably, to complex visual stimuli also. These types were there described as:

1. The *objective* type, who tends to make standard intellectual judgments on what he perceives.

2. The *physiological* type, who reacts to the stimulation, warmth or coolness, and brightness of colors.

3. The *associative* type, who reacts to colors in terms of pleasant or unpleasant image associations.

4. The *character* type, who tends not to prefer any particular color, and responds to his perception with an integral blend of personal and objective appreciation.

Herbert Read relates these four kinds of perspective reactions to Jung's functional typology: the objective type to thinking, the physiological to sensing, the associative to feeling, and the character to intuition.

In analyzing the styles of modern artists, Read also uses the Jungian model, although one may disagree with his particular interpretations and attributions. He distinguishes four main styles of modern art: (1) realism and impressionism, (2) surrealism and futurism, (3) expressionism and Fauvism, and (4) cubism and constructivism.

He relates *realism* and *impressionism* to the thinking function because this kind of art is oriented toward the external object or the sensory appearance of it, as in the case of impressionist art. One could also, however, I believe, with greater validity, relate these styles to the sensing function, with its predilection for the immediate data of sense experience. Impressionists were concerned with reproducing the here-now immediacy of visual sense impression. Realists are concerned with showing the way things actually look, reflecting again an attitude that is more sensory-realistic than mental. An empirical study by Knapp and Wulff (1963) demonstrated that sensing types prefer realistic, representational art, and intuitives prefer abstract art.

The art styles known as *surrealism* and *futurism* are connected by Herbert Read with the feeling function because they represent "a reaction from the external world toward immaterial (spiritual) values." Again, however, if we recall the characteristic future orientation and visionary flexibility of the intuitive-fiery types, this may represent a better correspondence to the surrealist vision. The prophetic and transformative values proclaimed by André Breton and other surrealists are intuitive visions of possibilities rather than oceanic-feeling experiences.

Expressionism and *Fauvism,* because they represent the externalization of the artist's inner, personal states, are related by Read to the sensation function. However, it is precisely this kind of expression that is the province of the emotional-feeling types. They, much more than the sensing types, are aware of their inner states and endeavor to foster and dramatize these subjective states and values. Expressionist art works in bold strokes and colors to maximize emotional impact; it does not have the detail and realism one would expect in the sensing attitude.

Cubism and *constructivism,* with their interest in the purely formal, abstract qualities of objects and materials, are related by Read to the intuitive function. It is, however, the mental level of functioning that is most involved in geometric and abstract patterns and designs. So again, the thinking function corresponds more closely with this kind of art than with realism or impressionism. The geometric vision in Picasso, Braque, or particularly Escher is a classic example of the abstracting power of mind: to bring out the purely formal inner structure of experience in an almost mathematical fashion.

From these observations, we see that the whole area of aesthetic expression and appreciation is one where objectivity and conceptual reliability are difficult to obtain. One possible line of cross-validating research would be to examine the astrological patterns of elemental emphasis in the horoscopes of painters of different schools, and determine if there is a consistent elemental, and hence functional, predominance correlated with the different art styles.

The Senses, the Elements, and the Arts

It is also possible to extend the analysis of types of creative expression to other forms of art besides painting. One can envision the following general system of correspondencies, as indicating which forms of art would primarily appeal to which area of personality consciousness.

TABLE 15
Functions, Arts, and Elements

Visual arts (painting, film)	—	intuition, perception; fire
Language arts (writing, drama)	—	thinking, mental; air
Music and poetry	—	feeling, emotional; water
Tactile arts (sculpture, crafts)	—	sensing, physical; earth

The visual arts, concerned with the qualities and effects of light and color, appeal of course primarily to the visual-sense modality—and to intuitive perception. In astrology, the visual artists are often predominant in the fire element, especially Leo.

The verbal, language arts have an obvious appeal to the thinking function. Sound, and hence auditory perception relate in general strongly to the air element, in part since sound waves are carried in air. Thinking-air types often respond strongly to music because it stimulates the emotional nature yet maintains a mathematical-structural component (or dramatic interest in the case of opera).

The effect of music on the emotions is legendary—and esoteric traditions, especially the Sufis, have developed the inspirational power of music to elevate the emotional nature to the level of mystical oneness. Poetry as musical prose also seems to have that power to stimulate the mental and emotional levels simultaneously.

The sensing function and the element earth in astrology are particularly related to the sense of touch. The earthy attitude seems to be that what is tangible is real. Touch can also be very sensual. Thus the arts that involve touching earth materials are especially relevant to this function. Movement arts, such as dance, would also be sensing because of the strong physical orientation.

These are of course very general correspondences, by no means intended to suggest that all sculptors would be earth-type sensors, or all musicians water-type feelers. Very probably, within each group of artists it would be possible to subdivide them according to functional-elemental preponderance. Certain kinds of music—for example, classical music, with its strong melodic lines—are more mental in their appeal. Romantic music, with its lush harmonies, seems to have a more emotional impact. Highly rhythmic music stimulates movement, whether dancing or marching. Similarly, different forms of literature are feeling oriented, or mental, or perceptual, or practical.

8

Psychiatric Character Types

The most widely accepted model of personality structure in the West in the past fifty years has been the psychoanalytic. Freud's findings and theories have dominated much of psychological and psychiatric thinking, as well as contemporary literature. A great deal of the terminology of psychiatry, derived from the study of neurotic and psychotic patients undergoing psychotherapy, has seeped into popular language. The categories and concepts developed to understand and treat people with severe emotional or mental disturbances are now routinely used by the average intelligent layman to interpret his own behavior and that of others. It is therefore necessary and appropriate to try to gain a clear understanding of what the major pathological character concepts are.

Development of Psychoanalytic Character Theory

Freud and the early psychoanalysts did not concern themselves very much with the nature of different character types. Their interest, as has often been pointed out, was primarily in the study of instincts or drives, their transformations and deformations in the various stages of psychosexual development. The symptoms of an adult neurotic or psychotic were studied for their content—that is, what defenses they represented, what childhood impulse or drive was disguised or distorted in them.

Among Freud's early followers, Carl Jung developed his well-known typology after breaking with his former teacher. Wilhelm Reich also was a pioneer in the study of character, as the relatively stable, long-lasting attitudes and traits. He made the important discovery that the character structure is deeply and pervasively correlated with the pattern of muscular tensions in the body. He described this pattern of muscular rigidities and tensions as an "armor," and stated his central thesis by saying that the muscular armor and the character armor are functionally identical. Reichian or bioenergetic therapy works directly, by means of physical manipulation on the body armor, while simultaneously working analytically on the character structure and defensive systems.

In his book *Character Analysis,* Reich gave several penetrating descriptions and analyses of some classical character types. Later students of his work, including Alexander Lowen and Elsworth Baker, have given detailed descriptions of the major character types and their particular body structures.

Reich described the body armor as being like a series of rings around a central elongated core of free-flowing plasmatic, or vegetative energy currents. There are seven of these ringlike segments, and their locations, interestingly enough, approximate those of the major energy centers of yoga psychophysiology. Different types of neurotic and psychotic characters have energy blockages in one or more of these segments. According to some Reichian therapists, they need to be worked with and dissolved from the top on down. The first is the ocular segment, which includes the eyes, ears, and central brain structures. The next is the oral, centered on the mouth; a cervical segment, covering throat and neck; a thoracic segment in the region of the chest and arms; a diaphragmatic segment in the area of the solar plexus; an abdominal segment; and a pelvic segment, which includes the legs. It is quite possible that the pathological symptoms traced to blockages in these segments of the body armor could be understood as distorted manifestations of the functioning of the energy centers.

The analysis of body structure and its deformations represents one approach to the descriptive diagnosis of character types. Another is in terms of developmental stages. Freud originally described the development of libidinal interest in the child as passing through three stages, corresponding to three erogenous zones: the oral, the anal, and the phallic. Later a genital phase was added to the end of the sequence, and an earlier ocular stage to precede or coincide with the oral.

Developmental analysis of this sort was carried further in the work of Erik Erikson, who delineated six stages of development, going all the way up into adulthood and old age. Each stage presents a characteristic choice between two alternative responses, the choice made then becoming a general mode of functioning—an attitude or a manner of relating. For example, according to Erikson, the phallic phase is one in which general "ambulatory and intrusive patterns" are developed, and the capacity to take initiative either established or prevented by excessive guilt.

Later researchers in the psychoanalytic tradition have led to the establishment of further stages and levels of development in adulthood, delineating the maturational crises and plateaus in the lives of women and men. The developmental ladder has also been extended down the age scale to prenatal life. Otto Rank was the first to emphasize the importance of the birth trauma as a possible source of psychopathology; and recently Stanislav Grof (1976), on the basis of findings from LSD therapy in which people frequently regress through their birth experiences, has proposed a four-stage schema of "perinatal matrices." These are characteristic experiences in four phases of the birth process—floating in the womb, feeling stuck in the birth canal, struggling down through the canal, and exiting—which lead to basic modes of experiencing the world. R. D. Laing, in his book *Facts of Life,* has taken the analysis even farther back, and writes (very poetically) of characteristic patterns of adult experience derived from the consciousness of the fertilized ovum on its passage down the Fallopian tube to implantation.

The twofold general theory that seems to be emerging is:

(1) that fixation can occur at one or another of these stages of development, leading to problems in handling the needs and demands of subsequent stages; and (2) that the more severe types of psychopathology are found with fixation at earlier stages of development. For example, autism and chronic psychosis may represent fixations at intrauterine phases, perhaps a refusal to be born. Such an analysis is not incompatible with a biochemical or organic theory of psychosis, as is often believed; in fact, biochemical abnormalities may well be responsible for a developmental fixation or weakness.

In an important contribution to psychoanalytic theory, David Shapiro (1965) has described what he calls "neurotic styles," general ways of thinking, feeling, perceiving, and acting that are characteristic of the different types of neurosis. They are not just symptoms and defenses, but consistent modes of functioning that are a part of the individual's basic makeup. In fact, as Shapiro points out, it is precisely these stylistic consistencies of functioning that determine what kinds of neurotic symptoms a person may develop or choose. "The disposition to one or another specific form of symptom may be regarded as essentially a problem of character, and character may be regarded as consisting of the configuration in an individual of just such general and relatively stable forms of functioning."

After these general remarks concerning the nature of character and its development in psychoanalytic theory, we may proceed now to a description and discussion of the main character types recognized in contemporary psychiatry.

The Hysterical Character

According to the official manual of psychiatric diagnosis, a hysterical personality is "characterized by excitability, emotional instability, overreactivity, and self-dramatization." The classical "conversion" symptoms of hysterical neurosis, such as partial anaesthesia or paralysis without organic cause, do not seem to occur nearly so often now as they did in the Victorian era when

Freud and his associates first described them. These kinds of symptoms were attributed to sexual repression, and so the change is not surprising in our present, more permissive cultural context.

The hysterical character style is more frequently, though not exclusively, found in women. It includes a reaction to external events that is emotional, impressionistic, diffuse, and not at all concerned with factual details or intellectual understanding. Such people are romantic, idealistic, sentimental, theatrical, and highly suggestible. They seem to be often "struck" by some vivid, colorful impression, "overcome" by an inexplicable mood, or "seized" by uncontrollable giggles. They are given to violent outbursts and sudden infatuations, but seem to have a kind of strangely bland, detached attitude toward their own emotions. Classically, one spoke of *la belle indifférence* of the hysterics toward their own symptoms, and there is that quality of dissociation, of insubstantiality. One has the feeling that they do not know who they are, and are creating a series of personal dramas to lend reality to their vague self-image.

In terms of developmental psychodynamics, the Freudians and the Reichians agree on the genital-oedipal phase as being the critical point of fixation of this type. They hypothesize that there was in childhood tremendous disappointment, and frustrated erotic attraction to the parent of the opposite sex; and that both the disappointment and the attraction are repressed. Hysterics are typically naïve about sex, but covertly seductive.

An additional interpretation has also been proposed, stemming from the meaning of the word "hysteria." This derives from the Greek word *hustera,* which means womb. For centuries it was believed that hysteria was caused by a slipping, or "wandering," womb; it was also associated with menstrual mood changes. A neo-Reichian view is that it is not the hysteric's own womb that is slipping, but that certain experiences in the mother's womb have led to a constant state of flight, of trying to escape from the grasp of the womb. From this could come the dissociation, the fugue states, the sense of tenuousness and diffuse distractibility (Boadella, 1976).

The Obsessive-compulsive Character

Wilhelm Reich described compulsive characters as "living ma-chines." They are noted for their rigid, narrow focus of atten-tion, their excessive concern for detail, and their overly consci-entious drive for technically correct forms of behavior. On the Rorschach ink-blot test they tend to describe innumerable small details around the edges of the pattern. As David Shapiro pointed out, they may in fact be excellent technicians, with good memory and precision skills.

The compulsive individual's rigid cognitive focus on details of external reality makes him unreceptive to intuition or hunches, and restricted in spontaneity of feeling or playfulness. They also tend to be insensitive to the feeling-tone of interper-sonal relationships or social encounters. They seem to be per-manently "driven," as if by an overstrict supervisor—actually their own "super-ego," in Freudian terms. They attempt to maintain control at all times, and worry and ruminate about an incessant stream of "shoulds" and "oughts." In extreme cases of obsessional neurosis, we may see complex trains of ritualistic behavior, often involving cleaning, or collecting things.

In classical psychoanalysis, Freud traced the origin of obses-sional neurosis to fixation at the anal phase of development. The traits of orderliness, stinginess, obstinacy, and control are thought to be the result of excessively strict toilet-training prac-tices, a "reaction formation" against the fear of anally letting go. This analysis seems to be generally accepted in psychiatry.

The Paranoid Character

The dominant trait of this character type is suspiciousness. Whereas the obsessive personality is focused on facts and de-tails, the paranoid personality is focused on "clues." They are forever looking for the hidden meaning, the masked motivation, or the coincidence that will confirm their suspicion that someone or something has hostile designs toward them.

There appear to be two subtypes of paranoid character: the arrogant, aggressive, and the furtive, apprehensive. Both operate from suspiciousness that appears to be a gross exaggeration of a basic attitude of guardedness and reserve. The paranoid style resembles the obsessive style in its constriction and lack of spontaneity or warmth, but for different reasons: While the obsessive worries about what he has to do, the paranoid is suspicious about what someone may do to him.

The paranoid character, like the obsessive, may actually have a rather good grasp on reality, and function effectively in many situations (if there is not a psychotic loss of reality contact). David Shapiro points out the paranoid is often right in his perception, but wrong in his judgment or interpretation of what he perceives, imposing "a biased and autistic interpretive scheme on the factual world."

It has been said the paranoid person lives in a "police state" consciousness. There is intense concern and sensitivity regarding authority and power relationships. He appears to be constantly on the lookout for a possible or probable invasion or infringement of his autonomy. Psychodynamically, Freud traced paranoia back to fears of homosexual attack. More generally, it is loss of control, or weakness, or surrender of any kind that seems to be the great fear. The favored defense mechanism of this type is projection onto the external world of threats and dangers that justify his expectation of harm or violence. Some paranoid ideas can take the form of "encapsulated delusions" that are internally logical and consistent, though still based on a subjectively distorted picture of reality.

The Masochistic Character

This type has some of the same characteristics as the obsessive-compulsive, and is also related by the Freudians to the anal stage of libidinal development. The dominant attitude is a whining, complaining submissiveness. To have such personality

THE BURDENED TYPE

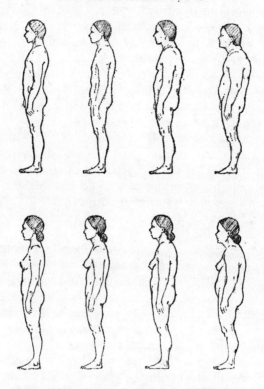

Note: Drawings of body types reproduced, with permission, from *The Body Reveals* by Ron Kurtz and Hector Prestera (New York: Harper & Row, 1976). In each sequence of four figures, the first figure, on the left, is approximately normal from a structural point of view. As the sequence progresses, the figures differ more and more from the normal, becoming finally an almost pure example of one of the types.

traits is not necessarily equivalent to having a masochistic sexual orientation.

While obsequious and submissive outwardly, the masochist is inwardly seething with spite, rage, and hostility; though these forces are strongly blocked and may not even be in his own awareness. He often feels trapped, bogged down, or burdened by overwhelming reality demands. Lowen has emphasized the role of feelings of shame and humiliation in the masochistic character structure. These feelings often seem to stem back to a mother who was sacrificial and smothering, and who placed much emphasis on the functions of the alimentary tract, eating and defecating.

In terms of the energy characteristics of the masochistic body structure, Lowen describes it as strongly charged, but tightly held in. They often look burdened, as if they are carrying a heavy weight, or are being compressed to the point of collapse. They are frequently short and thick-set, and the buttocks are usually tucked in and flattened, like a dog with its tail between its legs. They do not reach out to others with either sensitivity or feeling.

The Schizoid Character

This character type, who is not necessarily schizophrenic or even preschizophrenic, nevertheless has some of the features of that condition: the withdrawal from social-contact relationships, the split between feeling and thinking, the inappropriate expressions of affect, daydreaming, and fantasizing. The fantasy and illusionary thinking has not reached the point where ordinary reality perceptions are completely disorganized (as in schizophrenia). Rather, the realistic and autistic perceptions exist side by side.

Subjectively, the schizoid person may feel that the two sides of his body or the upper and lower halves of his body are very disparate. According to bioenergetics, this left-right and upper-lower discrepancy can be clearly observed in the structure of individuals of this type. Also, there is very weak charge in the extremities of the body—the hands, feet, face, genitals—as if energy is being pulled away from those means of contact with the world. This character type appears to occur mostly in ectomorphs.

The face of the schizoid individual is usually masklike, as if frozen in fear, and the eyes lack luster or radiance. The feeling of not wanting to be in the world is very strong. In terms of psychodynamics, this personality configuration is usually related back to early hostility and rejection by the mother, perhaps even during the uterine stage. The child does not feel wanted, and is terrified of the world as a place of overpowering and harsh sensations.

Feelings and relationships are avoided, and there is a tentative, almost disembodied quality to their consciousness. The schizoid feels as if he is living in more than one reality simultaneously and that he is trying precariously to balance and integrate them. One might say the schizoid personality has one foot in reality and one in another world; whereas the schizophrenic is completely in another world, entering into social reality only for fleeting moments, if at all. Schizophrenia was related by Reich to a severe energy blockage in the ocular segment, specifically at the crossover junction of the optic nerves from the two eyes.

The Dependent Character

This type is believed to be fixated at the early infantile oral stage of libidinal development, and is often referred to as "oral-dependent" or "oral character." The predominant qualities of this type are clinging dependence and low energy output. Their bodies are usually thin, elongated, sallow, and undercharged throughout. Arms and legs appear spindly and weak, the voice is thin and sad, speech is sparse and listless. They are reminiscent of the *pretas,* or "hungry ghosts" of Buddhist cosmology— beings with narrow throats and large bellies, forever unsatisfied.

THE NEEDY TYPE

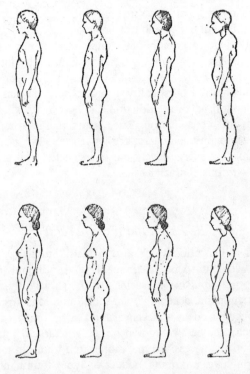

They give one the overall impression of being an empty bag, or bottomless pit of need and demand. They seem to suck and sap energy from other people, particularly from their parents and families. Often they feel the world owes them support, but some oral types may overcompensate by adopting a posture of independence. Even so, they never seem to be able to stand on their own feet.

Psychoanalysis traces this character attitude to a totally unsatisfying, disappointing early relationship with the mother. She may have been physically absent, or emotionally incapable of providing nourishment. Whereas the schizoid character reflects rejection by the mother, the oral-dependent type reflects deprivation of maternal affection or the loss of the mother or a substitute figure.

There is a deep, pervasive feeling of longing in these characters, and a fearful expectation of being abandoned, left helpless and lonely. Due to attempts at compensation, they may swing through alternating moods of depression and elation. The manic-depressive psychosis may be considered a more extreme form of this kind of personality disorder. Some psychiatrists associate alcoholism, drug addiction, and passive sexual promiscuity with this constellation. The "neurasthenic" or "psychasthenic" personality, characterized by chronic fatigue, lack of enthusiasm, low energy level, and oversensitivity to stress, also overlaps with this character type.

The Psychopathic Character

This kind of neurotic style is also termed "impulsive," and associated with antisocial, delinquent, and criminal behavior. However, the impulsive character may be sufficiently well integrated to function acceptably in social relationships; he may even be recognized as a decisive and daring "man of action." There appear to be two subtypes of this character: the domineering, active, aggressive type, more often found in males; and the manipulative, charming, seductive type, found more often in females.

Their consciousness is dominated by whims, immediate urges, and uncontrollable impulses. "I just did it, I don't know why" is a favorite phrase. They appear deficient in any long-range goals, plans, or interests. At the same time they may be quite adept at "conning," at seizing on another's weakness to exploit a situation for power or profit. Thus from one point of view, they do not relate to the future; yet from another they relate to present events only as they present opportunities or possibilities for exploitation or advantage. There is a tremendous drive to succeed, to control, to win, to be "on top." Underneath, there is a deep unacknowledged fear of being controlled.

Psychodynamically, Lowen and others relate this character disposition to a childhood triangle situation, in which one parent was sexually seductive, and yet basic emotional needs were not met. Thus there is a total denial of feelings of closeness, intimacy, or caring; sexuality is used as manipulation and conquest.

The two subtypes have different body structures. The dominating male, who seeks his objectives by threats, bullying, and overpowering, is structurally "top-heavy": The upper half of the body and head are overcharged, and sometimes oversized, whereas the pelvis and legs are undercharged and disconnected. The brain is overexcited, the eyes are watchful and distrustful.

TOP OR BOTTOM HEAVY TYPES

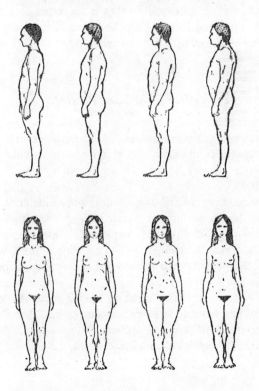

The seductive, female subtype tends to be "bottom-heavy," with a well developed and overcharged pelvic region that is disconnected from the upper half of the body. The chest and torso may be overly flexible, and the face may have the innocent "baby doll" appearance.

The impulsive character is notorious for his or her skill at manipulation and seduction. They are consummate "operators," conning and scheming to be one up on the world. In contrast to the other neurotic types, they are remarkably free of anxiety, and exude an air of confidence and social charm. They have an amazing capacity for insincerity and lying and absence of conscience regarding this or other forms of unethical behavior.

Some psychiatrists would include a "passive-impulsive" character with this type: These are individuals who seem to just "give in" to any impulsive idea that is suggested or proposed to them. Again, some forms of alcoholism, addiction, and promiscuity may be found with this character.

Other Character Patterns

These represent probably the major character types distinguished in contemporary psychiatry. There is, however, considerable disagreement about the classification of character patterns, both in psychoanalysis and within the bioenergetic tradition.

The official psychiatric diagnostic manual includes, in addition to the ones already described, personality disorders designated as "cyclothymic," "explosive," "asthenic," "passive-aggressive," and "inadequate." The asthenic is probably equivalent to the oral-dependent; and the passive-aggressive to the masochistic.

The *cyclothymic* is described as having recurring variations of mood, unrelated to external circumstances. Periods of elation, warmth, ambition, and optimism alternate with periods of depression, futility, worry, and pessimism.

The *explosive* personality is also called epileptoid personality disorder, although it is found only in *some* epileptics and also in nonepileptics. This type is marked by unexpected gross seizures of rage and violence that are out of character to the person's usual behavior. There are traits of rigidity, selfishness, seclusiveness, and religiosity.

The *inadequate* personality is described as ineffectual and inept in his responses to physical, social, mental, or emotional demands and relationships. Though not mentally deficient, he manifests poor judgment, instability, and nonadaptiveness.

Other psychoanalytic classifications of character patterns base themselves on Freud's theory of the erogenous zones of libidinal development, through which everyone is believed to pass. Many contemporary psychologists would question the rigidity of this developmental model, but it does appear to have some validity. In this kind of classification we have oral, anal, phallic, urethral, and genital characters.

The *oral* character, related to the sucking stage, has already been described as the dependent or passive type. Sometimes a secondary oral-aggressive type is distinguished, which represents a sublimation of the biting stage. This character is marked by aggressiveness, ambition, envy, and exploitation.

The *anal* character corresponds to the obsessive-compulsive character described previously.

The *phallic* or phallic-narcissistic character is described as arrogant, cold, aggressive, with violent hostility toward the opposite sex (the so-called "genital revenge").

The *urethral* character, infrequently described, supposedly represents a fixation and sublimation of urethral eroticism. He manifests the qualities of burning ambition, boastfulness, and impatience.

The *genital* character is a kind of mythically mature creature, not usually found in psychiatrists' offices. He has resolved the Oedipal complex, overcome narcissistic tendencies, integrated the libidinal interests of the previous stages, and is able to love and share mutually with another.

We have described the clinical picture found in many individuals whose personality functioning is in some way disturbed or distorted. This is not the gross kind of breakdown of personality structure found in schizophrenia or other forms of psychosis. Nor would people who manifest some of the traits and bodily features described necessarily be considered neurotic. As with all typologies, the complexity and uniqueness of the individual always eludes the conceptual net; but the net may nevertheless be found useful in helping us understand our own psyche and our relationships with others.

Character Disorders and Jung's Functional Typology

One might speculate about the possible relationship of these pathological types with the functional typology of Carl Jung described in an earlier chapter. Could one say that the neurotic styles are distorted, deviated expressions of the functional preferences and modes of relating to the world delineated by Jung?

The obsessive-compulsive, with his technical focus and concern for textural and factual details, parallels the sensing type, with his craftsmanship and precision. The paranoid type is more mental, logical, analytical, building systems of ideas, often brilliantly; he corresponds to the thinking type. The hysterical character is a feeling type, relating by way of emotion in exaggerated and distorted fashion. The impulsive, psychopathic character may well be an intuitive: Although incapable of long-range planning, his interests are in the possibilities and promises of situations, and he is capable of decisive, inventive, ingenious action. Astrologically, we may describe him as fiery. Recent research by Hans Eysenck has shown that some fire-sign personalities are high in extraversion *and* high in neuroticism—the typical pattern found in psychopaths.

The schizoid character would appear to be partly mental, partly perceptual-intuitive, but much more passive and introverted than the impulsive or paranoid. The oral-dependent character can be regarded as the passive, introverted emotional neurotic. The masochistic type is earth- and sense-oriented; he feels bogged down and trapped in physical realities, and burdened by work. Thus we appear to have a passive and active expression for each function in line with the introverted-extraverted polarity.

TABLE 16
Psychiatric Types and the Four Functions

FUNCTION	ACTIVE	PASSIVE
thinking/mental	paranoid	schizoid
feeling/emotional	hysterical	oral dependent
intuition/perceptual	psychopathic	passive-impulsive
sensing/physical	compulsive	masochistic

9

Types of Love and Sex

Few topics have exerted such enduring fascination over the minds of men and women, in all ages and countries, as the nature and meaning of love, and of its close relative, sexuality. Every generation seems to need to produce new psychological and philosophical works, providing definitions and analyses, as well as new works of literature, art, and popular music, providing evocative images and symbols of this most human of themes.

The apparently new definitions and poetic expressions usually turn out to be restatements of age-old truths and beliefs, however. *Love Story* and *Doctor Zhivago* are modern versions of the ancient theme of tragic, star-crossed lovers found in *Romeo and Juliet,* and, farther back, in *Tristan and Iseult,* and before that in the story of Dido and Aeneas. Contemporary theories and analyses do not surpass the subtle and sophisticated expositions of the ancient Greeks, Chinese, or Indians, although they do gain focus and relevance from an awareness of current patterns of social conditioning and social mores.

Many authors, throughout the ages, fall into the trap of identifying one kind of love as the "only" or "true" kind, and disparaging other kinds as "merely carnal," or perhaps "superficial." If we understand the value of recognizing different types of personality, we can also appreciate the importance of recognizing the different kinds of relationships without attaching either idealized or inferior evaluations to them.

Different Kinds of Love

The Greeks distinguished three kinds of love relationship: *eros, philia,* and *agape. Eros* was personal, emotional, passionate love, which included, but was not limited to, physical attraction. The sexual component has come to dominate in contemporary consciousness to the point where "erotic" now means "sexual." *Philia* was brotherly or sisterly love—companionate friendship, nonsexual affection and caring, nowadays sometimes referred to as *platonic* love. This kind of love can be extended to nonhuman forms of life also, as with people who love animals, plants, rocks, and minerals, or even objects and machines. We have love extended to whole groups (for example, the "Anglo*phile,*" lover of the English), or to objects (for example, a "biblio*phile,*" booklover), or to concepts (for example, *"phil*osophy," love of wisdom), or to humanity as a whole (*"phil*anthropy"). *Agape,* among the Greeks, was spiritual or cosmic love, a kind of all-embracing feeling of unity, totally nonexclusive, that culminates in and expresses a mystical experience of oneness with all of life. This kind of love was known as *caritas* in Latin, and translated as "charity" in English versions of the Bible.

In the cultural worlds of Rome and the Christian Middle Ages, *eros* became *amor,* the romantic love celebrated by troubadours and courtiers. Courtly, romantic love was personal and human, with a strong idealization of the beloved, but in some ways less physical and lusty than the *eros* of the ancients. Physical desire was *libido* in Latin, which was adopted by Sigmund Freud as the single term for the primal energy of all consciousness. *Caritas* became a religious concept: It was the love of God for man, and the love of man for God and his creations. This was the "love" in the commandment "Thou shalt love the Lord, thy God . . . and thy neighbor as thyself," the love that St. Paul and other theologians advocated as the Christian religious ideal.

In India and China much philosophic and religious writing was devoted to the analysis and description of different forms of interpersonal relationship, and the qualities of feeling and character associated with them. In the Indian tradition there is an interesting formulation of five stages of love, through which a devotee passes in his relationship to the Divine Being within him. In the first stage, the relationship is said to be like that of servant to master—loving obedience. The second stage is that of friendship, implying a relation between peers. In the third stage, the relationship is maternal: The devotee cultivates and nourishes the Divine Child within. The fourth degree of love was that of spouses for each other—much as in the West, a union both physical and spiritual. The fifth of this series of stages of love was considered analogous to passionate, illicit love—love outside the bounds of normal social structures. This was symbolized in the rapture of the women who followed the divine flute-song of Krishna and his dance. The notion of symbolizing the highest stage of divine love by illicit human love strikes many people as sacrilegious, even in India, but was done to emphasize the transcendent nature of this kind of devotion, which goes completely beyond the usual categories and forms of social conduct and conditioning. It was in this same spirit that Christ said, "And a man's foes shall be they of his own household" (Mat. 10:36).

In ancient China, the Confucian school described in detail the nature and rules of conduct for five main types of social relationships. The five relationships, slanted heavily toward the male side, were: between father and son, a relation of love; between husband and wife, a relation of faithfulness; between older and younger brothers, a relation of correctness and deference; between a ruler and his ministers-advisers, a relation of dutiful obedience; and between two friends, a relation of loyalty and affection.

An analysis of different types and styles of love relationships, based loosely on the Greco-Roman conceptions and on socio-psychological studies of contemporary American relationships, is propounded by John Alan Lee (1976) in his book *The Colors of Love*. Lee proposes a scheme, analogous to the color spectrum, in which there are three primary lovestyles, which he terms *eros, ludus,* and *storge;* three secondaries, compounded from the first three, called *mania, pragma,* and *agape;* and further secondary and tertiary mixtures, which he arranges in the forms of a star and a circle. The descriptions of the seven most common types of relationships were derived from actual interviews and tests involving several hundred couples.

1. *Eros* is defined as love of ideal beauty, in which there is the classic "falling in love" syndrome: strong physical attraction; deep, pervasive rapport; open and honest expression of intense feelings; and the willingness to take risks and make a total commitment.

2. *Ludus,* derived from the Roman poet Ovid's conception of *amor ludens* [playful love], is the kind of lovestyle in which relationships are seen as a sophisticated interpersonal game. This kind of lover seeks not "to get too involved," is not "ready to settle down," and generally moves rapidly from one partner to the other ("playing the field"). In this life-love style it is important to observe the rules and tactics of the game, which include (or used to) elements of flattery, coyness, coquetry, gallantry, and other devices to make social interactions smooth and harmonious but not too intense. The famous French film *Rules of the Game* portrays the situation where a group of players are relating according to the rules of love as a game, but one individual is painfully experiencing love as passion.

3. *Storge,* which is equivalent to the kind of love the Greeks referred to as *philia,* is love that grows gradually out of friendship, and primarily remains such. There is no sudden passion, no anxious and hopeful anticipation of future togetherness, just a gradual, relaxed coming together with shared interests and a strong family orientation.

4. *Mania* is obsessive, possessive, irrational, addictive love; the kind we are familiar with from numerous works of drama and literature, in which the lover is anxious, unhappy, distraught, preoccupied, and out of control to the brink of madness. Some people feel that this is *the true* kind of intoxi-

cating love, in which jealousy and self-abasement are seen as proof of the intensity of one's affections.

5. *Pragma,* as the name implies, is a practical, sensible, pragmatic type of relationship, based on a realistic assessment of compatible traits and qualities. Usually the relationship develops slowly out of shared interests and attitudes. Intense feelings and sexual passion are not prime factors in consideration, but factors of work skills and social status are important. Areas of incompatibility are treated by the partners as something to be "worked out."

6. *Agape,* totally selfless, altruistic love, was not found in his sample, according to Lee. "Storgic eros," which has some of the qualities of eros but is less possesive and demanding, comes closest to this kind of love as described in religious writings.

7. *Ludic eros* is another secondary type, not as exclusive and more playful than pure eros.[1]

It is important to remember that we are dealing here with styles of relationships rather than with types of people. A person may, in other words, experience in the course of their life history several of these different lovestyles. The same relationship may actually go through different stages also: For example, it may start off as playful, become more seriously erotic, and in time perhaps turn into a friendship; or sometimes a relationship that has been purely "storgic" for a long time, as with childhood companions, for instance, may at a certain time suddenly become erotic.

In a short but deeply meaningful essay called "On Love," Gurdjieff's student A. R. Orage presents a discussion of three levels of love, that Gurdjieff himself also touched on in his magnum opus *All and Everything.* This model, apparently derived from Tibetan doctrines, distinguishes "love of body," "love of feeling," and "love of consciousness." Gurdjieff said

[1] For more detailed discussions of these and other varieties of lovestyles, the reader is referred to Lee's book *The Colors of Love,* which includes two simple tests for evaluating one's relationships according to this typology. It should be noted that the study focused only on personal relationships (heterosexual or homosexual), and did not include parent-child, friendship, or other kinds of relationships.

love of body depends only on chemistry and polarity. In other words, physical, sexual attraction is a matter of chemical affinity, a purely physiological, instinctive process designed by God and nature for the preservation of the species.

"Love of feeling," according to Gurdjieff, "always turns into its opposite," referring to the universal human tendency for an erotic, emotional lover to project idealized images onto the beloved. When the inescapable facts of personality differences shatter these idealizations, the love feelings are bound to flip-flop sharply to dislike and/or hatred. Years of unspoken contempt and resentment, sudden separation and divorce, or even violent "crimes of passion" can result, in relationships based solely on this kind of feeling love.

"Love of consciousness," which would correspond to what has been called *agape* or *caritas* in Western philosophy, "is the wish that the beloved should arrive at his/her own native perfection, regardless of the consequences to the lover" (Orage). And, paradoxically, such love always evokes a similar attitude in the beloved. This kind of love, though it may be rare in contemporary personal relationships, as John Lee's research indicated, is probably more often an element in maternal or paternal love, if the latter does not remain at the level of possessive and idealized illusions. Perhaps conscious love also enters into the feelings of an enlightened teacher or therapist for the student or client they are helping to grow in self-understanding and self-reliance, and also into the feelings one has for animals and plants.

Five Types on a Desert Island—
A Test of Sexual Values

The following test in the form of a story is helpful in eliciting awareness of one's implicit value system in regard to personal relationships. It can also become the basis for discussion among couples or in therapeutic groups. The situation to be imagined is as follows. Five individuals have been shipwrecked on two desert islands, which are too far apart for swimming from one to the other to be practical. On one island, there is one man, A, and two women, B and C. On the other island are two other men, D and E. Prior to the shipwreck, the woman B and the man D, now separated by fate, were deeply in love.

B is eager to find a way to reach the other island to rejoin her lover, D. The only available boat belongs to A. When B goes to him to ask to borrow the boat, he tells her that he himself is also in love with her, and will only lend her the boat if she will consent to sleep with him. B is then thrown into a quandary, and goes to C, an old friend, for advice. C, after listening to her problem, says that she can't tell her what to do, and that the choice is hers to make.

B then decides to go to bed with A, does so, borrows the boat, and sails to the other island to rejoin her lover D. All is well, until D discovers the story behind how B managed to come to his island. Hurt and humiliated, since he feels she cannot really love him, he breaks off the relationship and asks her to leave. B is deeply disappointed and goes to E, to confide in him. After listening to her story, E feels strong sympathy for her and asks her to join him in his house and raise a family, which she accepts.

The task is to rank-order the five individuals, according to your personal moral evaluation of them—that is, to list which you consider most admirable, which next, and so on to the most reprehensible. It is suggested the reader do this, and write down the choices, before proceeding to the next paragraph. If this is done in a couple or a group, each should do his evaluation independently. One can then discuss the choices, and the reasons, attitudes, and values behind them; this often brings out a productive communication and exchange of views.

After the evaluations and discussions are completed, one can consider the following values, which represent the goals that motivate each individual. For A it is *power*—he has an advantage and uses it. B's primary value is *love sex,* or *eros*—this is what she consistently pursues. C is perhaps a Buddhist, practicing noninvolvement or *detachment;* she can also be seen as uncaring or *indifferent,* depending on one's point of view. D is a man of *moral principle*—he cannot continue the relationship if it doesn't meet his ideals of faithfulness. E's prime value is *home-family*—he is accepting and nonjudgmental over B's prior sexual history.

Some people may find that they would evaluate the situation differently if B were a man, and all the others were women. If this occurs in a couple or a group, it should be discussed, since it constitutes a significant double standard.

Personality Types and Sexual Behavior

While the researches of Kinsey and his associates accumulated voluminous data on the differences in sexual behavior among social-class and age groups, relatively little work has been done on the relationship between personality type and sexual behavior or attitudes. As discussed earlier, Freud and the psychoanalysts described developmental stages and different kinds of eroticism related to different erogenous zones (oral, anal, phallic), but the main assumption here was that everyone had to pass through these stages and reach a certain desired end point (the genital phase). Fixated development at one or another of these stages is conceptualized as leading to different kinds of psychopathology, different types of neurosis.

In research carried out in Germany and England, H. J. Eysenck correlated his personality dimensions of extraversion-introversion, and neuroticism and stability, with sexual behavior and attitudes in normal subjects. The following were some of the main findings.

1. Individuals who score high on extraversion have intercourse almost twice as frequently as those with high introversion scores. This was true of both men and women. Extraverts also tend to have more sex partners than introverts. Female extraverts have orgasm more frequently than introverted females.

2. When sexual attitudes were measured, it was found that extraverts tend to have more favorable attitudes toward promiscuity, and are relatively low on nervousness and prudishness

in sexual matters. Introverts, on the other hand, are more likely to stress the importance of virginity and fidelity, and to downplay the importance of physical sex. These appear to be two characteristic modes of sexual attitude, which, when carried to their extremes, become the *libertine* and the *puritan,* respectively. The extraverted males also expressed stronger preference for the busty, well-developed type of female body, whereas introverts select female pictures for attractiveness on other dimensions.

3. The research basically showed that it is important to distinguish between intensity of sexual drive (libido) and sexual satisfaction. The two are not necessarily correlated, and a person with one kind of personality and a strong sexually appetite may be no more satisfied or fulfilled sexual than someone whose interests involve less frequent and varied sexual activity. Satisfaction and fulfillment would seem to depend primarily on the congruence between one's expectations and outer experience.

Eastern Approaches to Sexual Typology

In the area of sexual satisfaction and compatibility, the West could learn much from the traditional teachings of India, China, and other Eastern countries, which have approached sexual relationships in a more matter-of-fact, realistic fashion than we, less subject to the ambivalent mixture of idealization, shame, and guilt so pervasive in Western culture. In these societies, at least until recent times, the majority of marriages were arranged at an early date, and partners were selected by the family in consultation with astrologers, giving careful attention to considerations of type and compatibility. Marital partnerships are based, in such a system, not on the inconstant vagaries of emotional love but on pragmatic considerations and evaluations of physical affinity. Conscious love was expected to develop gradually between the partners during the course of the marriage.

There existed in Indian and Chinese literature marriage manuals describing in detail the arts of erotic love along with instructions on housekeeping, food-buying, entertainment, home remedies, social etiquette, and so forth. Such manuals have been published only in very recent times in Western cultures. In India *kama,* the pleasures of the senses, was regarded as one of the four principal life-goals, the other three being *artha,* the acquisition and maintenance of property; *dharma,* fulfilling one's duty or chosen mission; and *moksha,* liberation by spiritual practice.

In the *Kama Sutra* of Vatsayana, the classic Indian sex and marriage manual, a sexual typology is outlined as the basis for compatible relationships. There are said to be three types of males, according to the size of the sexual organ—the Hare, the Bull, and the Horse; and three types of females, according to the size and depth of the *yoni*—the Doe, the Mare, and the Elephant. Classifications of this sort, sometimes with six or seven different types instead of only three, are still used in many Asian countries as part of the matchmaker's art.

	MALES	FEMALES
Small	Hare	Doe
Medium	Bull	Mare
Large	Horse	Elephant

According to Vatsayana, with the three types of men and women, nine different types of physical pairings are possible. Those between equal partners—that is, Doe-Hare, Mare-Bull, and Elephant-Horse—are held to be the best. Those in which the male is larger than the female—that is, Horse-Mare and Bull-Doe (referred to as "high union")—are said to be next best. The reverse situation, in which the female is larger than the male—that is, Bull-Elephant and Hare-Mare ("low union")—are less satisfactory. And the least satisfactory are said to be those in which the size difference is two steps—that is, Horse-Doe ("very high union") and Hare-Elephant ("very low union").

These classifications, though they may strike the Western reader as picturesque and quaint, have much to commend them. Western marriage manuals and sex-therapy programs are replete with discussions and advice concerning the importance (or irrelevance) of male genital size to female sexual satisfaction; and numerous programs and devices are offered to improve, or compensate for, supposed inadequate proportions. In view of this, simply paying attention to physical type compatibility, and choosing one's sexual partner with due consideration of these factors (along the lines of the *Kama Sutra* and similar oriental texts), would seem to be a natural and obvious way to counteract and prevent the whole aura of confusion and anxiety surrounding this whole issue.

A Circular Typology of Sexual Preferences

While numerous volumes have been written on the psychodynamics and sociological aspects of the various kinds of sexual proclivity, it remained for a San Francisco astrologer, Gavin Arthur, to propose a circular, clocklike model describing twelve basic sexual types. Arthur, in his book *The Circle of Sex,* published in 1962, wrote that his model aroused positive interest in such eminent sexologists as Havelock Ellis, Magnus Hirschfeld, and Dr. Alfred Kinsey.

The model, reproduced below, is based on the intersection of two dimensions: the male-female biological distinction, and the psychological qualities of masculinity-femininity, or *yang-yin.* According to Arthur, a key observation underlying his model was the close psychological similarity between the lesbian and the promiscuous Don Juan—alike in their single-minded adoration of the female body. He described the Don Juan as a "dyke" with a penis. An analogous parallel exists, according to this model, between the female promiscuous courtesan (called the "Lady C" type, after Lady Chatterley, in Arthur's scheme) and the male homosexual, whom he calls the "Dorian" type.

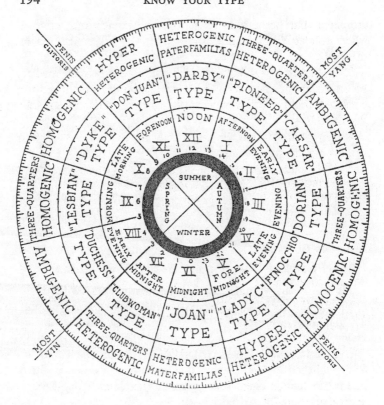

Circle of Sex.

The advantage of such a circular arrangement is that it allows one to place oneself, or other individuals, at a point on the circle—for example, quarter past two, or five-thirty—that reflects the subtle variations and shades among and within the twelve-type categories. A brief description of the six male types is as follows:

1. *The Father* ("Darby" type in Arthur's somewhat arch terminology) is the heterosexual husband-father, with a strong family orientation.

2. *The Pioneer* is very masculine, still predominantly het-

erosexual, but perhaps inclined to some homosexual contact when isolated from females, at sea, in the wilderness, or in prison.

3. *The Male Bisexual,* of which Julius Caesar was reputed to be an example, is equally attracted to men and women. Arthur considers this type very *yang,* although one might reasonably dispute this.

4. *The Active Male Homosexual* ("Dorian" type) mostly prefers men to women, but maintains a very masculine manner and appearance, and may in fact marry and have children.

5. *The Passive Male Homosexual* ("Finocchio" type), referred to in slang as "queen," often thinks of himself as a female in a male body, and may, on occasion, become transvestite.

6. *The Don Juan,* or "hyperheterogenic" type, is a woman-chaser or "lady-killer," who much prefers the company of women to men even socially, and is often mistrusted by other men. As mentioned above, Gavin Arthur places this type next to the "dyke," due to his dislike for the masculine physical form and idealization of feminine physical form. And yet, in another sense, this type is strongly polarized on the masculine side.

The six female types correspond to their male opposites, as indicated in the following descriptions:

1. *The Mother* (or "Joan" type) is, like the Father, monogamous and family-oriented.

2. *The Clubwoman,* or "woman's woman," is an active, energetic type of female, who excels at all women's activities, and who may be an organizer or executive. Arthur places her as more *yin* than the maternal type although most people would probably tend to see her as more active, and therefore slightly more masculine, or *yang.*

3. *The Female Bisexual* may outwardly be utterly feminine in style and manner, yet is also very active and energetic, and sexually is capable of relations with both women or men.

4. *The Lesbian* prefers women sexually, but still does not

look "mannish." She maintains femininity in appearance and style and may also marry and have children.

5. *The Dyke* abhors men physically, yet imitates their manner, roles, and appearance, feeling herself to be masculine.

6. *The Courtesan,* or "Lady C" type, vastly prefers the company of men to that of women. Like her male counterpart, the Don Juan, she tends toward promiscuity and relentlessly pursues sexual attention and experience.

Though one may disagree with certain of the descriptions and valuations that Gavin Arthur gives of his types, his system does enable one to visualize a person occupying a range of two or three of these categories, and being attracted to a range of several types. A person's type in this area, as with the different kinds of love relationships discussed above, may change at different stages of life.

Part of the difficulty with a typology of sexual behavior is that so much of what is called masculinity or femininity is bound up with cultural stereotypes. These collective images change from generation to generation, and are subject to ephemeral waves of fashion and popular culture, so the concepts and terminology are fluid and elusive. The dictionary is littered with outmoded terms descriptive of male-female sex roles from prior centuries. Current terms such as "queer," "gay," or "macho," may, in a decade or so, join this linguistic wastebasket of unused categories and sub-cultural labels.

The Development of Sexual Identities

Most cultures recognize that masculinity or femininity, as psychobiological characteristics, undergo various stages of development and transformation. One does not automatically become a "man" or a "woman" simply by reaching a certain age. The clusters of attitudes, feelings, motivations, and behavioral expressions that constitute masculine or feminine identity are subject to intense cultural and familial conditioning.

Many cultures have initiation or transition rituals and practices that mark the exit from one phase and entry into another. Ritual circumcision for boys or defloration for girls, puberty rites, wedding-night ceremonies, and childbirth rituals are examples of very widespread human practices relating to the development of sexual identities. Most societies seem to distinguish at least six general stages, although the age at which one typically enters a stage may vary quite widely. The male/female stages generally recognized are: (1) infant, (2) boy/girl, (3) adolescent youth/girl, (4) man/woman, (5) father/mother, and (6) old man/old woman.

As discussed earlier, psychiatrists and psychologists in Western society have often attempted to categorize and analyze different forms of disturbed sexual and emotional behavior by relating them to fixations at different stages of development. Thus, for example, a man might be said to be emotionally-sexually arrested at the "little boy" stage; or an adult woman relate to men on the basis of behavior patterns learned as an adolescent girl. Transactional analysis emphasizes the inner child as a constellation of feelings and attitudes maintained from childhood. Some psychologists have focused on the role played by sibling relationships and birth-order factors in determining the nature and quality of adult relationship patterns.

An example of this approach is the work of Alexander Lowen, a psychiatrist who has developed a body-oriented therapy known as "bio-energetics" based on Wilhelm Reich's work. Lowen, in his book *Love and Orgasm*, distinguishes four main sexual roles in women: sexual object, sister, romantic ideal, and mother. He relates these to four stages of psychosexual development: daughter, sister, sweetheart, and mother. Arrested development at the "daughter" level leads to a self-image as sexual object (the "baby doll" type), according to Lowen. Emotional fixation at the pre-adolescent sister level leads to an asexual, helpmate kind of relationship with men. Development arrested at the level of the adolescent sweetheart leads to romantic, idealized images of the male-female relationship, and hysterical behavior patterns. The fourth type plays a mother-martyr role in relationship to men. According to Lowen's formulations, the normal, mature woman can fill any and all of these roles (and, one should add, other roles as well) in a relationship, moving flexibly from one to the other. It is only fixated or arrested emotional development that leads to the neurotic distortions.

In the male, the corresponding roles are (1) the son, leading to the "playboy" attitude if carried into adulthood; (2) the brother, who relates to his woman as a kind, friendly "big brother"; (3) the romantic knight-hero, who views women in terms of phallic conquest; and (4) the fixated father figure, who may be either a rigid authoritarian or an indulgent "sugar daddy." Again, maturity of development implies progressive integration of the four stages and nonexclusive identification with the different roles in a fluid, flexible manner.

A somewhat different perspective on emotional-sexual development is provided by Jung's theory of the role of the contrasexual anima/animus figure in the process of individuation (Von Franz, 1964; Whitmont, 1969). According to the Jungian view, the anima can be experienced in a man's consciousness in several different symbolic forms, personified in mythological and literary figures, with some degree of correspondence to the four functional types discussed earlier (in Chapter 3). The anima figure in a man is an inner image that can be, and usually is, projected on to the external partner in relationships. At the same time, a woman may also "play the role" of that anima figure with such intensity and flair as to provide a natural external hook or screen for the man's projections. In women, the animus goes through parallel stages of development, and can be experienced as a negative, threatening force, or as a guide and mediator to inner sources of strength and initiative. It also enters, through projections, into the women's relationships with external males.

The anima corresponding to the level of instinctive, biological relations is symbolized by the figure of Eve, or may be pictured in dreams or art as a primitive woman, close to nature and of earthy sensuality (for example, Gauguin's Tahitian women). In a debased form, this anima figure may manifest in men as obsessive voyeurism or pornographic fantasizing. The animus counterpart to this level is the primitive, physical male

—the savage, the warrior or muscleman, expressing raw virility. If negative, he may be symbolized in dreams or collective art forms by a bandit, an outlaw, a sexual aggressor, or even a demon.

At the level of emotional love, we have the anima figure of idealized romantic beauty, as personified in myth by Helen of Troy or other legendary beauties, that can function in a man's consciousness as a guide to the receptive, feeling qualities of his psyche. If associated with negative attitudes and anxieties, this type of anima can become the seductive but dangerous *femme fatale*. The male counterpart to this figure is the animus archetype of the romantic man of action, energy, and initiative—the hero, the artist, or the knight. Again, he may have a dark, fateful attraction, as in stories and dreams of the mysterious stranger, or Bluebeard in his castle.

The mother and father figures described previously in the Lowen developmental typology can also be seen as anima/animus archetypes. A man who is bound to a mother anima will find himself in relationships with women who do indeed mother him; and will have to work out his feelings of dependency and helplessness. A woman dominated by the father animus will seek out men who are protective, strong, and supportive, but who may function to keep her in the role of little girl, stifling her growth and patronizing her own values.

At the mental level of relationships, there are several variations of the anima and animus. There is the hetaira, courtesan, or geisha type of anima, the woman who is intellectually gifted, cultured, aesthetic, capable. In her negative manifestation she is cold, promiscuous, untrustworthy, bright as a butterfly but fickle as the wind. A variation of this type, described by Whitmont, is the Amazon—a practical, realistic, supportive sisterlike figure, who may show her dark face as a domineering manager, critical and tradition-bound.

One animus counterpart at the airy-mental level is the *puer aeternus,* the eternal youth, flighty, spirited, brilliant, who "loves them and leaves them," and seems incapable of loyalty or constancy. Women bound to this animus in their psyche will repeatedly "fall for" this kind of man-boy. At another level, we may find here the archetype of the thinker-philosopher, who can appear in dreams or fantasies as the great writer or orator, political leader or creative pioneer—the guide to the world of ideas and knowledge.

Anima/animus figures may also manifest as spiritual guides, as mediators to the realms of intuitive wisdom and transcendent experience. Here we have the anima archetype of the medium or the muse, the psychic seeress who inspires visions and ecstatic revelations. Her dark aspect is hysteria, madness, chaos, frenzy, delirium. This anima may also appear as the prototype of religious devotion—the Madonna in Christianity, Kwan-Yin in China, or the compassionate Tara in Tibetan Buddhism.

On the masculine side, there is the animus of the wise man or magician, mediator of spiritual intuition and cosmic wisdom, who might be personified by human religious leaders, saints or yogis, or mythic gods such as Apollo or Osiris. The negative expression of this animus is the false prophet, the fanatic, the dark sorcerer, the corrupt guide.

We see here two models of the development of sexual identities. In the Reich-Lowen typology, sex roles are based on the network of expectations and attitudes provided by the family environment (child, sibling, parent). In the Jungian theory, the development of anima/animus goes through stages and levels that correspond approximately to the four functions discussed earlier: physical, emotional, mental, and intuitive or spiritual.

Self-Evaluation of Sexual Identities

The following test has grown out of seminars and discussions on masculine/feminine identity images as they are currently conceived by most adults in our culture. By asking oneself these questions and discussing one's answers with mates and friends, much can be learned about the sources of one's own sense of identity. It should be obvious that none of the answers is more "right" or "wrong" than any other. They simply reflect the kinds of social and personal-familial conditioning one has undergone regarding sex roles and how those conditioned self-images affect current attitudes, feelings, and behavior in relationships. The test is divided into two parts, Part A dealing with our images of masculinity and Part B with our images of femininity. It is suggested that both sexes answer both parts, but that women answer the femininity questions first, then go back to Part A for their men.

PART A. How masculine do you feel—or does the man you know best (either a mate or a friend) seem to you—in each of the following situations? Mark your responses X for somewhat, XX for very, and XXX for extremely masculine.[2]

1. in relationship to a woman—for example, in bed or while wooing a potential partner

2. competing with other men, defeating an opponent, or demonstrating superior skill or strength

3. in co-operative association with other men in such activities as hunting, fishing, drinking, or conversation

4. involved in work, achieving a goal, overcoming an obstacle, solving a problem, or meeting a challenge

5. involved in vigorous physical activity—for example, speed sports or sports involving physical danger

6. displaying and being recognized for some public display or performance of dexterity, strength, or wit

7. being a father

8. any other

PART B. How feminine do you feel—or does the woman you know best (either a mate or friend) seem to you—in each of the following situations? Mark your responses X for somewhat, XX for very, and XXX for extremely feminine.

1. in a sexual, intimate relationship with a man

2. competing with other women, showing superior beauty or attractiveness

3. associating co-operatively with other women in activities such as domestic arts, beautification, or communication

[2] There is, of course, no need to check all the items. For many people a given activity may not be associated with masculinity (or femininity) at all—that is, it may be neutral with respect to gender identity.

4. involved in work, achieving a goal, overcoming an obstacle, solving a problem, or meeting a challenge

5. displaying or being admired for appearance and form in public

6. involved in physical activities—for example, sports, movement, or dance

7. bearing and raising children

8. any other

In the seminars and groups using these questions, a number of interesting findings have emerged. Approximately 30 per cent, or almost one third, of men and women check the first alternative—that is, they derive their primary sense of masculinity or femininity from sexual relations. This finding correlates with the results of a similar survey conducted by the magazine *Psychology Today*.

Answer No. 4, relating to work and achievement, is chosen quite frequently by men, though not very often by women. This apparently reflects the widespread view that a man has to prove his masculinity by *doing* something, whereas women can be feminine just by *being*. Many women, especially liberated, active women, do, of course, practice and enjoy the activities listed in No. 4, but they don't feel particularly feminine when doing so. They don't necessarily feel unfeminine either; sexual identity is just not a part of that realm of experience for them. It often is, however, for men, as shown by the findings that businessmen whose business fails, or investors who suffer a stock loss, sometimes experience a temporary impairment of sexual potency.

A basic typological distinction for both women and men appears to be the difference between those who derive their sense of sexual identity primarily from experiences with the opposite sex (answer No. 1), and those who derive it from same-sex associations and affiliations (answers No. 2 and No. 3). In the former there is role learning through opposite polarization, while in the latter there is role learning through peer modeling and imitation. Same-sex associations can involve a strong competitive element (No. 2), or recreational and collaborative activities (No. 3). Men or women who are strongly and exclusively based in sexual identity roles per se (No. 1) tend to see other members of the same sex as actual or potential competitors, and avoid them. This factor was mentioned in the descriptions of the Don Juan and Courtesan types given above.

In answers to category No. 3, personal or emotional communication activities are most frequently chosen by women as being essentially feminine in nature; joint projects and enterprises were more often chosen by men.

Answers in category No. 5 have indicated that different qualities of physical activity were seen as "masculine" or "feminine." A man said his wife looked very feminine when she was swimming, because of the grace and beauty of her movements. In men, by contrast, it seems to be the power and endurance factors in sports that are more often associated with masculinity.

Interpersonal Relationship Balance

Jung's theory indicates that for the process of individuation to take place, a man must become aware of and come to terms with his *anima* or feminine component, and a woman her masculine *animus*. Esoteric and oriental systems of yogic and spiritual development have always taught that one must balance the male-female polarities within one's nature. In Chinese Taoism, the nature symbolism of *yin-yang* described this ideal, and in the Indian Tantra the mythology of Siva-Sakti symbolized this same inner balancing. In alchemy, the androgynous union of Sol and Luna (Sun and Moon) was depicted as the central procedure in the transmutation of metals from lead to gold— a process symbolic of the illumination of consciousness.

In Actualism, a contemporary Western teaching of consciousness transformation, the polarities are referred to as *dynamic* (expressive, outgoing, male, *yang*) and *magnetic* (receptive, incoming, female, *yin*). Every human being, male or female, has both dynamic and magnetic poles in his or her consciousness and body. The process of enlightenment involves bringing them into union and balance.

It should be noted that, contrary to the impression one might gain from Jungian writings, it is not always the feminine part of his psyche (*anima*) of which a man is unaware and that he must develop for inner balance. Some men (who are not necessarily effeminate or homosexual) lean strongly toward the magnetic side of their nature, due to their conditioning, and need to cultivate and express the male aspect. Similarly, some women (not necessarily either mannish or lesbian) are clearly dominant in their dynamic polarity, and for balance and wholeness need to become more aware of, and comfortable with, their softer, receptive, feminine side.

Our outer relationship situations provide a faithful reflection of the state of our inner balance or imbalance. A person unfamiliar with or uncomfortable with maleness, or masculine qualities in themselves (whether they be man or woman), will tend to avoid relationships or even encounters with external males, especially those in which masculine qualities are called for. Similarly, one who is out of touch with the feminine aspect of his or her psyche will tend to gravitate toward relationships with men or masculine females, and to avoid women.

Therefore, a simple self-test can give us valuable feedback on the state of male-female balance in our intrapersonal as well as interpersonal relationships. You simply make a list of the people you consider your friends. A good definition of "friend" is someone with whom you like to share time and space. You just write down all the names, and, when you are finished, count the numbers of men and women. You can, if you wish, make a separate list of past friends, whom you do not see now only for reasons of geographical location. Again, count the numbers of men and women. If there is a large inequality, it is worthwhile to examine what it is that causes one's discomfort with one half of the human species—what inner factors are blocking a free and mutual exchange with people of both sexes. An additional, often highly revealing, process for clarifying one's patterns of likes and dislikes is to make a list of the people *not* liked, people one would *not* enjoy being alone with; and again, to examine the list for inequality in the numbers of men and women.

Some people find it profitable and educational to make separate lists for (a) mental relationships, (b) emotional relationships, (c) working relationships, and (d) sexual or intimate relationships. In regard to the latter, it is of course sexual polarity per se that governs sexual preferences, and there is no indication that the balancing of inner polarities has to be expressed in physically intimate relationships with both sexes. Androgyny of consciousness does not imply or require bisexuality of body behavior. On the contrary, there is every indication that the more a person is inwardly balanced in terms of magnetic-dynamic, *yin-yang* polarities, the more essentially masculine or feminine their attitude and expression is in sexual relationships.

In Taoist and Tantric yoga of sex practices, a man and a woman practice inner union and communion, which is then expressed and grounded, in a sacramental-ritual manner, in the physical outer union of sex.

10

*Oriental and Esoteric
Typologies*

In this chapter we examine and discuss several personality type systems that are very different from those described so far. In Eastern philosophy and astrology and in Western esoteric teachings, we find perspectives on human nature and premises for understanding human differences that may appear obscure and alien to our rationally trained minds at first, but that can ultimately yield a fresh and fruitful harvest of insights. Human nature is what it is, and the different interpretive models and paradigms developed in different cultures and traditions have interesting points of contact and congruence, as one would expect when maps of the same territory are drawn by different explorers. We will discuss in this chapter the Indian theory of the three *gunas,* the twenty-eight lunar mansions of Hindu astrology, and the twelve-year cycle of Chinese astrology. We will also examine three modern esoteric systems: the theosophical teachings of the seven ray types, the Arica model of nine types, arranged in the form of an enneagram, and Gurdjieff's developmental typology. Another esoteric typology, based on the symbolism of numbers, will be treated in a separate chapter.

The Three Gunas

In the Samkhya branch of ancient Indian philosophic-religious teaching, it was held that the primordial universal substance or energy (*prakriti*) is divided into three strands or modes of activity, called *gunas*. Constantly interweaving and combining in different proportions, the *gunas* cause not only the different states and attributes of consciousness, but also the different properties of material substances. Indian philosophers often used the analogy of a rope, representing the totality of substance, made up of three spiral strands, representing the three *gunas*.

Emerging out of the dark field or matrix of unconsciousness, the three *gunas* represent the tendencies to awareness, to activity, and to inertia. *Sattva* is radiance, awareness, clarity, and calm; it reflects and magnifies light. *Rajas* is movement, energy, and activity; it transmits light outward and onward. *Tamas* is inertia, structure, and mass; it absorbs light.

These three general principles or moments of consciousness can be related to similar trinities found in many philosophic and scientific systems, as the following table (adapted from *Maps of Consciousness*) indicates:

TABLE 17
Three Principles in Different World Systems

Taoism	*Yang*	*Yin*	*Tao*
Hindu Tantra	Siva	Sakti	Brahman
Hindu Samkhya	Rajas	Tamas	Sattva
Gurdjieff	Affirming force	Denying force	Reconciling force
Alchemy	Sulphur	Salt	Mercury
Astrology	Cardinal	Fixed	Mutable
Actualism	Function	Structure	Consciousness/ energy
Einstein	Radiation (c)	Mass (m)	Energy (E)
Electricity	Positive (proton)	Negative (electron)	Neutral (neutron)
Natural Forms	Linear, angular	Curved, round	Radiating

In much Indian writing on the three *gunas* a definite value judgment is associated with them, making *sattva* the most desirable, *rajas* next, and *tamas* something to be avoided, associated with darkness, ignorance, and lethargy. Thus, for example, in Sri Krishna Prem's commentary on the *Bhagavad Gita,* the sattvic mind is described as clear and calm; the rajasic mind as restless, driven by impulses and desires; and the tamasic mind as slow, heavy, and obscure.

Yet from another point of view, one can see here a subtle denigration of both form and function, and an idealization of detached, pure awareness. If we recognize the three *gunas* as necessary and inevitable components of all consciousness and all matter, then it would be the excess or imbalance in any of the three that would lead to distortion or pathology. Looking at the emotional level, someone with an excess of *sattva* would be sensation-oriented, lustful, and overly curious; a person with excess of *rajas* is hyperexcitable, violent, passionate, even manic; and someone with excess of *tamas* would be prone to depression, lethargy, and indifference.

We previously noted, in the chapter on somatotypes, the striking parallels between this system and the threefold division of temperaments described by Sheldon, *sattva* corresponding to ectomorphy, *rajas* to mesomorphy, and *tamas* to endomorphy. Interestingly, in Indian psychophysiological writings *sattva* is correlated with the sense organs and the mind, *rajas* with the organs of movement and action (hands and feet), and *tamas* with the actual physical elements of the body.

James Hardt (1977), in reviewing experiments on ego strength and physiological arousal, suggests that the person low in ego strength and low in level of arousal, who has difficulty mobilizing enough energy to maintain a given level of activity, is predominantly tamasic in quality. On the other hand, low ego-strength people with a high level of arousal, who are energetic and excitable, can be described as rajasic. And high ego-strength people with a moderate, flexible level of arousal may be seen as sattvic. The last are the ones most likely to be able to learn to control their alpha-wave activity; the rajasic people are too restless, and the tamasic are too sluggish.

It is also possible to correlate the three *gunas* to three divisions of the nervous system: the calm, detached perception of *sattva* with the central nervous system and brain; the active energy of *rajas* with the sympathetic, fight or flight mobilization system; and the slow, even qualities of *tamas* with the parasympathetic relaxation and sleep system.

At another level of analysis altogether, *sattva* is the Spirit, *rajas* the mind and emotions, and *tamas* the body. Thus a sattvic person is aware of his or her Spirit, the source of light within. A rajasic person is identified with his or her thoughts and feelings, moving about restlessly. A tamasic person is identified with his or her body and involved in the pursuit of external, material goals and objects.

The nature and qualities of people expressed through the three *gunas* was probably the original basis for the divisions of the Hindu caste system before it became a hereditary system of rules and privileges. The sattvic person, because of his natural aptitudes and inclinations, was chosen and directed to become a teacher or priest (*brahmin*). The rajasic personality was guided into fields of action, such as administration and warfare (*kshatriyas*). The tamasic personality was encouraged to work in trade or commerce (*vaishya*). The original design here was thus a functional system based on natural capabilities, not an exclusionary system of antagonistic and hierarchical classes. It became an exclusive and separative system, by being compounded with hereditary and racial criteria, and those who did not fit any of the three groups, were made "untouchable" serfs and outcasts (*sudras*).

Originally, all three of the temperamental caste-types were considered essential for a harmonious social order; just as all three qualities of psychophysiology are essential components of the individual's constitution; and all three moments of consciousness are integral elements in the cosmic dance of energy.

To quote Sri Krishna Prem again: "The disciple must bend his energies upon transcendence of the *gunas* altogether. He must strive to see that all their play is objective to himself. . . . The movements of the Cosmos, shining with knowledge, passionately active, darkly inert, he sees with steady vision. His is the calm, immortal gaze of the Spirit, cool as the moonlight on a tropic lake. . . . Nothing that comes can be unwelcome to him; nothing that goes can be a source of grief. He knows that all is needed for a Cosmos, that in the darkest *tamas* shines the light."

The Lunar Mansions of Hindu Astrology

Indian astrology is different in many respects from Western. It uses a fixed, sidereal zodiac, rather than the movable, tropical zodiac preferred in the West, and emphasizes the Midheaven, indicative of social status, position and occupation, whereas Western astrologers emphasize the Ascendant, indicative of personal self-projection and appearance. Perhaps the most critical difference, however, is that Hindu astrology uses primarily a lunar zodiac, assigning secondary importance to the solar zodiac used in the West. This is interesting for several reasons, including the esoteric teaching that the oriental half of the planet is basically *yin,* feminine, or lunar, whereas the occidental half is *yang,* masculine, or solar.

Arabic, Chinese, and Hindu astrologers employ a system of lunar mansions, which divide the ecliptic or zodiac into twenty-seven or twenty-eight sections, each of which is about the length of the Moon's daily travel (approximately thirteen degrees). Thus, in Indian astrology, rather than asking which of the twelve signs of the solar zodiac the Sun occupied in a person's chart, one would ask first which of the twenty-seven *nakshatras* is occupied by the Moon, Sun, and planets. Each of the mansions or asterisms has certain specific characteristics, and questions of personal compatibility raised in marital counseling or arranging are most often resolved by referring to the qualities of these lunar mansions.

It should be noted that this typology of twenty-seven or twenty-eight divisions of the zodiac according to the Moon's daily motion is different from the twenty-eightfold system discussed in the chapter on planetary types; the latter is derived from the phase or angle relationship between the Sun and the Moon.

We give here a very abbreviated description of the twenty-seven *nakshatras,* which will allow one to identify which of these mansions one's natal Sun, Moon, or other planets occupy.[1]

1. 0°–13° Aries: *Aswini,* the Horseman, symbolized by a horse's head. Fiery imagination, need for movement. Favorable for merchants, physicians, and craftsmen. Intelligence, popularity, self-sufficiency, elegance.

2. 13°–26° Aries: *Bharani,* the Bearer, ruled by Venus, associated with Yama, god of Death. Aggressiveness, recklessness; also perseverance, health, determination in work.

3. 26° Aries–10° Taurus: *Kritika,* Commander of the Celestial Armies, symbolized by flame, associated with Agni and the Sun. Favorable for priests and teachers. Dignified, honorable, powerful emotions; but also sensual excess. Good practical instincts.

4. 10°–23° Taurus: *Rohini,* the Red Deer, symbolized by a wagon, ruled by the Moon, associated with Prajapati, the creator God. Associated with beauty in women, and with farming and animal care. Truthfulness, steadiness, kindness.

5. 23° Taurus–6° Gemini: *Mraga,* the Stag's Head, ruled by Mars. Anger, resentment in men. Religious aspiration in women. Timidity, capriciousness.

6. 6°–20° Gemini: *Ardra,* the Moist, symbolized by a gem, and associated with Rudra, the god of storms. Pride, cruelty, violence, ignorance.

7. 20° Gemini–3° Cancer: *Punarvasu,* the Two Together, ruled by Jupiter, associated with Aditi, the sky goddess. Intelligence, good fortune, devotion, amiability.

8. 3°–16° Cancer: *Pushya,* the Flower, symbolized by a crescent, ruled by Jupiter. Good for rulers and philanthropists. Social recognition, philosophic attitude, tenacity in action.

9. 16° Cancer–0° Leo: *Aslesha,* the Embracer, symbolized by a wheel, ruled by Mercury, associated with the serpent gods.

---

[1] It is suggested that readers who have their astrological chart determine which of the mansions is occupied by the Ascendant, the Moon, and the Sun. For example, the Moon in 29° Aries would be in *Kritika.*

Selfishness, lack of consideration, dishonesty; but also elevated mind.

10. 0°–13° Leo: *Magha,* the Mighty One, symbolized by a house. Favorable for wealth and position, but also jealousy, hostility, and restlessness.

11. 13°–26° Leo: *Purva Phalguni,* the Former Bad One, ruled by Venus, symbolized by a couch. For women, wealth and comfort; for men, impulsiveness, verbal facility, pride.

12. 26° Leo–10° Virgo: *Uttara Phalguni,* the Latter Bad One, ruled by the Sun, also symbolized by a couch or a bed. Good for warriors, intelligence, arrogance, popularity, sensuality.

13. 10°–23° Virgo: *Hasta,* the Hand, ruled by the Moon. Good for the arts, healing, commerce. Clever, verbal qualities, resourcefulness, industriousness.

14. 23° Virgo–6° Libra: *Chitra,* the Bright, symbolized by a lamp or a pearl, ruled by Mars. Favorable for crafts and music, beautiful objects. Charm, intuition, but indecisiveness.

15. 6°–20° Libra: *Svati,* the Good Doer, symbolized by a coral bead or pearl, associated with Vayu, god of winds. Deliberate, logical, willful individuals. Self-control, kindheartedness, modesty.

16. 20° Libra–3° Scorpio: *Vishaka,* the Branched, ruled by Jupiter, symbolized by a decorated gateway. Cleverness and religious tendencies, but also aggressiveness and overbearing manner.

17. 3°–16° Scorpio: *Anuradha,* the Successful One, ruled by Saturn, symbolized by a ridge. Favorable for women, giving a good mind and many friends; in men, secretiveness and guile.

18. 16° Scorpio–0° Sagittarius: *Jestha,* the Oldest, ruled by Mercury, associated with Indra, the sky god. Better for women than for men. Hypocritical, scheming, cheerful, irascible.

19. 0°–13° Sagittarius: *Mula,* the Root, symbolized by a lion's tail. Cleverness, diplomacy, shrewdness. Magnetic but stubborn personality.

20. 13°–26° Sagittarius: *Purva Ashadha,* the Former Unconquered, ruled by Venus, symbolized by an elephant's tusk. Conceit, pride, vulgarity, but loyalty in friendship.

21. 26° Sagittarius–10° Capricorn: *Uttara Ashadha,* the Latter Unconquered, ruled by the Sun. Honesty, sincerity, simplicity, intelligence. Favorable for warriors and hunters.

22. 10°–23° Capricorn: *Shravana,* the Ear, ruled by the Moon, symbolized by a trident. Humane, generous, kind, popular.

23. 23° Capricorn–6° Aquarius: *Dhanista,* the Most Favorable, ruled by Mars, symbolized by a drum. Rashness, ambition, strength; knowledge, abundance.

24. 6°–20° Aquarius: *Satabisha,* the Hundred Physicians. Associated with Varuna, goddess of waters. In women, respect and responsibility; in men, intelligence, moderation, and courage.

25. 20° Aquarius–3° Pisces: *Purva Bhadra-Pada,* the Former Beautiful Feet, ruled by Jupiter. High-strung, nervous, somber, clever, dignified, patient.

26. 3°–16° Pisces: *Uttara Bhadra-Pada,* the Latter Beautiful Feet, ruled by Saturn. Good for warriors and meditators. Wealth, intellignce, happy family life, sensitivity.

27. 16° Pisces–0° Aries: *Revati,* the Rich, ruled by Mercury, symbolized by a drum. Favorable for counselors; wealth, popularity.

The interpretations of these lunar *nakshatras* have come down to modern times from a very ancient period, in the centuries-old tradition of Hindu astrology.[2] They provide an intriguing and suggestive personality symbolism that complements and enriches the animal symbolism of the Babylonian, Greek, and Western solar zodiac.

The Twelve-year Cycle of Chinese Astrology

The twelvefold zodiac we know in Western astrology apparently originated in Mesopotamia, from where it spread westward to Greece and Egypt, and eastward to India and China. Some changes occurred in the symbolism in these diffusions.

[2] Readers who wish to study the lunar zodiac further are referred to the works of Robson (1923), Volguine (1974), and Oken (1976).

The sign known as the Twins (Gemini) in Western astrology is represented by a male/female couple in both Indian and Chinese astrology. Aquarius, the water-bearer, is symbolized by a pot or a vase in the oriental systems. In Egypt, the crab of Cancer is a scarab; and in China, the goat of Capricorn became a dolphin (in Babylonian astrology it is shown as half goat, half dolphin). However, the characteristics and qualities of the sign-symbols remained fairly similar and consistent in spite of these changes.

Chinese astronomers and astrologers also had a totally different symbol system of twelve animals, related to a cycle of twelve years. Mythologically, this series of animals is supposed to represent the order in which they came to pay homage to the Buddha on the day of his enlightenment. However, there is every evidence to indicate that the twelve-animal system is older than Buddhism. The Chinese system assigns one animal to each year, in a particular recurring sequence, that does not bear a neat one-to-one correspondence to the usual Western zodiac, although both have an ox or bull, a goat, a feline (tiger and lion), and a horse or centaur. The Chinese calendar year, being based on lunar months, begins on a different day of our calendar each year, ranging from mid-January to mid-February. One may ask if there is any astronomical phenomenon that could correlate with this series, and the cycle of Jupiter has been suggested: Since Jupiter takes about twelve years to traverse the entire zodiac, it takes about one year to pass through one sign. This fact raises the intriguing possibility that in former aeons, Chinese astrologers developed a whole human typology correlated with their observations of the changing positions of the planet Jupiter. In other words, this Chinese zodiac may be Jupiter-based, as the Western system is Sun-based, and the Indian Moon-based.

However, Jupiter's cycle is actually 11.8 years, not twelve exactly, and it does not enter a new sign around every January and February. Thus the relationship between the sign positions of Jupiter and the twelve-year animal cycle is a changing one. The Chinese used several other numerological and calendar systems, including the ten stems, the five elements, the twelve branches, and a sixty-year cycle, as well as the sixty-four *kua* of the *I Ching*. It did not trouble them that these different systems did not always coincide in a totally logical fashion. Rather, they treated them as different mappings of nature's complex patterns of recurrence and change.

Table 18 shows the Chinese animal years and the Jupiter sign positions for the years 1924 to 1995, illustrating how the patterns of correspondence change. From 1924 to 1927, Jupiter was mostly in one sign during the year; from 1928 to 1932, it generally occupied two signs, sometimes three; 1933 to 1935 were predominantly one-sign years again. A similar pattern prevailed in the next twelve-year cycle, from 1936 to 1947. In the next two cycles, from 1948 to 1971, almost every calendar year had Jupiter in two or more signs (even though it spent about one year's length of time in a given sign). By 1983 the pattern changes, so that Jupiter is now in Sagittarius in the Year of the Boar, after having been in Sagittarius in the Year of the Rat during the preceding six to ten cycles.

The following descriptions of the personalities born in the corresponding years give a brief indication of the nature of this typology, which is widely used throughout China, Japan, and Southeast Asia.

The Rat: intuitive, energetic, charming, meticulous, sociable, persistent, jolly, venturesome, sentimental, generous, honest; manipulative, greedy, petty, suspicious, tiresome, destructive, ambitious.

The Ox: patient, gentle, hard-working, familial, methodical, proud, eccentric, reserved, precise, strong, tenacious, long-suffering; slow, stubborn, conventional, authoritarian, rigid, vindictive.

The Tiger: generous, courageous, confident, meditative, noble, liberal, magnetic, sensitive, passionate, protective; suspicious, undisciplined, vain, rash, disrespectful, quarrelsome, impatient.

The Rabbit (sometimes called *The Cat*): discreet, refined, sociable, tactful, discriminating, forgiving, prudent, placid, de-

Rat	1924 ♐	1936 ♐	1948 ♐	1960 ♐/♑	1972 ♐/♑	1984 ♑
Ox	1925 ♑	1937 ♑	1949 ♑	1961 ♑/♒	1973 ♑/♒	1985 ♒
Tiger	1926 ♒	1938 ♒	1950 ♒/♓	1962 ♒/♓	1974 ♒/♓	1986 ♓
Hare	1927 ♓	1939 ♓/♈	1951 ♓/♈	1963 ♓/♈	1975 ♓/♈	1987 ♈
Dragon	1928 ♈/♉	1940 ♈/♉	1952 ♈/♉	1964 ♈/♉	1976 ♈/♉	1988 ♉
Serpent	1929 ♉/♊	1941 ♉/♊	1953 ♉/♊	1965 ♉/♊	1977 ♉/♊	1989 ♉/♊
Horse	1930 ♊/♋	1942 ♊/♋	1954 ♊/♋	1966 ♊/♋	1978 ♊/♋	1990 ♋/♌
Goat	1931 ♋/♌	1943 ♋/♌	1955 ♋/♌	1967 ♋/♌	1979 ♌/♍	1991 ♌/♍
Monkey	1932 ♌/♍	1944 ♌/♍	1956 ♌/♍	1968 ♌/♍	1980 ♍	1992 ♍
Rooster	1933 ♍	1945 ♍/♎	1957 ♍/♎	1969 ♍/♎	1981 ♎	1993 ♎
Dog	1934 ♎	1946 ♎/♏	1958 ♎/♏	1970 ♎/♏	1982 ♏	1994 ♏
Boar	1935 ♏	1947 ♏	1959 ♏/♐	1971 ♏/♐	1983 ♐	1995 ♐

TABLE 18

Chinese Astrology and the Jupiter Cycle.

tached, hospitable, clever; old-fashioned, pedantic, thin-skinned, devious, aloof, squeamish, melancholy.

The Dragon (or *Lizard*): scrupulous, sentimental, enthusiastic, shrewd, tenacious, vital, generous, spirited, artistic, autonomous; willful, demanding, irritable, loud-mouthed, impetuous, judgmental.

The Serpent: wise, cultivated, intuitive, amusing, sympathetic, elegant, soft-spoken, philosophical, calm, decisive; ostentatious, extravagant, presumptuous, possessive, vengeful, self-critical.

The Horse: amiable, eloquent, skillful, quick-witted, athletic, entertaining, independent, hard-working, sentimental, sensual; selfish, weak, ruthless, rebellious, pragmatic, tactless, impatient.

The Goat (or *Sheep*): elegant, creative, gentle, intelligent, tasteful, inventive, homespun, lovable, delicate, artistic, amorous, peace-loving; timid, pessimistic, capricious, intrusive, undisciplined, irresponsible.

The Monkey: intelligent, witty, inventive, affable, skillful, original, enthusiastic, lucid, youthful, clever; tricky, vain, deceptive, opportunistic, long-winded, unfaithful.

The Rooster (or *Cock*): frank, vivacious, resourceful, attractive, sincere, enthusiastic, conservative, industrious, stylish, adventurous; selfish, mistrustful, boastful, short-sighted, pompous, spendthrift, brazen.

The Dog: magnanimous, sincere, courageous, loyal, devoted, attentive, faithful, modest, altruistic, prosperous, discreet, dutiful; defensive, critical, pessimistic, cynical, stubborn, moralizing.

The Boar (or *Pig*): gallant, loyal, scrupulous, truthful, impartial, sociable, thorough, cultured, sensual, peaceable, profound, sensitive; naïve, insecure, willful, gullible, earthy, defenseless, short-tempered.

Chinese astrologers commonly consider the animal year of an individual first and subsequently look at the zodiacal position of the Sun within that year. This would theoretically yield 144 (12×12) types. It would be an interesting study to explore whether the symbolic meanings of the animal years are in fact related to the transits of Jupiter through the signs of the tropical zodiac, or whether we are dealing with an entirely different kind of recurring twelve-year cycle. This is a question that remains to be investigated by New Age astrologers and students of cyclic phenomena.

A similar situation exists with regard to the three-*guna* theory, and the lunar mansions. These age-old systems of classifying and typing personality, whether based on astrology or other esoteric doctrines, can provide valuable additions to the emerging synthesis of human psychological knowledge.

The Theory of the Seven Rays

The doctrine of the seven rays is an ancient esoteric teaching that was reformulated in the present century in the writings of theosophists such as H. P. Blavatsky and treated extensively in the works of Alice Bailey. The latter were stated to be the telepathic transmissions from a Tibetan initiate abbot named Djwhal Khul. Over a thirty-year period, Bailey wrote twenty-four volumes based directly or indirectly on the instructions of the Tibetan. The theory of the seven rays is developed throughout these writings, but especially in *Esoteric Psychology* and *Esoteric Astrology*. The doctrine is also summarized in Hodson (1973) and Bakula (1978).

The basic assumption is that all forms of life and matter are imbued with, or expressions of, certain basic types of energy, the rays, which give to every manifestation its particular quality. Traditional theosophy and Alice Bailey describe seven rays, although other teachings, including Actualism, work with more than seven basic energies. The number seven has a venerable history of significance in virtually every major sacred teaching of the world.

In regard to human typology, there is said to be a soul ray and a primary personality ray for each individual; in addition, there are secondary rays or energies that together with the primaries constitute the temperamental blend of that individual. Each of the rays has both negative and positive expressions, characteristic strengths and certain weaknesses that represent the developmental challenge of people of that type. The usual terms for the seven rays are as follows:

1. Ray of Will or Power
2. Ray of Love and Wisdom
3. Ray of Active Intelligence or Higher Mind
4. Ray of Harmony through Conflict, Beauty, and Art
5. Ray of Concrete Knowledge and Science
6. Ray of Devotion and Idealism
7. Ray of Ceremony, Order, and Ritual

The positive qualities of the *first ray* are said to be courage, will-power, leadership, independence, dignity, determination. They are typically expressed in strong statesmen, rulers, explorers, pioneers, soldiers, or executives. The personal defects of this type are arrogance, harshness, ruthlessness, egotism, aggression and rigidity. This ray is also known as the "ray of the destroyer." The basic polarity is strength vs. weakness. It is associated with the signs of Aries, Leo, and Capricorn, and with the planets Pluto and Vulcan.

The qualities of the *second ray* are patience, understanding, serenity, compassion, generosity, co-operation. People of this type may be healers, teachers, or reformers; they express a kind of impersonal, universal love. If negative, their defects are indifference, sentimentality, narcissism, self-pity, and martyr attitudes. The basic polarity is love vs. hate. The ray is also known as the "ray of synthesis." It is associated with the signs Virgo, Gemini, and Pisces, and the planet Jupiter and the Sun.

The *third ray* types exhibit sincerity, comprehension, clear and active intelligence, creative ideation, tact, and impartiality. They are often philosophers, scholars, diplomats, organizers, judges, and people with a flair for strategy and tactics. Their potential faults are coldness, aloofness, selfishness, deceit, obstinacy, and manipulation. The basic polarity is comprehension vs. mental blindness. This ray, also known as the "ray of intelligent activity," is correlated with the signs Cancer, Libra, and Capricorn, and Saturn and Earth among the planets.

The *fourth ray* has the special virtues of harmony, balance, sympathy, perceptive ability, generosity, rhythm. People of this ray may function as artists, mediators, interpreters, dramatists. Their negative expressions are restlessness, strong passions, extravagance, instability, conceit, self-indulgence, indolence. This ray is also called the "ray of struggle"—struggle between activity and inertia, and between beauty and ugliness. It is associated with the signs Scorpio, Taurus, and Sagittarius; and with Mercury and the Moon.

The *fifth ray* types are analytical, factual, precise, thorough, just, patient, and independent. They are typically scientists, mathematicians, lawyers, or teachers. Their faults tend to be narrowness of vision, prejudice, pride, criticalness, pedantry, and inquisitiveness. The ray is also known as the "ray of science and research." Its basic polarity is truth vs. falsity. It is correlated with the signs Leo, Sagittarius, and Aquarius, and the planet Venus.

The *sixth ray* positive qualities are devotion, loyalty, service, enthusiasm, reverence, one-pointedness, and love. People of this ray type become mystics, devotees, servers, helpers. Their defects may be excessive emotionalism, intolerance, superstition, dependency, blind devotion, impulsiveness. The core polarity is between unity and separation. The ray of idealism and devotion is associated with Sagittarius, Virgo, and Pisces, and the planets Neptune and Mars.

The *seventh ray* virtues are courtesy, nobility, grace, courage, attention to details, and perseverance. People dominant on this ray may become priests, ritualists, producers, synthesizers, politicians. Their weaknesses are formality, pride, bigotry, superficiality, ostentation, mechanical ritualism. The fundamental polarity is order vs. disorder. The seventh ray is associated with the signs Capricorn, Cancer, and Aries, and with the planet Uranus.

While the basic theory of rays or energies underlying personality characteristics appears valid and useful, the delineations of the different personality types in the available theosophical writings is not sufficiently clear and consistent to form the basis for a coherent understanding of human nature. There seem to be major gaps as well as overlaps in the different type portraits, although the basic theory is suggestive and interesting.

The Arica Enneagram of Types

Arica is an esoteric system of consciousness development brought to the United States in the 1970s by a Bolivian teacher named Oscar Ichazo. Many of the concepts of this school are evidently derived from the teachings of Gurdjieff, the Sufis, and other oriental philosophies. Much use is made of the enneagram, a nine-pointed figure inscribed within a circle, which was described by Gurdjieff as a major teaching symbol used by Asian esoteric schools. Also strongly emphasized in Arica is Gurdjieff's analogy of man as a machine, trapped in automatic, repetitive, mechanical patterns of thinking, feeling, and behaving.

The Arica model delineates nine types, each represented by a point of the enneagram and associated with a particular "ego fixation" or predictable pattern of reactions. This is analogous to Gurdjieff's idea of "chief feature," a kind of prime focus of the ego that is often obvious to others but not to the individual himself, who is too subjectively identified with it. In Arica, each ego fixation involves a particular trap, or habitual way of thinking that is the source of unhappiness. At the same time, each fixation is thought of as being a defensive system around a particular "divine idea" that can be used in meditation to draw the psyche out of ego into essence. These ideas are referred to as "psychocatalyzers."

Each of the nine types of fixations has a ruling passion. "He will feel all the passions at some time or another, but his predominant passion will set the emotional tone of his personality" (Lilly and Hart, p. 336). One is taught to counteract the typical passion by meditating on the corresponding virtue. The goal is to become aware of all nine points on the enneagram, not just the one on which one is fixated. As Oscar Ichazo states, "When the fixation is gone, the natural ego appears, and with the natural ego we are aware of the other eight points. Our psyche starts becoming richer. It begins to see the other eight possibilities."

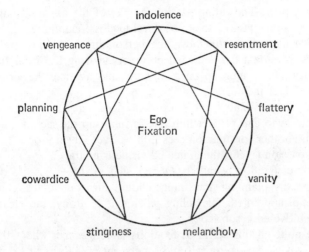

Enneagram of Fixations.

Beginning at the top of the enneagram and proceeding clockwise around the circle, the first fixation is called *indolence*. The corresponding character is described as overly nonconformist, a seeker who is always running from one outside solution to another. His ruling passion is laziness in searching within himself; his indicated virtue is action.

When the fixation point is *resentment,* the person is said to be over-perfectionist, resenting and criticizing himself and others for not being perfect. The dominant passion is anger, and the counteracting virtue is serenity.

The next fixation is called *flattery*. The person is dependent on others for constant approval, and yet is preoccupied with independence. The passion is pride, the virtue is humility.

The person fixated on *vanity* is preoccupied with position, importance, and efficiency. He is said to be over-efficient, thus defeating his purpose. His ruling passion is deceit, to cover his weaknesses, and the counteracting virtue is truthfulness.

The next fixation is called *melancholy,* where the person is constantly dissatisfied with what is, looking toward a happier future, a more authentic mate, a better reason. He is called the over-reasoner. The ruling passion is envy of the apparent happiness of others; the virtue to be developed is equanimity.

When fixated on *stinginess,* the personality withholds itself, prefers to remain the detached observer, viewing life from the sidelines. He is hung up on anonymity and avarice; the virtue he needs is detachment.

The person fixated on *cowardice* needs a strong leader, someone who can protect him. He is hung up on security, although another formulation sees him as over-adventurous. The ruling passion is fear; the indicated virtue is courage.

Another fixation is called *planning,* where the ego is always idealistically planning how things should turn out and is constantly disappointed. His ruling passion is gluttony; the virtue to be cultivated is sobriety.

The ninth of this series of fixations is *vengeance,* where the person takes revenge on self and others out of a feeling of outraged justice. He is also called the over justice-maker. His ruling passion is excess or lust, and his counteracting virtue is innocence.

The system of conceptual and psychological interrelationships portrayed in the various enneagrams is quite complex, and probably makes more sense to someone actually experiencing the meditation and training exercises taught in the Arica school. The two published descriptions of the nine types, on which the above outline is based, differ considerably in some of their formulations (Lilly and Hart, 1975; Ichazo, 1972). The interested reader is referred to these two sources for further information concerning the Arica typology and general philosophy.

Gurdjieff's Typology of Human Development

In his book *In Search of the Miraculous,* Ouspensky (1949) presented Gurdjieff's teaching concerning the evolutionary development possible for man. This is a particularly interesting formulation because it contains a basic typology of human nature, as well as the design for the progressive evolution of human nature. Three of the seven kinds of man are said to "constitute mechanical humanity on the same level on which they are born." The other four are stages of development that man goes through as he develops in an evolutionary way. Sometimes Gurdjieff would draw a diagram in which the first three were in a horizontal row, and the other four were in a vertical column.

According to this formulation, *Man number one* is the man whose center of gravity lies in the moving center. This center, located generally below the navel, actually has three centers within it: the moving, the sexual, and the instinctive. Thus man number one lives by his instincts, and his psychic life is dominated by the body and its needs for sensory gratification. Physical consciousness outweighs emotional or mental consciousness, and material considerations are more important than considerations of human sensitivity.

Man number two has his center of gravity in the emotional center. This center is generally dispersed throughout the region of the breast. He is dominated by emotional states, and pursues situations and events that are emotionally pleasing to him; material things may be sought, but more for the feeling of self-satisfaction they produce than for intrinsic interest. This kind of man is aware of his likes and dislikes and lives his life according to these personal valuations.

Man number three is centered in the intellectual center, located in the head, and governs his life according to theories, mental constructs, and ideas. He wants reasons and proofs for everything, and thinks things through from mental considerations that far outweigh emotional or material concerns.

It has been suggested that this threefold basic typology corresponds, in terms of temperament, to Sheldon's three somatotypes: number one to endomorphy, number two to mesomorphy, and number three to ectomorphy. While there is some parallelism here, there are also considerable differences. Sheldon's mesomorphs (or somatotonics) are more muscle-dominant than heart-dominant, more active than emotional; and the endomorphs (or viscerotonics) are earthy and practical, but also very feeling-oriented and emotionally sensitive.

An alternate correlation can be made with three of the Jungian functional types: man number one with the sensing type, number two with the feeling type, and number three with the thinking type. To some extent, the intuitives resemble Gurdjieff's man number four, to be discussed, who is already aware of human potentials and future development. Gurdjieff also spelled out that different systems of yoga or spiritual work were appropriate for these three basic types: karma yoga, the yoga of action and work, for man number one; bhakti yoga, the yoga of devotion, for man number two; and jnana yoga, the path of wisdom, for man number three.

Whereas these three types were said to be the groups that man was born into, *man number four* cannot be born, he can only develop. He is one in whom a permanent center of gravity has been established, based on his determination to develop, to become more conscious. He is the first non-mechanical man; he has some understanding of himself, and has a definite aim or purpose in mind. His centers are beginning to be balanced and function in harmonious interrelationship. He has a sense of cosmic purpose and personal destiny. He receives some insight and understanding from higher sources within himself.

Man number five is one in whom "essence has already been crystallized." He has a permanent "I," and therefore a sense of inner unity. He cannot change or go back as the other four types can; but, in very rare instances, he may be "crystallized on the wrong foundation," without having gone through the stage of man number four. In this case, such a prematurely crystallized being cannot develop further, unless, according to Ouspensky, he "again melt his crystallized essence, and intentionally lose his being of man number five. And this can be achieved only through terrible sufferings." Man number five has also developed, with awareness, his second or "kesdjan" body; this term literally means "vessel of soul," and probably corresponds to the astral body of Western occult doctrine. He is able to transcend the limitations of time and space, and has the ability to act from clear knowledge and total being.

Man number six and *number seven* are alike in what they have attained, the only difference being that number six has it intermittently, and number seven permanently. They have died and been reborn. They have a permanent and unchanging "I," individuality, immortality, purposeful will, and objective consciousness. People of this level of development are generally referred to as saints, avatars, or bodhisattvas.

While Gurdjieff and Ouspensky, in the published writings, present this system as a series of levels of development that a person who is consciously evolving would go through, it is also possible to see this as a description of the multilevel, multidimensional nature of man, as he actually is. There is a man number one, number two, and number three within everyone, each assuming dominance at different times. And also, men numbers four through seven exist within us as levels of being and levels of consciousness, but do not become actualized or manifest until we have learned the lessons and the laws of that phase of evolutionary development.

The Science of Idiotism

In his talks and meetings Gurdjieff also spoke of another developmental typology that he called the "science of idiotism." He apparently was referring here back to the original meaning of the Greek word *idios,* which meant something that was uniquely special and private—a meaning we still have in the word "idiosyncratic." At his famous dinner parties, Gurdjieff used to propose toasts to the different kinds of idiot, expressing to each kind a special affectionate recognition and acknowledgment. The following description is taken from J. G. Bennett's book *Gurdjieff: Making a New World* (pp. 157–59):

> In Central Asis ritual feasts are part of the Dervish way of life. The Chamodar, or Master of the Feast, is a very ancient institution, and Gurdjieff himself said that he had adopted customs that had favourably impressed him during his long sojourn in Turkestan. One of these customs was the ritual that Gurdjieff called the "Science of Idiotism." He explained that in a Sufi community, which he used to visit, a method of

teaching had been handed down from antiquity which consisted in tracing the path of man's evolution from a state of nature to the realization of his spiritual potential. I have put together the contents of many talks in the following account:

"There are twenty-one gradations of reason from that of the ordinary man to that of our Endlessness, that is, God. No one can reach the Absolute Reason of God, and only the sons of God like Jesus Christ can have the two gradations of reason that are nineteenth and twentieth. Therefore the aim of every being who aspires to perfection must be to reach the eighteenth gradation. You must understand that the people you know do not have any reason at all. They live in their dreams and have no connection with reality. Whoever has any contact with reality is called an Idiot. The word idiot has two meaning: the true meaning that was given to it by the ancient sages was *to be oneself*. A man who is himself looks and behaves like a madman to those who live in the world of illusions; so when they call a man an idiot they mean that he does not share their illusions.

"Everyone who decides to work on himself is an idiot in both meanings. The wise know that he is seeking for reality. The foolish think he has taken leave of his senses. We here are supposed to be seeking for reality, so we should all be idiots: but no one can make you an idiot. You must choose it for yourself. That is why everyone who visits us here and wishes to remain in contact with us, is allowed to choose his own idiotism. Then all the rest of us will wish from our hearts that he will truly become that idiot. For this alcohol was used by the ancient sages; not to get drunk, but to strengthen the power to wish."

Gurdjieff had a fixed ritual in proposing the toast of the idiots. The Director started with ordinary idiots, going on to the super idiot, then the arch idiot. The fourth, the hopeless idiot, was again and again chosen by Gurdjieff for an explanation of what he meant by dying an honourable death. The false hopeless idiot is satisfied with himself and does not see that he is a "candidate for perishing like a dog!" The true hopeless idiot sees his own complete nothingness and does not realize that this death of self is the guarantee of his resurrection. From this stage he becomes a compassionate idiot, whose reason has opened to enter into the sufferings of others. The sixth is the squirming idiot who is not yet ready for help. There are then three "geometric" idiots—square, round, and zigzag —who represent stages in the establishment of true reason, at first only momentarily, then comes the discovery of one's own identity and third the desperate struggle to break free. Gurdjieff said of him that he "has five Fridays in the week"—an example of a meaningless saying that communicates better than much good sense.

At the Saturday evening meals, the toasts seldom went beyond the zigzag idiot, unless he wished to associate someone present with the characteristics of one of the next series. These are the enlightened, the doubting and swaggering idiots. Beyond these again are idiots whose characteristics are deep in their essential nature. At each stage there is a death and resurrection before a new gradation of reason is attained.

Gurdjieff gave a most significant twist to the Science of Idiotism when he explained that no one could go beyond the enlightened idiot unless he had first "consciencely descended" to the first gradation of the ordinary idiot. His explanations made it clear that he was referring to the same secret as Jesus when he said: "Except ye become as little children, ye shall in no wise enter the kingdom of heaven." Having heard scores of times Gurdjieff's explanations of the idiot toasts, I can only marvel at the insights into human nature that he was able to express in such simple terms. His talks about the tragic situation of the enlightened idiot whom "even God could not help" invariably sent a shudder of horror down my spine. Nothing has done so much to convince me that we must totally shed any pretension to be "special people" if we hope to attain true freedom.

This account has several very interesting features. One of these is the reference to the different geometric types of idiots. We shall see again, in the next chapter, indications that it is possible to distinguish people on the basis of a geometry of consciousness—that there is a shape to an individual's mentality.

11

The Typology of Numbers

The meaning and symbolism of numbers have occupied the intellect and the imagination of humankind from the earliest times, and in virtually every culture. In China, numerical symbol systems evolved as ordering schema of cosmic and psychological processes, culminating in the magnificent and baffling *I Ching,* a computational handbook of universal cycles of change. Indian and Arab mathematicians worked out the bases of traditional number theory. Egyptian and Mayan astronomers and architects incorporated geophysical and numerical constants and proportions into their religious pyramid structures. Polynesian sailors navigated the globe without map or compass, using elaborate, ritualized counting procedures linked to changing celestial co-ordinates.

In Western civilization, it is generally Pythagoras and his school (in approximately 500 B.C.) who are credited with discovering and teaching the importance of numbers as fundamental ordering principles of nature. Pythagoras' studies reached into astronomy, with his doctrine of the harmony of the spheres, and into musical theory, with his discoveries of the numerical proportions underlying musical harmony and discord. The Pythagoreans are also said to be the originators of the study of the qualitative, or psychological, aspects of numbers, which lies at the base of modern numerology. Numerology and astrology may be considered the symbolic or psychological relatives of mathematics and astronomy, their more respectable, scientific sisters. In his monumental work *Synergetics,* mathematician-inventor Buckminster Fuller has a chapter on numerology, in which he writes:

> My intuition does not find it illogical
> That humanity has developed and retained
> The demisciences of astrology and numerology—
> *Demi* because they are
> Only partially fortified by experimental proofs—
> Which nonetheless challenge us tantalizingly
> To further explorations
> Within which it may be discovered
> That generalized scientific laws
> Are, indeed, eternally operative.
>
> [Fuller, pp. 727–28]

While modern mathematicians for the most part have focused their researches into number theory on the purely logical and quantitative aspects of number, especially in relationship to the physical sciences, some philosophers have been intrigued by a peculiar, irreducible quality of number that seems to relate it somehow to the structure of human consciousness. The striking similarities in the number symbolism of different cultures has attracted attention; for example, the interesting fact that certain numbers are always regarded as spiritual or sacred, others as material, some as masculine, some feminine, and so on. Numbers seem almost to have a certain personality of their own— for example, the forceful one, the pliable two, the solid four.

Anthropologist Alan Dundes (1968) has pointed out in a very persuasive essay that Western, especially American, culture has three as the predominant numerical pattern. This is in marked contrast to American Indian culture, which is strongly oriented around four; and South American as well as Chinese culture, in which five is the preferred ritual number. Dundes illustrates the symbolic and conceptual threefoldness of American culture with numerous examples from folklore, popular music, sports practices, games, names (of individuals and institutions), domestic practices, education, military rituals, religious conventions, and even scholarly and scientific theorizing. As an example, we may cite his amusing list of threefold folk speech patterns:

> beg, borrow, or steal; bell, book, and candle; blood, sweat, and tears; cool, calm, and collected; fat, dumb, and happy; hither, thither, and yon; hook, line, and sinker; hop, skip, and jump; lock, stock, and barrel; me, myself, and I; men, women, and children; ready, willing, and able; signed, sealed, and delivered; tall, dark, and handsome; Tom, Dick, and Harry; and wine, women, and song.   [Dundes, p. 407]

The Jungian Approach to Numerology

Carl Jung devoted much theorizing and writing to the place of number in the psyche, and the role of numerical symbols in psychological process of transformation. His student Marie-Louise von Franz has written a deep and subtle volume, entitled *Number and Time* (1974), carrying forward Jung's speculations and correlating them with the theories of modern physics and mathematics. Jung regarded numbers as *archetypes*—that is, as structural constants of consciousness. "It may well be the most primitive element of order in the human mind . . . thus we define number psychologically as an archetype of order which has become conscious" (C. Jung, "On Synchronicity," No. 870). Since number is also integrally involved in the basic structure of the material world, in the realms of crystals, plants, molecules, atoms, and subatomic particles, it is thought of as a bridging element between the material world and the psyche. "Numbers appear to represent both an attribute of matter and the unconscious foundation of our mental processes" (Von Franz, p. 52).

Von Franz also makes the interesting point that numbers are not merely static, abstract entities, but also enter in an energetic manner into the processes of the psyche. "Numbers, as archetypal structural constants of the collective unconscious, possess a dynamic, active aspect. . . . It is not what we can *do* with numbers but what *they* do to our consciousness that is essential" (op. cit., p. 33).

This active quality of numerical symbols makes it possible to use them as tools or aids in meditation and personal growth, much as astrological or Tarot symbols can be used; to let them evoke and resonate forces and elements in our psyche of which we are not aware. If we are to credit the reporting of the trance medium Jane Roberts, the channel for the Seth personality, Jung pursued his interest in numerology even in the afterlife. In her book *Psychic Politics* (1976), she quotes him as telling her, from the other side, that "great, as-yet-undiscovered correlations exit between the emotions and the numerology of the soul. . . . numbers, held unconsciously, as I now believe, have cellular connections that determine bodily health. . . . Magical type incantations of numbers could be used as an unconscious healing process" (pp. 73–74).

An illustration of the active, evocative quality of number symbols, which Jung discovered in alchemy and on which he wrote extensively, is the transition from three to four, from a trinity to a quaternity. In the process of individuation, the powerful but nonstable threefold organization gives way to the highly ordered *mandala,* a fourfold structure. For example, the three primary functions of personality are enriched and completed by the addition and inclusion of the fourth, initially unconscious, inferior function.

Again, in his posthumous communications, Jung carried this farther: "The number four signifies a secure framework in which the male and female principles are accepted. The number five can represent the birth of a new instability in the personality when it appears in dreams, for it represents an overswelling of the male or female element . . ." (Roberts, p. 74).

As a psychological symbol system, numerology is synchronistic, nonlinear, and nonlogical. Thus the process of reduction, or "theosophical addition," utilized in numerology to reduce all numbers to one digit of the primary-number series 1 to 9, has no mathematical or logical meaning; 234, 18, and 27 all have the same value in numerology, because they all reduce to 9, by simple addition of their component integers. The fact that mathematics and science can operate with number systems other than the familiar decimal system, such as the binary, which uses only two integers, and the duodecimal, which uses twelve, is irrelevant to numerology. Its elaborate network of symbolic associations ranges from the folklore of primitive tribes and modern cultures, to the arcane speculations of Pythagoreans, Alchemists, and Gnostics.

There is considerable congruence between numerology and astrology, especially in the interpretation of aspects, the angular relationships between planetary positions. In recent years, the research of John Addey on the use of harmonic analysis in astrology has given especial emphasis to this correlation. According to Addey, all aspects can be described as frequency harmonics of the fundamental circle. Thus oppositions represent the second harmonic, trines the third, squares the fourth, and so on. The meaning of the aspect is then derived from the symbolic meaning of the number, whose frequency harmonic it represents. In this way, astrological interpretations are essentially reduced to, or derived from, numerological ones. The position of a planet in a sign, for instance, is simply an expression of the twelfth harmonic. Readers are referred to Addey's work *Harmonics in Astrology* (1976) for further explanations and empirical findings supporting this particular interpretation.

The Polarities of the Numbers

The numerological systems of East and West agree in assigning a positive, masculine, dynamic polarity to the odd numbers, and a negative, feminine, magnetic polarity to the even numbers. It is as if the odd numbers have an outward-directed momentum, or inherent instability, compared to the resting, balanced, contained character of the even numbers. In the *I Ching,* one is *yang,* two is *yin,* three is creative, heaven, and four is receptive, earth.

We can regard straight lines as expressive of dynamic, *yang* force, as in the radiation of pure energy or light, and curved or circular lines as expressive of magnetic, *yin* energy, as in the shape of a magnetic field around a current flowing in a wire, or in the elliptical orbits of electrons around an atomic nucleus. This distinction is reflected, to a degree, even in the actual shape of the numerals of our primary-number series. The 1 is a straight, vertical line. The 2 is basically curvilinear. The 3 is usually mixed: straight above, curved below.[1] The 4 is a cross, and does not fit the pattern. The 5 is similar to the 3. The 6, a very feminine number, is very curved. The 7, a very dynamic number, is purely linear and angular. The 8 is two circles, a double magnetic. The 9 does not fit that pattern. (This distinction between straight-line and curved characters is used in graphology as an indication of masculine and of feminine traits.)

In astrology there is the twofold distinction between positive and negative signs, alternating around the zodiac. There is also the partially overlapping threefold distinction among cardinal, fixed, and mutable signs. A similar threefold pattern is also apparent in the number series: we can divide it into three groups of three, in which the third of each group has a mixed or balanced polarity.

1+dynamic	4—magnetic	7+dynamic
2—magnetic	5+dynamic	8—magnetic
3±mixed	6∓balanced	9±complete

Both the straightforward dual polarity of the numbers, and this threefold rhythm enter into the symbolic meaning of the numbers.

The Geometry of Consciousness

From the time of Pythagoras, numerologists have looked for the correlations between numbers and geometric shapes as further clues to their symbolic meanings. The *one* is usually shown as a point or a circle; the *two* as a line connecting two points, or two parallel lines; and the *three,* of course, as a triangle; *four* is a square, *five* a pentagram, and *six* the Star of David; *seven* is a seven-pointed star, *eight* a double square, and *nine* the sacred enneagram.

[1] Typographic and calligraphic styles may alter this form.

Some of these patterns are revealed when we examine astrological aspects in the light of number symbolism. A conjunction
(one) is a point; opposition (two) is a line. The other aspects
are triangles that divide the circle in various ways; into threes
(trine), fours (square), fives (quintile), sixes (sextile), and so
on.

The possibility arises of a geometric typology of states of
mind. We already recognize this when we speak of someone
having a linear mentality, or a "straight" attitude, or one-
pointed concentration. We say of someone that he is "square,"
if his thinking stays within the boundaries of traditional, conservative categories.

There are those whose mind moves like an arrow, along a
single track to a pointed goal; and those whose mentality seems
like a point with lines radiating outward. Some individuals'
thinking runs always in the threefold structure of dialectics—
thesis, antithesis, and synthesis; others are grounded in the
practical solidity of the square or the cross (for example, the
cross used in statistical co-ordinate systems). More complex
geometric structures are also found: pyramids, tetrahedra, net-
works or matrices, cubes, ellipses, and circles. One can surmise
that omnidirectional spherical consciousness would be an indication of psychic integration and wholeness.

Symbolism of the Basic Number Series

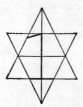

One is the number of unity, the prime source, the monad from
which all forms and energies emerge, the origin, the indivisible
whole, the fusion of opposites, the core, the center, the all-en-

compassing circle or sphere, the first cause, individuality. Psychologically it represents activity, initiative, assurance, willpower, originality, independence, leadership, attainment. A person with a strong *one* vibration is dynamic, progressive, courageous, assertive, capable, and confident. Since any quality can at times be found in an exaggerated and extreme form, we find the distorted *one* qualities in persons who are egotistical, overambitious, domineering, antagonistic, aggressive, impulsive, and headstrong. Biologically, *one* relates to the head and spine, the vertical axis of the body. In the Kabbala, *one* is the "Crown."

Astrologically, *one* is associated with the aspect of conjunction, in which two planets in close proximity fuse and emphasize their power. It's generally agreed that in terms of planets, *one* relates to the Sun, with its life-force radiance and power. In the Tarot, the number *one* is the Magician, the adept at multidimensional communication and expression.

Two is the number of polarization, symmetry, balance, reflection, awareness, alternation, rhythm. The basic components of matter are positively and negatively charged particles. In practically all mythologies, the threshold between two worlds, or realms of consciousness, is guarded by twin demons, beasts, or divine figures. Psychologically, the *two* manifests itself as receptivity, adaptiveness, association, co-operation, relationship, recognition (literally, "to know *again*"), awareness. A *two* personality is pliable, sensitive to others, emotional, friendly, tactful, fluid, gentle, and strongly oriented toward partnership and marriage. In negative expressions the person may appear vacillating, indifferent, separative, shy, anxious, spineless, overdependent, or deceptive. Biologically, *two* represents the two sides of the body and the bipolar symmetry of the mind-body continuum: male/female, left/right brains, sympathetic/parasympathetic systems.

Astrologically, the *two* symbolizes the aspect of opposition, 180 degrees, in which two planetary forces, at opposite ends of a line through the observer on Earth, mirror and reflect each other, bringing polarized awareness and recognition (with an "on-off" rhythm). Again, it's generally agreed that the *two* is related to the Moon, with its rhythmic alternations and fluctuating magnetic pull. In Tarot symbolism, the number *two* is the High Priestess, who teaches knowledge of Self in balanced relationship with another.

Three is the number in which the masculine one and the feminine two unite to produce an offspring, a third force. It is the number of creation, procreation, self-expression, conception (in any realm), birth, and growth. It is a number that betokens imagination, intelligence, ingenuity, inspiration, creativity, inventiveness, artistry. *Three* people tend to be sociable, clever, charming, highly verbal, playful, mobile, effective, and energetic. When distorted and extreme, they come across as scattered, verbose, superficial, nervous, critical, and boastful. Biologically, *three* is associated with the voice, throat, and lungs (cf. the "creative word" and "inspiration").

Astrologically, *three* represents the trine aspect, where two planets, 120 degrees apart, are relating for creative expression. The *three* is sometimes related to Jupiter, and sometimes to Venus. It clearly has many of the qualities of Mercury—versatility, intelligence, and wit. In the Tarot, the *three* is the Empress, the fruitful earthmother, generous and pleasing.

Four is the number that forms a cross and serves as a foundation for all building, whether physical or psychic. In every culture, the time-space world is measured by four coordinates: the four cardinal directions, the four corners of the Earth, the four winds of the American Indians, or the four elements of matter. In higher worlds of consciousness, there are four faces of God. Thus the *four* signifies construction, foundation, order, method, coordination, discipline, method, and work. *Four* personalities are practical, dependable, methodical, patient, grounded, exacting, conscientious, conservative, enduring. If expressing their negative traits, distortions of the above, they appear narrow, rigid, plodding, repressive, dull, resentful, and intolerant. Biologically, it is the *four limbs* that enable us to relate to the world in working and doing.

Astrologically, *four* is the square, a 90-degree angle between planets, that can symbolize either *con*struction or *ob*struction, depending on how it's handled. Some numerologists relate *four* to Uranus, some to Saturn; however, I cast my vote with those who relate it to the Earth, because of the earthy, foursquare quality of this number. In the Tarot, *four* is connected to the Emperor, builder of foundations, master of the material world.

Five is traditionally and always the number of man: a five-pointed star superimposed on a man with four limbs outstretched and the head. *Five* is also the fifth essence (quintessentia) of the alchemists, the sum and synthesis of the four elements, or psychic functions. *Five* is a very dynamic number, symbolizing change, freedom, variety, energy, activity, process, vitality, expansion, desire, and curiosity. *Five* people appear versatile, resourceful, free-spirited, adventurous, progressive, perceptive, alert, exciting, electric, amiable, flexible, and sensual. In a negative development, they come across as restless, impatient, irresponsible, careless, self-indulgent, inconsistent, and hot-tempered. Biologically, we have the *five senses* that relate us in a vital and ever-changing way to the energies of our environment.

Astrologically, the *five* can be associated with the quintile aspect (72 degrees), thought to be indicative of talents and will. In the planetary series, it's mostly correlated with either Mars or Mercury, although the free energy and excitement seem to me more congruent with the Mars consciousness. In the Tarot, *five* represents the Hierophant—the teacher or speaker who synthesizes and inspires.

Six is mathematically said to be a "perfect" number, and is traditionally associated with the perfection of beauty, symmetry, and balance. It is symbolized by the six-pointed star, composed of two perfectly matching, interlacing triangles, representing the perfect blend of spirit and matter. In the Kabbalistic Tree of Life, the *six* is called "Beauty." Psychologically, *six* is harmony, beauty, the happy home, health, love sex, service, adjustment, and responsibility. The *six* personality appears sympathetic, productive, balanced, poised, caring, fair, and domestic. In an exaggerated sense, he or she may appear self-righteous, complacent, conventional, sentimental, jealous, depressive, anxious, or perfectionist. Biologically, the *six* is associated with the heart, circulation, and the sexual system.

Astrologically, the *six* fits naturally with the sextile, or 60-degree aspect, indicative of productiveness and harmony. It's usually assigned to Venus, as one would expect, though sometimes to Jupiter. In the Tarot, *six* is the Lovers card, symbolic of perfect balance between male and female, higher and lower worlds, inner and outer consciousness.

Seven has, since time immemorial and in every tradition, been regarded as a sacred or mystical number. The seven "days" (actually, phases) of creation, the seven spirits before the Throne, the Seven Rays, the seven colors of the rainbow, the Seven Sages, the Seven Wonders of the World, the seven musical notes of the scale . . . there is an endless list of sevens in every conceivable physical and metaphysical context. Gurdjieff formulated an ancient Asian esoteric teaching according to which every evolutionary process of transformation or development, microcosmic or macrocosmic, goes through seven distinct stages, much like the notes of the octave. Thus *seven* is the number of spiritual transformation, of wisdom, science, the occult, research, observation, analysis, meditation, of visions and dreams. People with a strong *seven* vibration are introspective, discriminative, silent, dignified, philosophical, earnest, seeking, and refined. They may also be aloof, cold, melancholy, suspicious, skeptical, and isolated. Biologically, we have the *seven* major endocrine glands.

Astrologically, *seven* could be correlated with the septile aspect, very rarely used; or with the quincunx, a 150-degree aspect that suggests some stress, but also clarification. Authors differ widely on which planet goes with *seven:* Neptune, Mercury, and Uranus have all been proposed. The occult insightfulness and scientific interests seem to fit best with Uranus. In the Tarot, *seven* is the number of the Chariot card, symbolic of the interrelationship of body, mind, and soul.

Eight is twice four, which is foundation, thus: double foundation, both in consciousness and in reality. The two circles, like the Tibetan double *vajra,* symbolize inner and outer power and method. Psychologically, the *eight* symbolizes organization, success, achievement, authority, judgment, management, involvement with money. The *eight* personality is efficient, generous, self-reliant, responsible, ambitious, a powerful organizer. Expressed in a negative fashion, this person may come across as hard, materialistic, power-hungry, demanding, deceitful, intolerant, or even cruel. In the body, the *eight* is correlated with the skeletal system, providing structural integrity, and the muscular system, providing strength and endurance.

Astrologically, the *eight* can be associated with the complex aspect pattern known as a T-square, in which two planets are in opposition, and third is square to both of them: It's an aspect of strength and achievement. In terms of the planets, we find the *eight* related to Saturn, the great organizer and taskmaster. In the Tarot, *eight* is the Strength card, which symbolizes the unifying of inner experience with outer expression.

Nine is traditionally the number of completion, since it completes the first basic cycle of numbers. It is a number of destiny and its fulfillment; of the global perspective and humanitarian aspiration; of universal brotherhood and benevolent compassion. The *nine* individual is generally spiritually oriented, often a teacher—idealistic, inclusive, intuitive, humane, forgiving, dedicated, and co-operative. Expressed negatively, he or she may be impractical, aimless, condescending, vague, fickle, bigoted, or self-idealizing. Biologically, the *nine* is associated with the structures and functions of assimilation and elimination.

Astrologically, the *nine,* since it's three times three, can be associated with the Grand Trine, in which three planets all make trines with each other, forming a pattern indicative of internalized self-sufficiency. Numerologists relate the *nine* either to Mars, Neptune, or Jupiter, the latter being most congruent with the expansive idealism of that number. In the Tarot, the *nine* represents the Hermit, who is devoted to the perfecting and completion of his mission on Earth.

While this completes the basic number cycle, in numerology the numbers 11 and 22 are generally not "reduced" to 2 and 4, but left as special higher-octave symbols, usually written 11/2 and 22/4; sometimes the 33/6 is also used. One must decide on an individual basis whether the basic number or the higher-octave overtone is being expressed. It should be mentioned also that the numerology of the Tarot, being based on a series of 22 symbols (the Major Arcana), rather than 9 or 11, does not necessarily coincide exactly with the basic number symbolism laid out here, except in some instances.

The *eleven* symbolizes the mystic, psychic, or visionary. Intuitive, prophetic, and inspiring, the *eleven* person is a dreamer and seeker of revelations. Negatively, *eleven* can express itself as dishonesty, deception, illusion, glamor, shiftlessness, and fanaticism. The planet Neptune has many of the qualities associated with this number. In terms of aspects, the Stellium, in which several planets are clustered in multiple conjunction, is a rare configuration appropriate to this situation.

The *twenty-two* is said to be the number of the "master builder," whether of physical structures, groups, corporations, or churches. Here is someone with tremendous leadership potential, a teacher, coordinator, promoter, organizer. In a negative expression, they may be corrupt, blind, grudging, resentful, and secretive. Astrologically, this has much in common with the qualities of Pluto. The Grand Cross aspect configuration (double opposition and four squares) has many of the high-potential, high-tension characteristics of this symbolism.

TABLE 19
Numerology Symbolism

NUMBER	ASPECT	PLANET	TAROT	BODY
1	Conjunction	Sun	Magician	Head and spine
2	Opposition	Moon	High Priestess	Two sides of body
3	Trine	Mercury	Empress	Throat and lungs
4	Square	Earth	Emperor	Arms and legs
5	Quintile	Mars	Hierophant	Senses and nerves
6	Sextile	Venus	Lovers	Heart and sex
7	Quincunx	Uranus	Chariot	Glands
8	T-square	Saturn	Strength	Skeletal and muscular systems
9	Grand Trine	Jupiter	Hermit	Assimilation and elimination
11	Stellium	Neptune	————	————
22	Grand Cross	Pluto	————	————

Life-cycle Numbers

The basic technical principle to remember in numerology is that of reduction: Every number is reduced to a single digit, by simply adding up the component digits. Thus 1977 is $1+9+7+7=24=2+4=6$. Thus, *all* numbers become one of the basic nine numbers. The only exceptions are 11 and 22, which are considered special, higher-octave numbers, and are retained together with their reduction to 2 and 4. They are usually written 11/2 and 22/4 in numerology charts. Some numerologists also use 33/6 as a third power factor.

There are literally dozens of numbers in our reality worlds which can be and are used by numerologists to derive significant number symbols, including age, birth date, street address, telephone number, Zip Code, and others. For the purposes of personality typology the two most important numbers are those derived from the date of birth, often called *life-cycle, life-path,* or *destiny* numbers; and those derived from the person's name, called *expression, personality,* or *identity* numbers.

1. The *Life-path number* is simply the reduced numerical digit of the date of birth. Thus if a man was born on September 12, 1949, his life-path number is $9+12+1949=9+1+2+1+9+4+9=35=8$. This indicates that his life path or destiny is characterized by the "vibration" or symbolism of the number *eight.* Much of the activity and concerns of this person's life would revolve around achievement, authority, management, organization, and possibly finances. His life would be marked by lesson learning in those areas: The choices and decisions he makes would mold and shape his personality systems. His evolutionary purpose is to manifest the highest spiritual qualities of the *eight* archetype.

The basic assumption here, as in astrology, is that the date of entry into incarnation is no accident, but is chosen at the level of Individuality to accord with, and synchronize with, specific planetary and numerical vibrations or symbolic patterns. The numbers and planets are not related by way of causality to personality and life development, but by synchronicity in consciousness.

2. *Life cycles.* The basic life-path number can be broken down into three component numbers, which yield numerical symbols for three major life cycles. Cycle I, also known as the *formative cycle,* governs the first third of a person's life. It is indicated by the number of the birth month. In the above example, with September, it is *nine.* This person's childhood and youth would be marked by searching idealism and a broad range of experience.

Cycle II, also known as the *productive cycle,* governs the middle third of life. It is indicated by the number of the birth day; in the example, this was $12=1+2=3$. His productive cycle, which is also thought to indicate profession, is governed by *three.* This person could function as a communicator, or verbalizer in education, the media, the arts, the professions, or business.

Cycle III, also called the *harvest cycle,* governs the last phase of life. It is indicated by the number of the birth year; in the given example, this was 1949, which reduces down to 23=5. His harvest cycle is marked by the qualities of five: change, variety, freedom, growth.

The sum of the three subcycle numbers again adds up and reduces to the life-path number. In the example given, $9+3+5=17=8$. If we wish to be more precise than simply estimating a division of the life path into three broad phases, there are several different approaches to calculating the beginning and ending dates of these cycles. Some say the first two cycles are each exactly twenty-seven years long, the third one lasting till death. Others relate the cycles to the astrological cycle of the transits of Saturn. These can occur anywhere from age twenty-seven to thirty-three for the first transit (Cycle I to Cycle II), and fifty-four to fifty-nine for the second transit (Cycle II to Cycle III). Yet another group of numerologists asserts that the first cycle ends and the second cycle begins in the *one* year (explained below) closest to the twenty-eighth birthday; and the second cycle ends in the *one* year closest to the fifty-seventh birthday.

This writer's personal preference leans toward using the Saturn cycle, but also to not being too concerned with the exact date of transition, which can in any case last quite a while.

3. *The Nine-year cycle.* Astrology has the twenty-seven-year cycles of Saturn and the progressed Moon, the twelve-year cycle of Jupiter, and many others. Numerology has an all-important nine-year cycle. Starting with the birth date, we can compute the number of each birthday, year by year. This will go through nine steps to completion, and start again with a 1. In the above example, the person born in an *eight* phase would go to a *nine* on his first birthday, and begin a new cycle (with a *one*) on his second birthday.

The number governing any year, often called the "Personal Year," can be easily computed from birthday to birthday. For example, the person of the above example, on his birthday in

1975, entered a *seven* year (9+12+1975=34=7), which ran till his birthday in 1976, when he entered an *eight* year. In 1978 he will begin a new personal year cycle with *one*. (For the Tarot, these numbers are computed somewhat differently, since here the number base is 22, for the twenty-two Major Arcana. Thus the birth date and birthday numbers are not reduced to the nine primary digits.)

Personality (Name) Numbers

The use of these numbers, computed on the basis of an individual's name, implies that the name given to the child at birth is not simply a personal whim of the parents, but reflects in some way the nature of the personal qualities to be brought to Earth by the incarnating Spirit. Many cultures have practices involving personal names that are suggestive of this kind of attitude, such as seeking one's name in a vision quest, or a special religious naming ceremony (for example, in Catholic confirmation and Judaic bar mitzvah rites). Some cultures, including the modern Greek, attach more importance to a person's name day (the day of the saint of that name) than to the actual birthday.

Each sound of the language, and especially names, has a particular quality of vibration. These vibratory qualities resonate with the person all his or her life. Our name is probably the most emotionally charged sound that we know. One may suppose that the reason nicknames are used, or people change their names altogether, is to signal a personality role or expression that is more congruent with their nature. Some American Indian cultures believed that disease can be caused if a person's name does not fit his nature.

While there exists a separate system of symbolic correlates with each letter-sound of the alphabet, in numerology the symbolism of the name is based on the numerical value of the component letters. It is important to use the full name *as given at birth;* the numerical equivalent of later modifications, or the names actually used, can then also be calculated separately.

(The importance of one's original name is analogous to the importance of the exact date and time of birth in astrology: Both systems are synchronistic with the birth moment.)

a b c d e f g h i / j k l m n o p q r / s t u v w x y z
1 2 3 4 5 6 7 8 9 / 1 2 3 4 5 6 7 8 9 / 1 2 3 4 5 6 7 8

Thus, for example, the name John Smith would be computed as follows:

$$\begin{array}{cc} \text{J o h n} & \text{S m i t h} \\ 1+6+8+5 & 1+4+9+2+8 \end{array}$$

which comes out to $20+24=2+6=8$. It is suggested that the reader compute the numbers of his or her name, and begin to consider and meditate on the symbolism of these numbers.

Numerologists generally compute the number derived from the vowels in the name, and the number derived from the consonants, separately. In the above example, the vowels o and i are $6+9=15=6$. The consonants are $1+8+5+1+4+2+8=29=11/2$. The number derived from the vowels and that of the consonants should, of course, add to the total; in the example given, 6 (vowels)$+2$ (consonants)$=8$ (total). The number derived from the vowels is variously said to be symbolic of the "soul urge," "inner self," or "heart self," and the consonant number is called "latent self," or "quiescent self." The rationale for this appears to be that the consonants are relatively quiet, or nonvocal, hence "quiescent," or "latent."

It is worth considering the distinction between the vowels and consonants more carefully. In acoustic theory it is generally stated that the vowels provide the energy for verbal language, whereas the consonants provide the intelligibility or information ("in-*form*ation"). Vowels are the primary sound outflow, with the consonants providing a kind of package or vehicle for the sound. Vowels without consonants are formless and very emotional, as in cries, moans, laughter, or shouts. On the other hand, consonants without vowels are, if not totally soundless, at least flat, dry, and lacking in the power to evoke, to call. Consonants provide the texture, the differentiated forms and edges of words and names.

Therefore, in terms of psychological symbolism, while it makes sense to regard the vowels as corresponding to inner motive, emotional force or energy, I do not see the consonants as indicating latent self, or secret dreams, or heart, but rather the form qualities of personality, the structural patterns and habits of thought, feeling, perception, and behavior. In line with this interpretation is the correlation some numerologists make of the consonant number with outer physical appearance.

To put this another way, the vowels represent the inner, functional energy, and the consonants the outer, structural patterns; and the two together constitute the *personality expression,* the fusion of form and function. An interesting sidelight on this polarity comes from the observation that in every Indo-European language the word for "1" starts with a vowel, and the word for "2" starts with a consonant. People presented blindly with the pairs of words can almost always tell which of the pair means "1" and which means "2."

SANSKRIT	GREEK	LATIN	FRENCH	SPANISH	GERMAN	RUSSIAN
eka	*en*	*unus*	*un*	*uno*	*eins*	*odyn*
dva	*duo*	*duo*	*deux*	*dos*	*zwei*	*dva*

Research in the area of speech pathology and speech therapy, which I learned of after arriving at the above formulations, sheds further light on these distinctions. Clyde Rousey (1974) has pointed out that in the first six months of an infant's life, the predominant sounds are vowels, and during this stage, drives and emotional states are the presumed dominant elements in the child's consciousness. In the next six months, all the consonants appear, and in the same period we have greatly intensified development of ego functions such as perception, discrimination, articulation, and structured movement.

In his work as speech therapist Rousey found that adults who have difficulties with vowels, which is relatively rare, have problems with drives and primary instincts; whereas difficulties with consonants reflect problems with ego development and impulse control. It is even hypothesized that the different consonants can be related to different stages of psychosexual development: some to the oral stage, some to the anal, and some to the phallic period.

Thus, to summarize, psychologically the vowels are correlated with emotional drives and needs, and the consonants with learned, adaptive ego-structures, defenses, and habit patterns. This is congruent with the inner-outer distinction presented above, where vowels are *yang,* energetic, like "ones," and consonants *yin,* structural, like "twos."

In working with number symbolism as meditative tools, one would use all three of the numbers (vowel, consonant, and total) derived from the name, and study how they interrelate and what this implies for the inner and outer balance and integration of the personality.

Certain other numbers are also computed by numerologists and added in to the number chart. One of these is called the "key," and is the number value of the first name, the one the person hears most often and is probably most closely identified with. (It is perhaps analogous to the ascendant in astrology.) The numerical value of the first letter of the first name is also considered important, and is referred to as the "foundation" or the "cornerstone." If one adds the value of the key (first name) to the value of the birthday (from the life-cycle numbers), one obtains a number referred to as "method of approach," or "angle of eccentricity"—said to be indicative of how the personality solves problems.

Many numerologists construct what is called an inclusion table, in which one counts the frequency with which the different letters, and their numbers, appear in the name. The most frequent letter-numbers are said to indicate ruling tendencies; and missing letter-numbers are supposed to indicate "karmic lessons." This technique is questionable on the basis of the fact that the natural frequencies of the letters in the English language are not equal. The number 5, for example, because it is correlated to the letter "e," would appear as ruling tendency far too frequently.

Simply the number (count) of letters in the name—for example, five for "Smith"—is another value often calculated; or the initials of the names added together; or the sum of the life-path number and personality number, considered a basic life or power number. Numerologists construct complex charts in which one can then estimate the dominance of certain values, and the lack or scarcity of others.

For people who change their names, it is particularly valuable to calculate the old and the new names and examine the shift in numeric-symbolic value that occurred at that time. Women who marry and adopt their husband's name will often find significant changes in consciousness, indicated by number changes, brought about by the marriage, as one would expect. For example, a woman with no sevens in her basic numbers married a man whose last name reduced to seven, in her life experience, the man brought in and stimulated in her the functions of spiritual growth, meditation, scientific observation, analysis, and discrimination.

Since most people have three or more names, the question arises as to the meaning of the different names. Some relate these to body, mind, and soul, the traditional psycho-theological threesome. It seems most valid to relate the last or family name to the body: This is the name that we share with other members of the family and that's tied to heredity and therefore constitution and physical consciousness. The first name is the one by which we are known by most people, and *called:* It relates to the mind and the senses. The middle name is more hidden. Only close family and friends generally know it. Thus it represents the emotional aspect or level of our nature.

If there are four names instead of three, we have the first name as the mental, the second as the emotional, the third as the perceptual, and the fourth as the physical name. Nicknames should be computed separately and treated as extra identity roles, or "handles."

The Inner or Soul Name

As indicated above, many cultures attach great magical or spiritual significance to the name. It is believed that there is a special virtue or power inherent in a person's true, inner name, so that someone who knew that name would have power over that person. This belief is at the root of numerous name taboos in many cultures: Some believe that it is dangerous to speak the name of the dead (we call them "the deceased"); others prohibit the naming of certain deities, or spirits, or demons; in China it was forbidden to speak the name of the Emperor; and in some cultures certain specially feared or revered animals are never named directly.

In ancient Egypt and other civilizations one's soul had a secret name that became known to the initiate only after certain visions or experiences. American Indian youths went on vision quests to find their secret name, their special mission and their animal or spirit ally. In recent times, many people have also chosen to adopt a new name that reflects and expresses more of the spiritual qualities that they are hoping to develop and manifest.

The other side of the secrecy surrounding one's actual, inner name is the practice of adopting multiple names. Western societies take the father's family name as the common social identity label; and many cultures relate the name to the ancestral lineage in some way. In some Indian tribes, for example the Kwakiutl, people had a summer name and a winter name. The use of pseudonyms by authors or aliases by criminals are other expressions of this camouflaging of identity by multiplication of names.

While some numerologists do calculate numbers that they consider symbolic of the soul, my understanding is that this is misguided, and that the vibrations of soul and Spirit are hidden in the inner worlds of consciousness. They may have an expression or out-picturing in the personality domains of the mind, the feelings, the perceptions, and the body, but are themselves veiled from ordinary awareness.

There is a numerology of the soul, just as there is an astrology of the soul, but it is different from the personality and reality numbers and horoscopes. It is something as yet to be (re)discovered. People do have inner names: actual, true, inner names, numbers, and symbols of the soul and Spirit. But these are things to be discovered by the individual in his or her own inner searchings, through meditation, dreams, or visions. This inner name can then be used by the individual as a kind of *mantra:* an inner sound with the power to evoke the qualities of soul and Spirit, and cause the personality systems to resonate to these higher dimensions of our Being. Among the ancient Egyptians, the following beautiful prayer-wish was addressed to the recently deceased individual: "May your name flower again."

12

Types of
Consciousness—the
Actualism Approach

Actualism is a process of enlightenment training in which one
learns to work with internal sources of light-life energy. The
teachings were originated and founded by Russell Paul
Schofield, based on over thirty years of group and individual
research. The core of the process is a graduated series of powerful inner tools and techniques that bring about the enlightening of different levels of consciousness in a step-by-step manner. These techniques provide the means for direct experiential
validation of the evolutionary teachings.

Actualism stands in the tradition of Western esoteric transmissions. It has philosophic, though not technical, ancestry in
the teachings of European alchemists and Gnostics concerning
evolutionary transformations of human consciousness. Farther
back in time, it has parallels to light-fire teachings and techniques known in Vedic India (*agni yoga*), in Taoist China
("circulation of *chi*"), in Tibetan Buddhism (*vajrayana*), as
well as in Persia, Greece, Egypt, and numerous other cultures.[1]

[1] The philosophy of Actualism has been previously described in my book
Maps of Consciousness, and in *Basic Principles of Actualism* by Russell
Schofield.

The world view of modern science recognizes man as living within a vast complex of interdependent energy relationships with all life forms and environments on planet Earth. The Einsteinian equation $E=mc^2$ tells us that, within the relativistic framework of our time-space world, matter and energy are convertible one into the other. In other words, the basic process of the universe manifests either as free radiation (for example, light) or as embodied in form, in matter. All forms of matter, from atoms and cells, to animals and men, to planets and galaxies, are complex aggregates of energy systems, that are unceasingly involved in energy transformations, and in the reception and transmission of energies to and from other energy systems, both macrocosmic and microcosmic.

In the history of science, the range of energies that have been recognized and studied has expanded greatly, from the narrow segment of the electromagnetic spectrum visible to our unaided eyes, to the much broader spectrum (including infrared and ultraviolet) that can be detected by recording devices of increasing power and sophistication. Scientists are only now beginning to explore aspects and ranges of energies that may exist on farther reaches of the electromagnetic spectrum, and on other energy spectra, not yet identified by science.[2]

Sensitivity and the Human Energy Field

Individual clairvoyants and esoteric teachings have long maintained that human beings, and other life forms, are surrounded by a living envelope of light-energy, or aura, that pulsates and changes in color, in brightness, and in extent. On the one hand, this energy field is the medium for the complex, subtle, nonverbal communications that pass between people—the processes popularly described as "picking up vibrations." On the other hand, the energy field also seems to reflect and ex-

[2] For reviews of this kind of research, on the energy fields and radiations of living systems, the reader is referred to Tompkins and Bird (1973); Gallert (1966); Mann (1973); and White and Krippner (1977).

press, to those able by nature or training to observe it, the feelings, thoughts, and physical condition of the person.

The external planetary energy fields, both the environmental (air, water, earth) and the human, are incredibly polluted. "We live in a sea of energy, moving throughout the planetary field. Where planetary energy-flow is polluted by misdirected thinking, explosive outbursts of mixed emotions, conflicts and hostilities, the energy systems of man's physical body degenerate into non-productive stagnation" (Schofield, 1974). Techniques of light-fire are used to purify and cleanse the consciousness, functions and structures of the personality energy systems, so that they become less vulnerable to the destructive forces that produce stress, tension, and malfunction.

The energy field is a system of perceptual antennae, enabling one to sense into the vibrations of a room, a group, or a person. This faculty is known as *sentience,* or clairsentience if it is highly developed and clarified, and is our basic means for detecting differences in vibratory rates. "The response capability for perceiving the many subtle shadings in frequency and intensity of incoming stimuli is heightened by the degree of enlightened awareness with which one is relating to the condition or situation" (Schofield, op. cit.).

The higher frequency energies that a person learns to experience and channel from sources within themselves, are at first low intensity sensations; they are subtle, delicate experiences, that gain in power and vividness, becoming high intensity as well as high frequency, as awareness and sensitivity increase.

The Human Being as an Energy System

According to Actualism, every human being is a multidimensional being of light-energy, the Actual Self, who has created energy systems at the different dimensions of energy and consciousness, for self-expression and manifestation. These dimensions or plane of energy/consciousness differ from one another in vibratory rate, with the physical, or time-space dimension, being the lowest frequency—that is, the densest matter. The lower four levels—physical, perceptual, emotional, and mental—constitute the personality systems, and correspond to the subtle bodies of esoteric psychology.

Above these four levels (that is, at higher frequencies) are the unobstructed worlds—dimensions of energy/consciousness where light-energy is received and expressed freely, without any hindrance or obstruction due to personality conditioning. These higher frequency dimensions have been given various names in esoteric literature. In Actualism they are, in ascending order above the mental: the *soul* or solar dimension; the *angelic* dimension or Eden consciousness; the *archetypal* dimension; and the *Infinity* level of formless form, which transcends all dimension.

The personality systems of human beings function as step-down transformers of the very high frequency energies flowing from the unobstructed worlds within, bringing them down into time-space, for here-now expression. Human beings may function also as step-up transformers, raising the vibratory rate of their physical bodies, or earth-level energy systems, using the transmutational power of light-fire energies to uplift the form and substance of this level.

The first of these processes, bringing light down into the physical world, has been described and taught in many spiritual traditions, and is symbolized in numerous legends of the light-bringer or fire-bringer. Prometheus brings fire to mankind, at the price of becoming enmeshed in material form, bound to the rock of matter. Siva dances with a ring of fire surrounding him, and channeling the mighty River Ganga down to Earth through the streaming locks of his hair.

The second process, transforming earth-level consciousness, was symbolized in alchemy by the transmutation of "lead" (heavy, dark, obstructed states of consciousness) into "gold" (purified, refined, illumined states of consciousness). The rising of the kundalini serpent-power is another symbolism for the process of transmutation; as is the changing of water into wine in the Christian tradition.

According to Actualism, by *earthing* the light from higher sources within, down throughout the personality systems, and raising them in frequency rate, man can accomplish his evolutionary purpose: to become a clear, lighted vehicle for the manifestation of the Being of Light that he actually is.

These kinds of communication and interaction between different frequency levels, or dimensions of consciousness, may be described as vertical energy exchanges. Horizontal energy transactions occur where we as human beings, through our personality systems, or *self-extensions,* interact with other human personality systems or with energy systems embodied in the other life forms of this planet (animal, plant, or mineral).

Actualism distinguishes two basic polarities of energy relationships, *dynamic* and *magnetic.* The dynamic pole is outgoing, expressive, giving, masculine, *yang.* It is focused in the right side of the body and energy field. The magnetic pole is incoming, receptive, feminine, *yin,* and focused in the left side of the body and field. In addition, the front is polarized dynamic, as we move forward into the world; and the back is polarized magnetic, as we take loads and burdens on our backs (for example, someone may be "a pain in the neck").

In a broader sense, the dynamic aspect of consciousness is *functional* and the magnetic is *structural.* Function moves through structure, and is given body or form by structure. Energy (dynamic) is embodied (in-formed) into matter (magnetic). Some examples of this principle are: the flow of electric current (dynamic) through a conductor (magnetic); the flow of life energy through the human body; and the structuring of sound energy into meaningful verbal patterns. An unstructured dynamic expression is random and incoherent; a magnetic without dynamic function is an empty and powerless structure.

Applied to human relationships, the magnetic-dynamic polarity parallels in many ways the introversion-extraversion distinction described by Jung and others. The extraverted personality is most focused on, and aware of, the dynamic flow of psychic energy and communication from himself or herself out into the world; he or she is less conscious of the return flow from the world back, and hence less receptive and sensitive to inner realities. The introverted personality is more focused on the

magnetic, receptive aspect of consciousness, and, as Jung
pointed out, often feels the world to be somehow impinging on
his or her awareness; with this orientation there is deficiency in
the ability to project energy and communication outward. One
aspect of the process of achieving wholeness is the balancing of
these two polarities, both within oneself (the inner marriage)
and in relationships with others. This intrapersonal and interpersonal balancing and integrating of polarities needs to be
done at each of the different levels or dimensions of consciousness for reciprocal, mutually productive, and creative
relationships.

Types of Personality Consciousness and Their Polarities

Table 20 presents in summary form the parallels among the
Actualism formulation of the personality levels of consciousness, the Jungian typology of functions, the astrological
symbolism of the elements, and the traditional esoteric terminology of inner planes.

TABLE 20

ESOTERIC PLANES	ACTUALISM DIMENSIONS	JUNGIAN FUNCTIONS	ASTROLOGICAL ELEMENTS
manas	mental	thinking	air
astral	emotional	feeling	water
etheric	perceptual	intuition	fire
material	physical	sensation	earth

The inner bodies (or self-extensions) at each of the personality
dimensions of consciousness are energy systems that have certain characteristics common to all energy systems. There is always an input, or receiving modality, and an output, or transmitting modality; and between these two there are energy
exchanges and transformations. This design has been succinctly
summarized in the formula "in-mix-out." From the point of
view of the organism or system, the intake is clearly a recep-

tive, *yin,* magnetic function, whereas outflow from the system is an expressive, *yang,* dynamic function. We can recognize the three aspects or phases of energy-system function (intake, transformation, outflow) at each of the levels of personality consciousness (physical, perceptual, emotional, mental).

Different individuals will tend to be fixed or dominant in one or another of these phases, yielding a typology of human consciousness somewhat analogous to (though also different from) the Jungian typology of functions. One could say that people are "at home" more often in particular, characteristic levels or aspects of consciousness. This is where they usually live, how they usually experience the world. The other areas are there, but are somewhat like unoccupied or unused rooms in one's house.

1. At the *physical-physiological* level of the human energy systems, we have on the magnetic or receptive pole the intake of nourishment, in solid and liquid form as food and drink, and in gaseous form as breath. Then we have manifold metabolic transformations, the exchange of substances, as foodstuff is broken down (catabolic processes), nutrients extracted and assimilated, reassembled, and distributed (anabolic processes). On the dynamic pole of the system, we have (a) the expenditure of energy in muscular activity or work,[3] including speech activity; and (b) the elimination of that which cannot be used by the system as waste matter.

It is well known that a condition of regenerative health and efficiency is maintained in the physical body if, and only if, the processes of assimilation, transformation, and elimination are functioning in a balanced and coordinated fashion. Weakness of the assimilative, intake capacity leads to nonabsorption of essential nutrients. Weakness of the eliminative functions leads to self-poisoning through toxic accumulation. Impairment of the kinetic muscular energy output leads to paralysis, ranging from mild inhibitions, cramps, and blocks to comatose cessation of function.

---

[3] This is the *kinetic energy* of physics, defined as the work done by a physical system in changing from one state to another state.

Individuals who are strongly focused on the physical level of consciousness are the sensing types of the Jungian typology. They are both sensible and sensual. In astrology they correspond to the Earth signs of the zodiac. They use good practical common sense in dealing with material realities, and operate effectively within the time-space coordinates of our physical world. Those who are dynamic on the physical are objective realists, who function actively and assertively in the material world. Those who are magnetic at this level are receptive to material energy—they are able to attract resources, including financial supply, to gather things around them, as well as being able to organize and structure physical enterprises and activities.

2. On the *sensory-perceptual* level of consciousness, in the energy systems of perception, we can recognize the stimulus input, carried by afferent nerves from sense receptors all over the body, as well as from the fine lines of the energy field extending out into the environment. Then we have the processing of this sensory input, much of which is carried out in the thalamus and related midbrain structures: the comparing, evaluating, recognizing, discriminating, communicating, appraising, and assimilating of sense *in-formation*. On the output side there are the outgoing sensory transmissions carried by efferent nerves to sense organs and muscles, and via the energy field into the environment. Psychology has long recognized that perception is not just the reception of stimuli, but also an active, creative function. In its most extreme form we see this in the *projection* of images, as in hallucinations, dreams, or visions and in projective tests.

Ordinary language seems to implicitly preserve the distinction between the two aspects of perception. We speak of "seeing," which connotes the passive, receptive intake of visual stimuli; and "looking," which suggests a more dynamic, active kind of probing, visually moving and reaching out into the environment. In the auditory sphere there is "hearing," which is a purely passive reception of sound impressions, and "listening," which carries a dynamic force of intention. In the olfactory range, perhaps "smelling" and "sniffing" would be the equivalent pair (dogs are particularly dynamic in this perceptual modality). In tactile perception, we distinguish obviously between being touched and touching.

Individuals who have highly developed perceptual functions correspond to the intuitives of the Jungian typology and the fire signs of the zodiac. They experience the world primarily in direct patterns of perception, whether by means of the usual five senses, or by extended sense perception. If they are dynamic in perception they are active and vital at this level of consciousness: They come across with a great deal of fiery energy and enthusiasm. They probe, test, and challenge their environment. Those who are primarily magnetic on this level often strike one as "sensitive" but perhaps somewhat dreamy—caught up in the receptive perception of interior impressions, or preoccupied with the satisfaction of a hunger for sensation.

As perception develops with enlightened awareness we have *clairsentience,* the clear sensing of the subtler frequencies of life-energies in the energy field or aura of living beings. Clairvoyance and clairaudience may be thought of as specialized extensions of that basic function of clairsentience. This kind of perception is referred to as clear because by comparison ordinary perception is obstructed or clouded. By way of analogy we can think of ordinary perception as a black-and-white photograph, and clear perception, clairsentience, as a color picture of the same reality—that is, with the more sensitive perception more of the subtle frequencies of color and shade are included.

3. On the *emotional-feeling* level of human consciousness and relationship, we observe and experience a similar threefold energy process. We have the reception, the acceptance of feelings, focused primarily in the left area of the breast and the heart—the inflow of emotion that we take in from others. Whether we are aware of it or not, we tend to "take things to heart." Within our emotional nature, feelings are mingled and mixed, as they collide or blend with other feelings and are transformed by being lifted up into high energy states of joy, euphoria, or excitement, or churned into lower emotional energy states such as anxiety, resentment, depression, and grief.

On the output polarity of the emotional energy systems, we

have the outpouring of feeling toward another, the dynamic expression of emotion. While this may be structured or accompanied by verbal output, it need not be; emotional energy radiates out directly, mostly from the region of the right breast and liver, but also strongly through the eyes. A person may not be aware of what his emotional nature is transmitting or broadcasting to others; frequently it's easier for another person to read one's emotional expression than it is for oneself.

When a person is emotionally fixed on one polarity or the other, frustration and conflict inevitably enter into both intrapersonal as well as interpersonal relationships. Those fixated on the dynamic side may have difficulty accepting, and therefore expressing, the softer, receptive emotions. Being uncomfortable with their own femininity, they tend to adopt a "hard," even aggressive, emotional posture. This corresponds to the choleric temperament of the alchemists. Those who are emotionally dynamic, but not in an extreme or fixated manner, come across with the warmth of feeling and sympathy that characterizes the sanguine temperament of the ancients.

On the other hand, those fixated on the receptive side are in a posture of emotional dependency, sometimes to the extreme of sapping others' emotional energy. Being uncomfortable with their own dynamic, masculine feelings, they have trouble asserting themselves, and they find it difficult to project any enthusiasm into emotional situations or relationships. They correspond to the melancholic temperament of the old alchemical classification. Those who are mildly or moderately polarized on the emotional magnetic are receptive to emotional energy from others, but are not that expressive, much like the phlegmatic type described by the alchemists.

In recent years, psychologists have developed therapeutic approaches designed to specifically overcome both these kinds of imbalances: sensitivity training for those who need to cultivate and enhance their emotional receptiveness, and assertiveness training for those who need to develop the ability to stand up and speak up for their own feelings and values.

The projection of emotion is a very physical, even physiological process: We can bask in the glow of someone's warm feelings toward us, or shiver at the iciness of emotional rejection. In the alchemical-astrological symbolism, emotions relate to the water element and the fluid components of the body. Under the influence of conditioned images of ourselves and others, we tend to react to emotional stimuli or situations in a fixed, habitual manner, with instant like or dislike, sympathy or antipathy, feeling resonance or dissonance. Shafica Karagulla (1967), in her book on the observations of the sensitives that she worked with, reported that in concerts or performances the emotional energy field of the performer would expand to contact and merge with the emotional fields of the audience. If this did not happen, the performance didn't work; the artist was perceived as "not coming across."

Working with enlightened awareness, the emotional nature can be lighted and lifted to higher expressions of joy and enthusiasm. The enlightened individual maintains a light heart in emotional relationships of all kinds. This does not mean that his or her relationships are shallow or frivolous, it means that he or she does not get pulled into other people's emotional turmoil or sentimental dramatics. Keeping dynamic/magnetic polarities balanced, one can assimilate what is communicated emotionally, and project a lighted outflow of feeling that affects and touches others. Thus a balanced mutuality of emotional interrelationships is maintained, externally as well as internally. There is a simultaneity of giving and receiving, a circulation of love and affection.

4. On the *mental* level of functioning, the three aspects of energy exchange are also evident. We take in thoughts, information, data, and concepts—that is, mental input—in the form of spoken or written words, or graphic symbols and designs. One should allow also for the nonverbal, nonsensory, direct reception of ideas or patterns as shown in telepathy experiments, of the kind performed by J. B. Rhine. After reception, thoughts are submitted to a large variety of transforming processes in the brain's biocomputers. We speak appropriately enough of "digesting information." This kind of mental metabolism includes the *analytic*, "taking apart" functions (which correspond to catabolic processes in the body), and the *synthetic*, "putting

together" functions (corresponding to anabolic processes in the body). In recent years, brain researchers have proposed that these different brain activities are located in different cerebral hemispheres—the analytic more on the left, the synthetic more on the right (see Chapter 6).

Mental output may take the usual physical form of the written or spoken word, or graphic images and patterns. The direct, nonverbal projection of thought to another person is sometimes referred to as mental suggestion, sometimes as telepathy. The latter has an implication of transmission across a distance (*tele*="far").[4] It is probable that this kind of nonverbal, nonphysical communication occurs all the time, rather than only with a certain few gifted individuals, or under selected circumstances. When we think of someone, we are in effect sending a thought-form, a mental energy packet, to that person. Conversely, what is it that makes us unexpectedly think of someone, if not their thought energy directed toward us?

Whether these mental transmissions are consciously received or not would depend on the clarity and one-pointedness of both the receiver's and the transmitter's instruments—that is, minds. Evidently, some individuals are able to tune in so powerfully, screening out the distracting chatter of other thoughts, that they are able to receive and decode accurately and consistently. Recent experiments have shown, and yogic traditions have long maintained, that these abilities can be developed through training.

In terms of individual differences, the mental-thinking level of consciousness corresponds to the air signs of the zodiac, and

[4] A note on terminology is appropriate here. To be precise, the word *telepathy* would best be reserved for emotional communication at a distance since "-pathy" refers to feeling states, as in sympathy, apathy, or pathetic. Perhaps *telegnosis*, "far knowing," would be the best word for mental communication at a distance. (Compare "diagnosis" and "prognosis.") Thus the reception and transmission of feelings of love or anxiety between two people at a distance would be telepathic ("far feeling"); whereas the transmission of actual thoughts, words, or images would be telegnostic. Perception of visual scenes at a distance is now referred to in parapsychology as "remote perception"; this would correspond to the perceptual, rather than the mental level. At the physical level, the accepted term for physical action at a distance is, of course, *telekinesis*.

TABLE 21
Functions of the Human Energy Systems

	INTAKE	TRANSFORMATIONS	OUTFLOW	ACTION AT A DISTANCE
physical	food & drink; breath	metabolism (catabolic, anabolic)	muscular work; elimination	psychokinesis telekinesis
perceptual	afferent sense stimulation	perceptual processing (recognition, discrimination)	efferent sense projection; imagination	remote perception
emotional	acceptance of feelings	emotional blending; exchange of feelings	emotional pro-jection; sympathy	telepathy
mental	reception of ideas, words, symbols	analysis & synthesis	expression of ideas, words, symbols	telegnosis

the thinking function in the Jungian system. Some mentally oriented individuals are clearly predominantly magnetic or receptive in their mental activities: these are the readers, researchers, the gatherers and compilers of information. If psychically gifted, they may be telegnostic receivers. Others are mentally dynamic: They initiate, originate, investigate, and communicate ideas and thoughts actively and vigorously. If psychically gifted, such individuals may turn out to be talented telegnostic senders.

On Transcending One's Type

The more one becomes aware of the different levels of function and consciousness within oneself, the more one also becomes aware of the characteristic attitudes and consciousness of another. As we know ourselves, we can know others. As we gain awareness of our own feelings, we can have empathy and perhaps telepathy for the feelings of others. As we extend and enlighten sensory awareness of our own perceptions, the sense recognition of our own interior states, our sentience and clairsentience of others become more vivid and accurate. As we bring more enlightened awareness into the structures and functions of our own physical body, we also become more sensitive to both the natural and the distorted body-type expressions of others.

The conditioning processes of culture generally do not foster or develop this kind of enlightened awareness of self and others. Instead, ill-conceived and unnatural educational practices set up conditions in which the development of personality consciousness proceeds in an unaware, unenlightened, and imbalanced manner. The flow of life energy through the personality systems becomes, to a greater or lesser degree, distorted and deviated from its actual inner design. On the mental level these conditions bring about fixed attitudes, mental blocks, and lack of objectivity; on the emotional level they cause inhibitions, emotional conflicts, and frustrations; on the perceptual level, fixed biases and prejudices based on appearance; and on the physical level, ill health or lack of well-being, due to the accumulation of toxic elements or other kinds of energy blockage in the body.

The process and objective of Actualism enlightenment training involves the practice of channeling the different life energies that the human being can channel, with different energies being used in different situations, according to need and purpose. One learns that as various states of discomfort, whether mental, emotional, nervous, or physical, are indicative of energy deficiency or distortion, and that one can channel the appropriate kind of life energy to the energy systems that are calling for help.

Each individual tends to be a naturally gifted channel for one or more of the basic life energies, expressing them through the magnetic and dynamic aspects of personality consciousness that we have been describing. For example, those who naturally channel healing energy are recognized as gifted healers, though they may or may not have medical training to supplement their natural gifts. Those who are naturally strong on the energy of creative expression usually become active artists or inventors. Those who are natural channels of wisdom energy function as thinkers, designers, or scientists. Those gifted in the energies of perception may become psychic or clairvoyant, whatever their chosen field of endeavor. Those whose natural energies are focused in the physical realm may develop athletic or dance or mechanical skills to a high degree.

Through enlightenment training any human being has the potential for learning to channel all the various kinds of energy with increasing intensity and breadth of scope, and to do so at all levels of consciousness; in other words to function multidimensionally, and with the total spectrum of energies. This is the process of moving toward wholeness by rounding out our talents, and developing the functions and capacities in which we are naturally less strong.

Individuals who are expressing their inner-essence energies in a relatively free, unobstructed manner are recognizable by the seemingly overabundant outflow of creative vitality that we find in the genius or adept. However, more commonly, the outer manifestation of the essence energies in personality function is inverted, obscured, and obstructed by numerous layers of image conditioning, compensation, suppression, and idealization. These overlays and underlays of illusion and delusion in the consciousness of human personality systems are referred to in the esoteric literature as the veils of *maya*.

In the process of enlightenment training one learns to channel, focus, and direct the different light-fire energies, to process through the obstructions and inversions, and to dissolve these veils of illusion. As this proceeds in a step-by-step manner, the personality systems gradually awaken to the inner presence of the Actual Self—in all the many aspects of Actual Self: the teacher-knower within, the physician within, the warrior-of-light aspect, the creator aspect. The realization comes that the Actual Self, or Higher Self, has *chosen* to experience the personality of a particular type, and the particular personal and cultural conditioning patterns.

Through the process of expanding and enlightening awareness a gradual but pronounced shift in self-perception and self-understanding takes place. We come to recognize certain patterns of thinking, feeling, perceiving, and acting as *typical* of our particular temperament. These are our reality-filters, as it were, and other people have theirs. The filters of type-conditioning give the characteristic colors and shapes to the reality worlds in which we each live.

Being aware of, and becoming centered in the essence energies of our nature, the actual inner beingness, we can begin to transcend the limitations of type. We learn to withdraw identity from the type-given characteristics of our nature. We are then no longer totally subjective in them, but aware of them objectively, while remaining aware of the subjective states of consciousness also. We generally find that as soon as we recognize a particular feature within ourselves, we can then also perceive and recognize it in others in a nonjudgmental way. This would be the point of Christ's admonition to focus on the beam in our own eyes before being concerned with the mote in another's.

This kind of learning represents a shift in point of view—

from the relatively set perspective of the personality, embedded as it were in type, to the fluid awareness of presence, creatively living and *being* within and throughout the personality. It can be likened to the knowing and recognition of the builder/owner of a building rather than merely the physical building itself, or its many inhabitants (the many personality selves or egos). This experience is at first a glimpse or vision, and in time becomes more continuous and certain.

A Greek alchemist named Olympiodorus, quoted by Jung, wrote the following beautiful statement of this process:

> If thou wilt calmly humble thyself in relation to thy body, and thou wilt calm thyself also in relation to the passions, and by acting thus, thou wilt summon the divine to thyself, and in truth the divine, which is everywhere, will come to thee. But when thou knowest thyself, thou knowest also the God who is truly one.[5]

In the body, we become more sensitive to its shifting states and messages, more aware of its strengths and limitations, as we withdraw identity from it. We then recognize the body's identity as the beloved creation of the Actual Self. As Actual Self, we experience being *in* the body, but not *of* it; in the world, but not of it. In the same way, as we recognize and acknowledge our perceptual, emotional, and mental experiences, but do not identify with them, we become more aware of them. We also become more aware of potentials as yet neither experienced nor expressed by the personality.

We then move into and live increasingly in the consciousness of the designer-creator of personality structure and functions: the consciousness of the Mother-Father within, to whom the personality is as the prodigal son. This prodigal son personality at first loses and then redeems the rich heritage of the light-world of his/her beginnings. The descent into form is followed, in the end, by the return ascent to the Spirit.

[5] C. G. Jung, "The Philosophical Tree" *Collected Works*, Vol. 13, *Alchemical Studies*. (Princeton, N.Y.: Princeton University Press, 1967), p. 285.

Epilogue

by Russell Paul Schofield

All members of the human race are members of one family. As in any family, there are those who are older and those younger; those who have had more experience in form and those souls who have not progressed as far along the evolutionary path.

Whether more or less experienced in form, each individual Being chooses the type of physical, sensory, emotional, and mental capabilities needed for the learning experience required to reach their objectives and accomplish the evolving purpose of their life. The particular type reflects the choice made by the Beingness, the *I AM* that each one is.

What we term type might be perceived from another perspective as specialization of expression by way of specific nerve, brain, glandular, muscle, bone, and other tissues in a variety of combinations, to afford the learning experience provided by each combination. Some of the combinations found useful throughout history are described in the text of this book.

Within the framework of each type the predictable inclinations and tendencies may be modified within widening boundaries as each individual actualizes the great potentials of his or her lighted Self. The manifestation of these potentials is bound by genetic and environmental conditioning imprints, as Prometheus is bound to the rock. The most tragic result of this conditioning has been the separation in consciousness of personality self from the royal heritage of Actual Self.

In numerous ancient legends and writings, seen as sacred in their time and place, there appears a common theme that, simply stated, says, "in those days there were giants in earth," or "in those times the gods dwelt among men." In modern times we refer to such highly evolved incarnations as "genius." Those rare individuals we call genius serve as radiant examples of the inner light of the giant Being within, shining through in a particular area. Their work has taken form in art, science, philosophy, and religious revelation. They have been the heralds of new ages of enlightenment for humanity, in past and present times. Just as artistic and scientific technology has been advanced by these forerunners, there has also been a less known advance in inner technology—technology to free the conditioning-bound Promethean nature so that there may again be recognition, acknowledgment, and experience of the giant-in-earth that each human being actually is. The Buddha demonstrated in his way the impact upon humanity of a giant in earth, as did Laotse, Pythagoras, and others, each in his own way.

The questions and purposes of life and death have always plagued mankind. The most illumined answer to the paradoxical mystery of life and death was indelibly demonstrated by the Christ, in the victory of immortal life over mortal death, and the lifting up of the visible form into the invisible realms of life. This was also demonstrated in more ancient times by the prophet Isaiah and others. However, Christ left these encouraging words to one who works with the radiant consciousness of his lighted Self:

. . . the works that I do shall he do also; and greater works than these shall he do . . . [Jn. 14:12].

So as the human family works together in the dawn light of the New Age, united with the source of life within, we can move beyond the limitations of type, alter and modify the inclinations and tendencies prescribed by type into a balanced expression of total Beingness. Meanwhile, preparation for moving beyond the specializations of a particular type requires bringing

out the fullest expression possible of each one's unique qualities. As we utilize the talents afforded by type in an enlightened
manner, we earn the freedom to move from exclusive experience of one type or another, to the inclusive experience of the
wholeness that is the goal of evolution. This is the progression

> from point of light
> to brightening Star
> to radiant Sun of manifestation.

Appendix

A Typology of Ways of Growth

Many strategies have been used by the teachers and way-showers of mankind in present and past ages to bring about the personality changes required to free consciousness from the regressive imprints and images that keep it in an unenlightened, unawakened condition. We can distinguish among these methods, according to which of the four energy systems or levels of function they primarily focus on. There is also a fifth group of methods that utilize pure energy and energy-transformation throughout the psychological and physical structures and functions of consciousness.

1. The *physical* methods are those that seek to change consciousness by directly altering the physical energy input of the body. This includes special diets of all kinds (e.g., macrobiotics), fasting (no diet), and the use of special herbs, plants, or drugs (such as *bhang* or *soma* in the East, peyote or LSD in the West). It also includes breathing exercises (*pranayama*), and various kinds of movement and physical disciplines (*hatha yoga, tai chi,* martial arts, sacred dances). In the West, physical methods include systems such as structural integration (Rolfing), Feldenkrais work, Alexander technique, and several other types of awareness-oriented body work.

One would also have to include in this group the use of special devices or instruments to alter awareness and perception: traditional esoteric and magic teachings describe the use of psychically charged amulets and talismans; modern experimenters have devised or re-invented pyramid structures, orgone accumulators, psychotronic generators, and other tools of healing and energy enhancement.

As a therapeutic technique, behavior therapy also belongs in this category, since it is an approach that considers only the energy input (stimulus) and the energy output (response) relevant to behavioral description and change. Though not an awareness modality, it is definitely an effective approach to the learning and unlearning of habitual behavior patterns.

Many of these methods of course affect more than just the physical nature of man, even though the primary change agent is of a physical or physiological nature. Also, many of the new-old holistic healing methods, such as homeopathy, acupuncture, polarity therapy, or laying-on-of-hands, that aim at bringing about wholeness in the human being include physical modalities in their approach along with attention to attitudes, feelings, and lifestyles. Generally, in most yogic traditions, the physical methods are regarded as preparation for, or supportive to, other approaches of a more meditative kind.

2. As far as *sensory* or *perceptual* methods are concerned, spiritual traditions have historically been sharply divided over the best strategy to deal with sense experience. In one powerful branch of religious and esoteric teachings, both Eastern and Western, the *ascetic* attitude has prevailed: It was held that the most appropriate way to deal with the fascinating, glamorizing pull of sense experience was to deny or negate it. Monastic seclusion, desert or mountain hermitages, and more extreme forms of abnegation and renunciation are expressions of this attitude. In modern times, the samadhi tank technique pioneered by Dr. John Lilly may be considered a radical, scientific approach to total withdrawal from external sense experience.

A totally opposite approach to the problem was taken by the *tantric* tradition in India, China, Persia, and cultures: Here the goal was liberation from the pull of the senses by sensory enhancement and cultivation, by the use of sensory rituals and sacraments. The tantric movements developed the use of *yantras* (geometric designs) for visual concentration, *mantras* for focusing on subtle inner sounds; and special rituals involving stimulation of the sense of smell (incense), taste (ritual food), and sexual touch (*maithuna*).

In recent years in the West, certain approaches which cultivate and develop sensory awareness (for example, that of Charlotte Selver), would fall in this category; as well as various forms of chanting, and exercises devoted to improving perceptual sensitivity. One might also consider the use of biofeedback in this group—where a physical instrument is used to establish internal sense communication with a part of the body, that was previously outside the range of the person's awareness. Music is of course a sensory modality that has a direct and powerful effect on the emotional nature, and has been used for that purpose in many religious traditions, especially those of a devotional orientation.

3. Methods that focus on the *emotional* nature specifically include all the various forms of *bhakti* or devotional yoga in the East; devotional prayer and dancing in the Sufi and the Hassidic Jewish tradition; the Greek Orthodox Christian "prayer of the heart"; Christian gospel singing; and many other expressions of this—probably the most widespread kind of yoga all over Earth.

In Western psychotherapeutics, methods such as encounter group work, gestalt therapy, psychodrama, and client-centered therapy would be included in this group. Many of these developed specifically in reaction to the overly analytic approach of previous therapies. In encounter work for instance, the cardinal rule is to follow the feelings, and to ignore the ideas and thoughts.

4. At the *mental* level of consciousness we find a long tradition of methods aimed at redirecting one's thinking, out of destructive or self-defeating patterns, to healthier and more enlightened perspectives. In the East there are the various forms of wisdom (*jnana*) yoga. Some of these use complex symbolic meditations. Others, such as Zen, advocate simply an

"emptying" or "stilling" of the mind (analogous perhaps to sensory deprivation or physical fasting). The aim here is to allow awareness to rise up out of (or sink down below through) the chattering frequencies of everyday random associative thought. The Western world also has a long history of mental and philosophical approaches to enlightenment, ranging from the elaborate metaphysics of the theologians to the arcane symbolism of occult schools and secret societies.

In the area of psychological therapeutics, we have known the rather complex analytic systems such as the Freudian, or transactional analysis, as well as the simple (some would say simplistic) use of positive thinking, autosuggestion, cybernetics, mind control, and others. These therapeutic methods, while they may work in the sense of bringing about positive changes in a person's life, do not appear really to touch the inner core of being, or to awaken man to his higher potential.

Yet other methods, such as those of Gurdjieff and the Southern Buddhist *vipassana* practices, involve the person learning to simply observe his thought processes, without judgment or attachment.

5. The fifth group of methods might be called *pure energy* techniques. Here the individual is trained to work directly with inner sources of life energy. He is taught how to tap into sources or focal points of "light-fire energies," and to channel and direct these energies, by means of sentience and awareness, into and throughout the personality systems, down to and including the physical.

These techniques are called light-fire energies because light and fire are basic manifestations of the primordial sea of energy in which everything moves and exists. The light aspect of life-energy is used to illuminate the darkened areas of consciousness, and to awaken the personality systems to the Higher Self or Essence within. The fire aspect of life-energy is used like a consuming fire to burn up and eliminate the crystallized imprints and images that have come to overlay and distort man's consciousness at the various levels.

Light-fire methods of this kind were known in ancient India as *agni yoga*, the yoga of fire. In Tibet they were referred to as *dumo,* "inner heat," used by the practitioners of the *vajrayana,* the "diamond lightning-bolt way," also known as the "path of direct enlightenment." Chinese Taoists cultivated many methods for developing *chi* or primal energy, among which acupuncture and *tai chi* are the best known. Phrases such as "fire-breathing dragon," and "circulation of light" referred to specific energy techniques. The secret orders of *kahunas* in Hawaii and Polynesia called the life energy *mana* and practiced light methods and teachings that they referred to as the "rainbow path." American Indians, both North and South, had their secret initiations in which they were taught methods of working with "shields of light." Many cultures practiced sun worshiping as a symbolic means for getting in touch with the illuminating fire of the inner sun. European alchemists used the "fire of transmutation" to extract the golden essence of truth from the black dross of false conditioning.

Schools and teachings in this tradition of light-fire differ from most current meditative systems in emphasizing the need to ground or earth the light-energies within the physical body and the everyday consciousness of the personality. It is not sufficient to *transcend,* i.e. rise above, negative, dark states of consciousness; they must be *transmuted,* i.e. raised in vibratory rate, in order for true change or transformation to take place.

Schools of enlightenment in ancient Egypt, Greece, and Persia were often referred to as "mystery schools," and people came to believe that they practiced concealment and deliberate veiling of the truth. The fact is that these schools taught and revealed the so-called mysteries to the students who attended them, who took the training in the experiential techniques. There was no more concealment or mystery than there would be in a contemporary school of physics or astronomy or architecture. Any discipline with specific technical terms used in its training is bound to sound somewhat esoteric to an outsider, to one not engaged in that study.

Examination of the historical record will show that it was actually the mystery schools, while primarily engaged in teaching methods of enlightenment and liberation, that kept alive the spirit of scientific inquiry and preserved the findings of the sciences in times of civilizations' collapse. In the West, the last major open mystery school was that of Pythagoras, the descendants of which (Gnostics and Hermeticists) went under in the holocaust of the Dark Ages. From the East and the North came the Mongolians, the Vikings, the Goths, the Teutons— invading the Roman Empire and its European colonies, robbing, pillaging, destroying. Only a few of the monasteries were able to preserve some of the learning and wisdom of the ancients.

In the Arab world, enlightenment teachings were evidently preserved somewhat longer, in the elusive and whimsical ways of the Sufis, and in colleges that maintained and developed the sciences of mathematics, chemistry, and astronomy. In India secret groups in all three major religions—Hindu, Buddhist, and Moslem—carried on with enlightenment teaching, referred to as Tantra, right into the late Middle Ages. In the last several hundred years, such work has gone almost completely underground in all parts of the world, under the intellectual onslaught of scientific rationalism.

As we move into the Aquarian Age and through the turmoil times of the present century, it has become evident that numerous seekers and sensitives are again searching for a path of enlightenment, and a way to re-establish the awareness and union with the higher aspects of human nature.

Down through the ages, some schools and teachers have found it expedient to utilize what might appear to be brutal tactics, apparently in order to shock the students into awakening to their inner resources. We might mention, for example, the use of physical ordeals, such as standing in a snake pit, in some American Indian initiation practices. Prolonged isolation and entombment were part of the training in the Egyptian schools. Some of the Tibetan *vajrayana* orders practiced the deliberate evocation of demonic entities to test and sharpen the awareness and psychic warrior skills of the initiate. In modern times we could cite G. I. Gurdjieff, who used insult and ridicule to activate self-images based on vanity or egotism. The semi-legendary Yaqui Indian sorcerer Don Juan, described in the books by Carlos Castaneda, employed tactics of "controlled terror" in his attempts to awaken his student to alternate realities.

In contrast to this approach, there are the profoundly influential teachings symbolized in the legends of the Graal, or Holy Grail, a name that derives from root meanings of "gradual." This refers to the gradual, step-by-step process of expanding awareness and extending perception into higher dimensions of consciousness and simultaneously earthing or grounding higher frequency energies in the body and personality. The Grail, thought of variously as the chalice used at the Last Supper or the cup that caught the blood of Christ on the cross, was throughout the Middle Ages the great symbol for the actual living experiential teaching of Christ—as distinct from the official dogmas of the Christian Church, which had long since deviated and distorted much of the original meaning.

All the enlightenment teachings, whether in a religious-devotional framework or in a psychological training framework, have had the same core message and goal: that the direction for man's quest and searching is within. Light-fire techniques are used to awaken personality consciousness and identity to the point where we can experience, *and manifest* the inner radiance of our actual essence nature.

References

INTRODUCTION

Adorno, T. W., et al. *The Authoritarian Personality*. New York: Harper & Brothers, 1950; discussed in Chapter 7 of the present book.

Friedman, M. *Type A Behavior and Your Heart*. New York: Alfred A. Knopf, 1974.

Melville, Leilani. *Children of the Rainbow: Religions, Legends and Gods of Pre-Christian Hawaii*. Wheaton, Ill.: Theosophical Publishing House, 1969.

Metzner, Ralph. *Maps of Consciousness*. New York: Collier-Macmillan, 1971.

Osmond, H.; Siegler, M.; and Smoke, R. "Typology Revisited: A New Perspective," *Psychological Perspectives*, Vol. 8, No. 2, 1977, pp. 206–19.

CHAPTER 1   *The Three Body Types*

Cortes, J. B., and Gatti, F. M. *Delinquency and Crime: A Biopsychosocial Approach*. New York: Seminar Press, 1972.

————. "Physique and Self-description of Temperament," *J. Consult. Psychol.*, Vol. 29, 1965, pp. 432–39.

Hall, C. S., and Lindzey, G. "Sheldon's Constitutional Psychology," in *Theories of Personality*. New York: John Wiley & Sons, 1970.

Huxley, Aldous. *The Perennial Philosophy*. New York: Harper & Row, 1970. (1944).

Lenski, Robert. "An Introduction to European Constitutional Psychology," in *Body and Mind* (A Journal of Constitutional Psychology), Vol. I, No. 1, Dec. 1976 (P.O. Box 4815, Washington, D.C. 20008).

Oliver, Ruth Hale. *Physique, Temperament and Psyche—An Astrological Approach*. Hollywood: RGO Publishing, 1977.

Sagan, Carl. *The Dragons of Eden.* New York: Random House, 1977.

Sheldon, W. H. *The Varieties of Human Physique.* New York: Harper & Brothers, 1940.

————. *The Varieties of Human Temperament.* New York: Harper & Brothers, 1942.

Simeons, A. T. W. *Man's Presumptuous Brain.* New York: E. P. Dutton & Co., Inc., 1961.

Whiteside, Robert L. *Face Language.* New York: Frederick Fell Publishers, Inc., 1974.

CHAPTER 2 *The Four Humoral (Emotional) Types*

Eysenck, H. J., and Eysenck, S. B. G. *Personality Structure and Measurement.* San Diego: Robert R. Knapp, 1969.

Eysenck, H. J., and Wilson, G. *Know Your Own Personality.* Baltimore, Md.: Penguin Books, 1976.

Klibansky, R.; Panofsky, E.; and Saxl, F. *Saturn and Melancholy.* New York: Basic Books, 1964.

Roback, A. A. *Psychology of Character.* London: Kegan Paul, 1952.

Steiner, Rudolf. *The Four Temperaments.* New York: Anthroposophic Press, 1944.

CHAPTER 3 *The Jungian Typology*

Arroyo, Stephen. *Astrology, Psychology and the Four Elements.* Davis, Calif.: CRCS Publications, 1975.

Bulletin of Research in Psychological Type. Vol. 1, No. 1, 1977. Palo Alto, Calif. Consulting Psychologists Press.

Dean, Douglas, and Mihalasky, John. *Executive ESP.* Englewood Cliffs, N.J.: Prentice-Hall, 1974.

Eysenck, H. J., and Eysenck, S. B. G. *Personality Structure and Measurement.* San Diego: Robert R. Knapp, 1969.

Gauquelin, M.; Gauquelin, F.; and Eysenck, S. B. G. "Personality and Position of the Planets at Birth: An Empirical Study," *Brit. J. Soc. and Clin. Psychol.,* in press, 1979.

Journal of Geocosmic Research, Vol. 1, No. 3, 1975. Special section on Astrology and the Work of C. G. Jung. Tempe, Ariz.: *American Federation of Astrologers.*

Jung, Carl. *Psychological Types* (originally published in 1921).

Collected Works, Vol. 6, R. F. C. Hull. Princeton, N.J.: Princeton University Press, 1976.

Jungian Type Survey—The Gray-Wheelwrights Test. San Francisco, Calif.: Society of Jungian Analysts, 1964.

Lectures on Jung's Typology. I. *The Inferior Function* by M. L. von Franz. II. *The Feeling Function* by James Hillman. Zurich: Spring Publications, 1971.

Lim, R. "Zodiacal Sign Polarities as an Index of Introversion-Extraversion," M.A. Thesis, San Francisco State University, 1975.

Malone, Michael. *Psychetypes.* New York: E. P. Dutton, 1977.

Mann, H.; Siegler, M.; and Osmond, H. "The Many Worlds of Time," *Journ. Analyt. Psychol.,* Vol. 13, No. 1, 1968, pp. 33–56.

Mayo, J; White, O.; and Eysenck, H. J. "An Empirical Study of the Relation Between Astrological Factors and Personality," *J. Soc. Psych.,* 1978, Vol. 105, pp. 229–36.

Metzner, R. "Symbolic Components of Individuation and Social Change," *Astrology Now,* Vol. 2, No. 15, 1976, pp. 25–30.

Metzner, R.; Holcombe, R.; and Holcombe, J. "Astrological Elements and Personality Types: An Empirical Study," to be published, 1979.

Myers-Briggs, Isabel. *Manual—Myers-Briggs Type Indicator.* Palo Alto, Calif.: Consulting Psychologists Press, 1962.

Osmond, Humphrey. *Understanding Understanding.* New York: Bantam Books, 1974.

Osmond, H., Siegler, M., and Smoke, R. "Typology Revisited—A New Perspective." *Psychological Perspectives,* 1977, Vol. 8, No. 2, pp. 206–19.

Strickler, L. J., and Ross, J. "An Assessment of Some Structural Properties of the Jungian Personality Typology," *J. Abn. Soc. Psychol.,* 1964, Vol. 68, No. 1, pp. 62–71.

Wheelwright, Joseph. *Psychological Types.* San Francisco: C. G. Jung Institute, 1973.

CHAPTER 4 *The Evolutionary Typology of the Zodiac*

Arroyo, S. *Astrology, Psychology and the Four Elements.* Davis, Calif.: CRCS Publications, 1975.

Bailey, A. *Esoteric Astrology.* New York: Lucis Trust, 1951.

De Santillana, A., and von Dechend, H. *Hamlet's Mill.* Boston: Gambit, 1969.

Ebertin, R. *The Combination of Stellar Influences.* Aalen, Germany: Ebertin-Verlag, 1960.

Fagan, C. *Astrological Origins*. St. Paul: Llewellyn Publications, 1971.

Gammon, M. H. *Astrology and the Edgar Cayce Readings*. Virginia Beach, Va.: A.R.E. Press, 1967.

Gauquelin, M. *Scientific Basis of Astrology*. New York: Stein & Day, 1969.

Gleadow, R. *The Origin of the Zodiac*. New York: Atheneum, 1969.

Greene, L. *Relating*. New York: Samuel Weiser, 1977.

Jocelyn, J. *Meditations on the Signs of the Zodiac*. Blauvelt, N.Y.: Multimedia, 1970.

Metzner, R. *Maps of Consciousness*. New York: Collier-Macmillan, 1971.

Oken, A. *As Above, So Below*. New York: Bantam Books, 1973.

Rudhyar, D. *The Pulse of Life*. Berkeley, Calif.: Shambhala, 1970.

Sakoian, F., and Acker, L. *The Astrologer's Handbook*. New York: Harper & Row, 1973.

Stone, Merlin. *When God Was a Woman*. New York: Harcourt, Brace, Jovanovich, 1976.

Tyl, N. *Principles and Practice of Astrology*. (12 vols.). St. Paul, Minn.: Llewellyn, 1976.

Van Deusen, E. *Astrogenetics*. Garden City, N.Y.: Doubleday & Company, 1976.

West, J. A., and Toonear, J. G. *The Case for Astrology*. Baltimore, Md.: Penguin Books, 1973.

CHAPTER 5   *Planetary Types*

Anonymous. *The Mystery of the Ductless Glands*. Oceanside, Calif.: The Rosicrucian Fellowship, 1940.

Bieler, Henry G. *Food Is Your Best Medicine*. New York: Random House, 1966.

Busteed, M.; Tiffany, R.; and Wergin, D. *Phases of the Moon*. Berkeley, Calif. and London: Shambhala, 1974.

Collin, Rodney. *The Theory of Celestial Influence*. London: Vincent Stuart, 1958.

Gammon, M. H. *Astrology and the Edgar Cayce Readings*. Virginia Beach, Va.: A.R.E. Press, 1967.

Gauquelin, Michel. *The Scientific Basis of Astrology*. New York: Stein & Day, 1969.

———. *Cosmic Influences on Human Behavior*. New York: ASI Publishers, 1978.

Lieber, Arnold L., and Agel, Jerome. *The Lunar Effect*. Garden City, N.Y.: Anchor Press/Doubleday & Company, 1978.

Meyer, M. R. *A Handbook for the Humanistic Astrologer*. Garden City, N.Y.: Anchor Press/Doubleday & Company, 1974.

Rudhyar, Dane. *The Lunation Cycle*. Berkeley, Calif. and London: Shambhala, 1971.

Swedenborg, Emanuel. *Earths in the Universe*. London: The Swedenborg Society, 1860 (repr., 1970).

Yeats, William B. *A Vision*. New York: Collier-Macmillan, 1956.

CHAPTER 6 *Styles of Thinking*

Bakan, Paul. "Dreaming, REM Sleep and the Right Hemisphere: A Theoretical Integration." Burnaby, B.C.: Psychology Dept., Simon Fraser University, 1975.

Bandler, R., and Grinder, J. *The Structure of Magic*. Cupertino, Calif.: Meta Publications, 1977.

Barron, Frank. *Creativity and Personal Freedom*. New York: Van Nostrand, 1968.

Delacato, C. H. *The Diagnosis and Treatment of Speech and Reading Problems*. Springfield, Ill.: Charles C Thomas, 1963.

Domhoff, G. William. "But Why Did They Sit on the King's Right in the First Place?" *Psychoanalytic Rev.*, Vol. 56, 1969, pp. 586–96 (repr. *The Nature of Human Consciousness: A Book of Readings,* ed. Robert Ornstein. San Francisco: W. H. Freeman, 1976).

Eysenck, H. J. (ed.). *The Measurement of Personality*. Baltimore, Md.: University Park Press, 1976.

James, William. *Principles of Psychology*. New York: Holt & Co., 1891.

Lee, Philip R., et al. *Symposium on Consciousness*. New York: Viking Press, 1976.

Ornstein, Robert. *The Psychology of Consciousness*. San Francisco: W. H. Freeman, 1972.

Richardson, Alan. "Verbalizer-Visualizer: A Cognitive Style Dimension," *Journ. Mental Imagery*, Vol. 1, No. 1, 1977, pp. 109–26.

Shouksmith, George. *Intelligence, Creativity and Personal Style*. London: Batsford, 1970.

Tomkins, Sylvan. "Left and Right: A Basic Dimension of Ideology and Personality," in White, R. W. (ed.), *The Study of Lives*. New York: Atherton Press, 1963.

CHAPTER 7 *Political, Occupational, and Aesthetic Typologies*

Adorno, T. W.; Frenkel-Brunswik, E.; Levinson, D. J.; and Sanford, R. N. *The Authoritarian Personality.* New York: Harper & Brothers, 1950.

Di Renzo, Gordon J. (ed.). *Personality and Politics.* Garden City, N.Y.: Anchor Press/Doubleday & Company, 1974.

Eysenck, H. J., and Wilson, G. *Know Your Own Personality.* Baltimore, Md.: Penguin Books, 1976.

Hockert, S. A. "The Relationship between Personality Type and Choice of College Major." Ph.D. Dissertation, University of Minnesota, 1975.

Holland, John L. *Making Vocational Choices: A Theory of Careers.* Englewood Cliffs, N.J.: Prentice-Hall, 1973.

————. *The Self-directed Search: A Guide to Educational and Vocational Planning.* Palo Alto, Calif.: Consulting Psychologists Press, 1970.

Knapp, R. H., and Wulf, A. "Preference for Abstract and Representational Art." *I. soc. Psychol.,* 1963, *60,* pp. 255–62.

Maccoby, Michael. *The Gamesman: The New Corporate Leaders.* New York: Simon & Schuster, 1976.

Myers-Briggs, Isabel. *The Myers-Briggs Type Indicator.* Palo Alto, Calif.: Consulting Psychologists Press, 1962.

Read, Herbert. *Education Through Art.* New York: Pantheon, 1974.

Spranger, E. *Types of Men.* Halle: Max Niemeyer Verlag, 1928.

Strong, E. K., and Campbell, D. P. *Strong-Campbell Interest Inventory.* Palo Alto, Calif.: Consulting Psychologists Press, 1974.

CHAPTER 8 *Psychiatric Character Types*

Baker, Elsworth F. *Man in the Trap.* New York: Macmillan, 1967 (Avon paperback, 1974).

Boadella, D. "Organ System and Life Styles." *Energy and Character,* 1976, Vol. 7, No. 3, pp. 27–39.

Diagnostic and Statistical Manual of Mental Disorders (DSM-II). Washington, D.C.: American Psychiatric Association, 1968.

Erikson, E. *Childhood and Society.* New York: Norton, 1964.

Grof, Stanislav. *Realms of the Human Unconscious.* New York: E. P. Dutton, 1976.

Hinsie, Leland E., and Campbell, Robert T. *Psychiatric Dictionary*, 4th ed. New York: Oxford University Press, 1970.

Kurtz, Ron, and Prestera, Hector. *The Body Reveals*. New York: Harper & Row, 1976.

Laing, R. D. *The Facts of Life*. New York: Random House, 1968.

Lowen, Alexander. *Bioenergetics*. New York: Coward, McCann & Geoghegan, 1975 (Penguin paperback, 1976).

Reich, Wilhelm. *Character Analysis* (1933). New York: Orgone Institute Press, 1949.

Shapiro, David. *Neurotic Styles*. New York: Basic Books, 1965.

CHAPTER 9 *Types of Love and Sex*

Arthur, Gavin. *The Circle of Sex*. New Hyde Park, N.Y.: University Books, 1966.

Eysenck, H. J. "Introverts, Extraverts and Sex," *Psychology Today*, Vol. 4, No. 8, Jan. 1971.

Lee, John Alan. *The Colors of Love*. New York: Bantam Books, 1976.

Lowen, Alexander. *Love and Orgasm*. New York: Signet Books, 1967.

Orage, A. R. *On Love*. London: Janus Press, 1966.

Vatsayana. *The Kama Sutra*. Many editions.

Von Franz, Marie-Louise. "The Process of Individuation" in C. G. Jung (ed.), *Man and His Symbols*. Garden City, N.Y.: Doubleday & Company, 1964.

Whitmont, Edmund. *The Symbolic Quest*. New York: G. P. Putnam's, 1969.

CHAPTER 10 *Oriental and Esoteric Typologies*

Bakula, J. S. *Esoteric Psychology: A Model for the Development of Human Consciousness*. Seattle, Wash.: United Focus, 1978.

Bennett, J. G. *Gurdjieff: Making a New World*. New York: Harper & Row, 1973.

Carus, Paul. *Chinese Astrology*. La Salle, Ill.: Open Court, 1974 (orig. publ. 1907).

Hardt, James. "Psychophysiology and the Three Gunas," *Rediscovery of the Body*, ed. Charles Garfield. New York: Laurel (Dell), 1977.

Hodson, G. *The Seven Human Temperaments*. Adyas, India: Theosophical Publishing House, 1973.

Ichazo, Oscar. *The Human Process of Enlightenment and Freedom.* New York: Arica Institute, 1972.

Lilly, John C., and Hart, Joseph E. "The Arica Training," *Transpersonal Psychologies,* ed. Charles T. Tart. New York: Harper & Row, 1975, pp. 329–51.

Logan, Daniel. *Your Eastern Star: Oriental Astrology, Reincarnation and the Future.* New York: William Morrow & Co., 1972.

Oken, Alan. *Astrology: Evolution and Revolution.* New York: Bantam, 1976.

Ouspensky, P. D. *In Search of the Miraculous.* New York: Harcourt, Brace & Company, 1949.

Prem, Sri Krishna. *The Yoga of the Bhagavad Gita.* London: John M. Watkins, 1958.

Robson, Vivian. *The Fixed Stars and Constellations in Astrology.* New York: Weiser, 1923.

Speeth, Kathleen R. *The Gurdjieff Work.* Berkeley, Calif.: And/Or Press, 1976.

Volguine, A. *Lunar Astrology.* New York: ASI Publishers, 1974.

White, Suzanne. *Book of Chinese Chance.* Greenwich, Conn.: Fawcett Publications, 1976.

CHAPTER 11   *The Typology of Numbers*

Addey, John. *Harmonics in Astrology.* Green Bay, Wisc.: Cambridge Circle, 1976.

Avery, Kevin Quinn. *The Numbers of Life.* Garden City, N.Y.: Doubleday & Company, 1977.

Dundes, Alan. "The Number Three in American Culture," *Every Man His Way,* ed. A. Dundes. Englewood Cliffs, N.J.: Prentice-Hall, 1968.

Fuller, Buckminster. *Synergetics: The Geometry of Thinking.* New York: Macmillan, 1976.

Heline, Corinne. *The Sacred Science of Numbers.* La Canada, Calif.: New Age Press, 1971.

Murphy, Gardner. "Pythagorean Number Theory and its Implications for Psychology," *American Psychologist,* Vol. 20 (1967), pp. 423–31.

Norris, A. G. S. *Transcendental Astrology.* New York: Weiser, 1970.

Jung, Carl. "Synchronicity: An Acausal Connecting Principle," *Collected Works of C. G. Jung,* Vol. 8. New York: Pantheon (Bollingen Series), 1960.

Roberts, Jane. *Psychic Politics*. Englewood Cliffs, N.J.: Prentice-Hall, 1976.

Roquemore, Kathleen. *It's All in Your Numbers*. New York: Harper & Row, 1975.

Rousey, Clyde L. "A Theory of Speech" in *Psychiatric Assessment by Speech and Hearing Behavior*, ed. C. L. Rousey. Springfield, Ill.: Charles C Thomas, 1974.

Von Franz, Marie-Louise. *Number and Time*. Evanston, Ill.: Northwestern University Press, 1974.

CHAPTER 12 *Types of Consciousness—the Actualism Approach*

Burr, Harold S. *The Fields of Life*. New York: Ballantine Books, 1972.

Gallert, Mark. *New Light on Therapeutic Energies*. London: James Clark & Co., 1966.

Karagulla, Shafica. *Breakthrough to Creativity: Your Higher Sense Perception*. Los Angeles: De Vorss Press, 1967.

Mann, W. Edward. *Orgone, Reich and Eros: Wilhelm Reich's Theory of Life Energy*. New York: Simon & Schuster, 1973.

Metzner, Ralph. *Maps of Consciousness*. New York: Macmillan, 1971.

Schofield, Russell Paul. *Basic Principles of Actualism*. Los Angeles: privately published, 1974. (Available from: Actualism, Valley Center, Calif. 92082.)

Tompkins, Peter, and Bird, Christopher. *The Secret Life of Plants*. New York: Harper & Row, 1973.

White, John, and Krippner, Stanley. *Future Science*. Garden City, N.Y.: Doubleday & Company, 1977.

Index

Actualism, 203–4, 219, 255; Actual
   Self, 257, 270, 271; emotional body,
   82, 258; enlightenment training,
   269–70; human personalities as
   energy systems, 257–60, 269–70;
   mental body, 82–83, 258; other
   higher levels, 83, 258; perceptual
   body, 81–82, 258; physical body, 81,
   257–58; transcending one's
   personality type, 268–71
Addey, John, 235
Adler, Alfred, 11, 71
Adorno, T. W., et al., 153
Alchemy: air element, 83; earth
   element, 81; fire element, 82; water
   element, 82
Alexander, 144
All and Everything, 187–88
Allport-Vernon test, 19–20, 61, 155–56
Anatomy of Melancholy, The, 39
Angularity, 115–16
Archetypes, 9–10
Arica, 222
Arica enneagram of types, 222–24; ego
   fixations, 222–24; psychocatalyzers,
   222
Arroyo, S., 81
Arthur, Gavin, 193–96
Ascendant, 80–81, 115, 116, 117, 211
Astrogenetics, 76
Astrological influences, 5, 45, 107–9;
   Edgar Cayce on, 118–19; Gauquelin,
   research of, 116–17, 126, 130
Astrological language, alphabets of,
   77–79
Astrological theories of human life:
   evolutionary, 77; humanistic, 76;
   physical-causal, 76; symbolic, 76
Astrology, 75–76; Ascendant, 80–81,
   115, 116, 117, 211; body types and,
   33–34, 52; Chinese, 214–19;
   Descendant, 81, 115, 116; Eastern
   (lunar), 211–14; four elements in,
   81–84; glandular hypothesis, 119,
   121, 123, 126, 127, 128, 130, 131,
   132; grouping of signs, 83–84;
   humoral types and, 52; Jungian
   types and, 71–73; Moon, importance

of, 80, 111–15, 121–22, 211;
   numbers in, 236, 237–45*passim,* 247;
   planetary prominence, indicators of,
   115–16; planetary rulers, 117–18;
   planetary types, 111–33; Sun,
   importance of, 79–80, 111–13,
   120–21, 124–25, 126
Authoritarian Personality, The, 153
Autobiography of a Yogi, 12

Bailey, Alice, 4, 77, 80, 118, 122, 123,
   219
Bakan, Paul, 140, 143, 146
Baker, Elsworth, 166
Bakula, J. S., 219
Bartlett, Frederic, 137
Bennett, J. G., 227–30
Berman, Louis, 45
Bhagavad Gita, 1, 29, 209
Bieler, Henry, 119
Bioenergetics, 173–74, 197–98
Blavatsky, H. P., 219
Body characteristics, measures of,
   17–18; dysplasia, 17;
   gyandromorphy, 18; textural aspect,
   18; trunk index, 17
Body types, 13–36; and astrology,
   33–34; distinctions among, 28–36;
   and evolution, 31–33; racial types
   and, 30–31; and religion, 29–30;
   temperamental attitudes correlated
   with, 18–20
Bogen, Joseph, 140
Breton, André, 162
Brown, Barbara, 137
*Bulletin of Research in Psychological
   Type,* 61–63
Bullough, Edward, 160
Burton, Robert, 39, 49–50
Busteed, Tiffany, and Wergin, 115
"But Why Did They Sit on the King's
   Right in the First Place?", 150

Case for Astrology, The, 76
Cayce, Edgar, 4, 45, 77, 94, 118, 120,
   121, 123, 125–26, 128, 129, 130–31,
   132

Cerebrotonia. *See* Ectomorphy

Character, 6

Character Analysis, 166

Circle of Sex, The, 193–96

Clairsentience, 257, 263

Collin, Rodney, 119, 121, 123, 126, 130

Colors of Love, The, 186–87

Combination of Stellar Influences, The, 76

Constitution, 7

Corporate management types: company man, 159; craftsman, 159; gamesman, 159–60; jungle fighter, 159; resemblance to Jungian functional types, 159

Cortes and Gatti, test derived from, 18–19

Dean, Douglas, 62

Descendant, 81, 115, 116

Development of functions, 68–70

Differentiation, in functions, 68–69

Disposition, 7

Djwhal Khul, 219

Doman-Delacato system, 146

Domhoff, William, 150

Dragons of Eden, The, 32

Dundes, Alan, 232–33

Dysplasia, 17

Earths in the Universe, 120

Ebertin, Reinhold, 76

Ectomorphy, 13, 26–28, 32

Education Through Art, 160–62

Eisenhower, Dwight, 160

Ellis, Havelock, 193

Elsenhans, 40, 47

Embryonic development, 20–22

Endomorphy, 13, 23–25, 31

Energies, 255, 256–68, 269–70

Energy field, human, 256–57; clairsentience, 257

Environment, 4

Erikson, Erik, 167

Esoteric Astrology, 219

Esoteric Psychology, 219

Evolution, body types and, 31–33

Extraversion and introversion, 55–57, 138; parallel to magnetic-dynamic polarity of Actualism, 259–60; unconscious energy flows of, 56–57; weaknesses of, 56

Eysenck, Hans J., 3, 4, 47–49, 51, 56, 62, 138, 154, 180, 190–91

Facts of Life, 167

Fagan, Cyril, 86

Feldenkrais, 144

Food Is Your Best Medicine, 119

Ford, Gerald, 160

Franz, Marie-Louise von, 69, 233–34

Freud, Sigmund, 11, 63–64, 71, 103, 165–66, 167, 169, 170, 171, 179, 184, 190

Fromm, Erich, 153

Fuller, Buckminster, 91, 232

Functional types, Jung's eight: extraverted feeling, 64–65; extraverted intuition, 67; extraverted sensation, 66; extraverted thinking, 63; introverted feeling, 65; introverted intuition, 67–68; introverted sensation, 66–67; introverted thinking, 63–64

Functions, Jung's four, 55, 81, 82; and time-space relationships, 59–60; typology by, 57–59

Galin, David, 140

Galton, Francis, 135–36, 143

Gandhi, Mahatma, 85

Gauquelin, Michel, 76, 116–17, 126, 130

Gazzaniga, Michael, 140

Genotype, definition of, 4

Glands of Personality, The, 45

Glueck, Sheldon and Eleanor, 19

Gray-Wheelwrights Type Survey, 60–61, 70, 72–73

Greene, L., 81

Grof, Stanislav, 167

Gurdjieff, G. I., 187–88, 222, 242; idiotism, science of, 227–30; typology of human development by, 224–27

Gurdjieff: Making a New World, 227–30

Gurdjieff-Ouspensky teachings, 119, 224–27

Gyandromorphy ("g index"), 18

Hamlet's Mill, 75

Hardt, James, 209

Harmonics in Astrology, 235

Harvey, William, 39

Heindel, Max, 45

Heredity, 4

Hirschfeld, Magnus, 193

Hockert, S. A., 158

Hodson, G., 219

Holcombe, Richard and Jean, 71–73
Holland, Dr. John, 156–57, 158
Human consciousness, typology of, 260–68; emotional-feeling level, 263–65; mental level, 265–68; physical-physiological level, 261–62; sensory-perceptual level, 262–63
Human energy systems, 257–68; according to levels of personality consciousness, 260–68; dynamic-magnetic polarity of, 259–60; horizontal interactions, 258–59; vertical energy exchanges, 258–59
Human types: descriptions of, 1–2; traits making up, 2–3
Humoral types, 37–54
Humors: body, 37–41; emotional balance affected by, 50–51; and endocrine types, 45–47; and feeling states, 40–41; relationships and, 51–52; temperaments according to, 42–45; typology by, 47–50
Huxley, Aldous, 29

Ichazo, Oscar, 222
I Ching, 231, 235
Idiotism, science of, 227–30
In Search of the Miraculous, 224–27
Individuality, 7
Individuation, 198, 203, 234; definitions of, 68
Inquiry into Human Faculty, 135
Inter- and intrapersonal relationships, balancing, 203–5

James, William, 136, 143
Johnson, Lyndon, 160
Jung, Carl, 3, 5, 9, 71, 138, 166; anima/animus theory in individuation, 198–200, 203; eight functional types of, 63–68; and four functions, 55, 57–59, 81; and numerology, 233–35; typology of, 11, 55–73
Jungian type system, correlation of: with occupational and value classifications, 157–58; with pathological character disorders, 180–81
Jungian typology, 11, 55–73, 156; and astrology, 71–73; balancing of functions through relationships, 70–71; development of functions in, 68–70; eight functional types of, 63–68, 157, 262, 263, 268; four

functions of, 55, 57–59; Gurdjieff typology, correlation with, 226; measurements according to, 60–63; parallelism with Actualism, 259–60; Read, Sir Herbert, and, 161

Kagan, Jerome, 138
Kama Sutra of Vatsayana, 192–93
Kant, Immanuel, 39, 64
Karagulla, Shafica, 265
Kennedy, John F., 160
Kinsey, Dr. Alfred C., 190
Knapp, R. H., and A. Wulff, 161

Laing, R. D., 167
Lee, John Alan, 186–87, 188
Lenski, Robert, 30–31
Levels of consciousness, 83
Lieber, Arnold L., and Jerome Agel, 122
Lim, R., 72
Love, 183–88; kinds of, 184–88
Love and Orgasm, 197–98
Lowen, Alexander, 166, 173, 177, 197–98, 199, 200
LSD, effects of, on mental processes, 137, 167
Lunar Effect, The, 122
Lunation Cycle, The, 113
Lunation cycle, typology of, 111–15

McClelland, David, 20
Maccoby, Michael, 158–60
McKinnon, 62
MacLean, Paul, 32–33
Making Vocational Choices, 157
Mann, Harriet, Miriam Siegler, and Humphrey Osmond, 59
Man's Presumptuous Brain, 32
"Many Worlds of Time, The," 59–60
Maps of Consciousness, 76, 208
Mayo, White, and Eysenck, 72
Mesomorphy, 13, 25–26, 31–32
Metzner, R., et al., 72
Midheaven, 115, 116, 117, 211
Moon, importance of, 80, 111–15, 121–22, 211
Myers-Briggs Type Indicator, 60–63; Manual for, 61–63

Nadir, 115, 116
Names: inner or soul, 252–54; numerology of, 248–52
Nixon, Richard, 160
Number and closeness of aspects, 116
Number and Time, 233–34

Numbers: and geometric shapes, correlations between, 236–37; importance of, 231–33; Jung and, 233–35; life-cycle and life-path, 245–48; personality (name), 248–52; polarities of, 235–36; symbolism in basic, 237–44; symbolism in higher-octave, 244–45

Oliver, Ruth Hale, 33
Olympiodorus, 271
"On Love," 187–88
Orage, A. R., 187–88
Oriental and esoteric typologies, 207–30; Arica enneagram of types, 222–24; Chinese astrology, twelve-year cycle of, 214–19; Hindu astrology, lunar mansions of, 211–14; human development, Gurdjieff's typology of, 224–27; idiotism, science of, 227–30; seven rays, theory of, 219–21; three *gunas*, 208–11
Ornstein, Robert, 140
Osgood, Charles, 149
Osmond, Humphrey, 11, 59, 70–71
Osmond, Siegler, and Smoke, 11
Ouspensky, P. D., 224–27

Perception, 81–82
Perennial Philosophy, 29
Personality, 6, 7; four sources of, 4–5
Personality types and sexual behavior, 190–91
Phases of the Moon, 115
Phenotype, definition of, 4
Planetary typology: Jupiter type, 128–29; by lunar phase, 111–15; Martial type, 126–27; mental types of Mercury-Sun cycle, 124–25; Mercurial type, 122–24; Neptunian type, 131–32; Plutonian type, 132–33; Saturnian type, 129–30; by solar or lunar prominence, 120–22; Uranian type, 130–31; Venusian type, 125–26
Plato, 1–2, 118, 152
Polarities: dynamic-magnetic, of human energy systems, 259–60; left-right, in culture and lore, 147–50; of numbers, 235–36; of types of personality consciousness, 260–68
Prem, Sri Krishna, 209, 210–11
Prototypes, 8–9
Psychiatric character types:

dependent, 174–76; hysterical, 168–69; masochistic, 171–73; miscellaneous, 178–80; obsessive-compulsive, 170; paranoid, 170–71; psychopathic, 176–78; schizoid, 173–74
Psychic Politics, 234
Psychoanalytic character theory, development of, 165–68; Reichian body armor, 166
Psychology Today, 202
Pythagoras, 231

Rajas, 30, 208–10*passim*
Rank, Otto, 167
Read, Sir Herbert, 160–62
Reich, Wilhelm, 3, 71, 166, 170, 174, 197, 200
Reincarnation, 4–5
Religion, body types and, 29–30
REM sleep, 143, 144
Republic, The, 1–2, 152; forms of government described in, 152
Rhine, J. B., 265
Roberts, Jane, 234
Roe, Anne, 136
Rolf, I. P., 144
Rosicrucian School, 45, 119, 123, 125–26
Rousey, Clyde, 250–51
Rudhyar, Dane, 76, 111, 113, 124

Sagan, Carl, 32
Santillana, Georgio de, and Hertha von Dechend, 75
Sattva, 30, 208–10*passim*
Schofield, Russell Paul, 81, 255, 273–75
Self (Higher; Creator), 5, 6, 7, 10, 12, 77, 79, 270
Semmes, Josephine, 140
Seven rays, theory of, 219–21
Sexual identities, development of, 196–200; emotional fixations, 197–98; initiation or transition rituals, 196–97; Jung's anima/animus theory in individuation, 198–200
Sexual identities, self-evaluation of, 200–3
Sexual typology: chart of, 193–96; by Eastern standards, 191–93
Sexual values, test of, 188–90
Shapiro, David, 168, 170, 171
Sheldon, William, 3, 4, 11, 13–18, 19, 20, 22, 24, 26, 27, 29, 30, 31–33, 209,

225
Simeons, A. T. W., 32
Singularity, 116
Solar progressions, 107–9
Somatotonia. See Mesomorphy
Somatotyping, 13, 18–36, 209, 225;
    embryological hypothesis in, 20–23
Sperry, Roger, 140, 141
Spirit. See Self
Spranger, Eduard, 155, 156
Steiner, Rudolf, 4, 42, 43, 45, 94
Stereotypes, 8
Strickler and Ross, 61
Strong Vocational Interest Test, 61,
    156
Sun, importance of, 79–80, 111–13,
    120–21, 124–25, 126
Swedenborg, Emanuel, 83, 86, 120,
    123–24, 127, 128–29, 130
Synergetics, 232

Tamas, 30, 208–10passim, 211
Tarot card associations, 86, 87, 95,
    98–99, 104, 106, 121, 125,
    238–44passim, 248
Temperament, 6–7
Temperaments according to humors,
    choleric, 43; melancholic, 44–45;
    phlegmatic, 43–44; sanguine, 42–43
Textural aspect (t component), 18
Theory of Celestial Influence, The,
    119
Theosophists, 119
Three gunas, 1, 30, 208–11
Tomkins, Sylvan, 149–50
Trunk index, 17
Tyl, Noel, 80
Type, factors relating to, 151–64;
    aesthetic styles, 160–62; executive
    and managerial styles, 158–60; other
    arts than painting, 162–64; political
    attitudes, 152–55; vocational and
    occupational interests, 155–58
Typing systems, 1–12; interpersonal
    view of, 10–11; intrapsychic view of,
    11–12

Typology by aesthetic style, 160–62;
    cubism and constructivism, 162;
    expressionism and Fauvism, 162;
    realism and impressionism, 161;
    surrealism and futurism, 161–62
Typology by styles of thinking:
    convergent and divergent thinking,
    139–40; field dependence or
    independence, 139; left-right
    polarity in culture and lore, 147–50;
    levelers or sharpeners, 138–39;
    reflectivity or impulsivity, 138;
    split-brain thinking, 140–47; visual
    vs. nonvisual, 135–38

Uexküll, von, 59
Umwelt, 59, 60
Unconscious, 69–70

Van Deusen, Edmund, 76
Viscerotonia. See Endomorphy
Vision, A, 114–15

West, J. A., and J. G. Toonear, 76
Whitmont, Edmund, 199
Witkin, 139
Wundt, Wilhelm, 40, 47, 50

Yeats, W. B., 114–15
Yogananda, Swami, 12, 101

Zodiac, characteristics by sign of:
    Aquarius, 86–87; Aries, 95–97;
    Cancer, 89–91; Capricorn, 100–2;
    Gemini, 87–89; Leo, 97–99; Libra,
    84–86; Pisces, 93–95; Sagittarius,
    99–100; Scorpio, 91–93; Taurus,
    102–4; Virgo, 104–6
Zodiac, typology of, 75–109; air signs,
    84–89, 266; earth signs, 100–6, 262;
    fire signs, 95–100, 263; water signs,
    89–95
Zodiacs: Chinese, 214–19; Hindu
    lunar, 211–14; sidereal, 79; tropical,
    77